SUSTAINABLE URBANISM

Sustainable Urbanism:
Urban Design with Nature

Douglas Farr

To Patrick,

A true Sustainable Urbanist! Carry the flag.

Alexandria 07

Doug Farr

BICENTENNIAL
1807
WILEY
2007
BICENTENNIAL

John Wiley & Sons, Inc.

Published by John Wiley & Sons, Inc.,
Hoboken, New Jersey

Published simultaneously in Canada

For general information about our
other products and services, please
contact our Customer Care Department
within the United States at (800)
762-2974, outside the United States at
(317) 572-3993 or fax (317) 572-4002.

Wiley also publishes its books in a
variety of electronic formats. Some
content that appears in print may not
be available in electronic books. For
more information about Wiley products,
visit our web site at www.wiley.com.

Graphic Design (interior); Sam Silvio,
Silvio Design Inc.,Chicago

Wiley Bicentennial Logo:
Richard J. Pacifico

Library of Congress
Cataloging-in-Publication Data:

Farr, Douglas
  Sustainable urbanism: urban design
with nature/Douglas Farr.
     p. cm.
  Includes bibliographical references
and index.
  ISBN 978-0-471-77751-9 (cloth)
1. Urban ecology. 2. Urban ecology –
United States. 3. City planning –
Environmental aspects. 4. Sustainable
development. 5. Neighborhoods.
I. Title. HT241.S8736 2008
307.76–dc22

                  2007029064

Printed in the United States of America
10 9 8 7 6 5 4 3 2 1

To Gail, Will, my inspiring
colleagues at Farr Associates, and
the good Kingdom of Upnot

Contents

The time has come, the Walrus said,
To talk of many things:
Of shoes—and ships—and sealing-wax—
Of cabbages—and kings—
And why the sea is boiling hot—
And whether pigs have wings.

Lewis Carroll (1872)
Through the Looking-Glass

And so indeed, the time has come. This was the year when the Intergovernmental Panel on Climate Change's report converged with "An Inconvenient Truth." The boundaries of our playing field are now visible. The vast and amusing game called the American Lifestyle has limits after all!

What shall we do now?

Well, with about forty years' worth of dedicated publications, there is certainly a lot of know-how available. For example, on my office's "green" bookshelf, the 1963 edition of Olgyay's *Design with Climate* sits 3 feet away from last year's edition of Schaeffer's *Solar Living Sourcebook*. My collection may be impressive—but I am not its equal. When I count which ones of these many books I have managed to really study, the honest answer is...*just one:* Christopher Alexander's *A Pattern Language*.

Surely, this cannot be entirely my fault, for I am known to be a disciplined and interested reader.

The problem may lie with the books themselves. It seems that when I try to read the hortatory ones, I get their point well before the last page; and the technical ones are just too tedious to get through. Besides, both of these kinds of books are usually too specialized, with each author implying that their particular silver bullet is *the* important one to deal with the world's environmental problem.

And so it has been for decades: waves of books asserting the importance of safeguarding habitat; or the danger of atmospheric pollution; or the demise of water quality; or the dreaded holes in the ozone layer; or the need for conservation, recycling or alternate energy; or the urgency of reinstating the production of local, organic agriculture; or green building.

Taken together these books offers a complete body of knowledge, but no single volume has been holistic (or legible) enough to induce my expertise...with the unique exception of *A Pattern Language*.

Why then, having Alexander's book already in hand, should we welcome Doug Farr's? It may be, ironically enough, because *A Pattern Language* is too beautiful; too much a work of art. It is an epic, worthy of being the foundation myth of a great, ethical, intelligent, pleasurable civilization—one I would delight to inhabit. Alas, however, most Americans have come to mistrust intuition as a basis for action. Our leaders trust technique, not mystique. *unfair* They require "studies" to provide them with "metrics" that support "accountability." Happily, Doug Farr's manual responds well to this situation. While it is similar to Alexander's in that it propounds the full range of elements necessary for a sustainable future, it is potentially more convincing because it does so technically.

Also, like *A Pattern Language,* this manual designates the human settlement pattern— and not just the dwelling—as the crucial variable in the environmental equation. This makes a great deal of difference, as the absence of the community scale in the environmental literature has been masked by the recent obsession with "green" building—the latest of the silver bullets. But this is a long story, beginning with Ian Mc Harg's early *Design with Nature,* which did not make a proposition regarding what was to be built once the where had been determined.

The primacy of the settlement pattern is demonstrated by what can happen when it is overlooked: Take the ecologically-sited headquarters to which every employee must daily drive a long distance; or the green Wal-Mart that depends on a trade area of 35 miles; or the chic "model" house in the desert with "solar" glass walls of impossible expense. With this manual, such absurdities are shown for what they are.

Without dismissing the techniques involved, Farr corrects the equation. The book's presentation has a refreshing bias towards the practical and the pleasurable, and it also avoids case studies that are dependent on the sort of socialized subsidies that disqualify many marvelous European models from widespread influence in this country. No less important, he is practiced enough to avoid the imposition of austerities and inconveniences as a condition of securing a sustainable dwelling. Americans will not voluntarily tolerate suffering.

But there is nothing in this manual that recommends a neo-medieval nightmare. It may advocate a simplification, but that could lead to a more pleasant, elegant and meaningful life, and one relieved of the spiritual pall that comes from harming the planet which nurtures us.

Andrés Duany

This book celebrates the magical power of design and of an emerging pattern of human settlement—Sustainable Urbanism—that holds the promise of strengthening the interdependence of all life on earth. We humans are now a "superspecies," making personal and national choices that together will determine the world our children will inherit and the fate of the world's other species. Many progressive leaders now envision and champion a win-win balance between humanity's needs, both social and economic, and those of nature. An increasing number of those leaders recognize the power of thoughtful urbanism to induce people to voluntarily live a more human-powered and less resource-intensive lifestyle. A small but fast-growing number of leaders are now beginning to recognize opportunities to enhance the inherent sustainability of a walkable, diverse urbanism integrated with high-performance buildings and infrastructure.

This book is a pioneering first effort to understand and document this emerging design movement called sustainable urbanism. This book grew out of the questions we at Farr Associates have encountered trying to fulfill our firm's mission to design sustainable human environments. It started as a modest project to develop a manual of practice that would bridge the differing scales of sustainability efforts practiced by our firm's amazingly hardworking and talented planners and architects. It has grown to involve some of the best designers, consultants, researchers, and developers in the United States and beyond. Despite the knowledge and high quality of work represented here, it is hard not to think of this book as a first draft, destined to be written over and over as our collective knowledge, achievements, and sense of urgency increase.

This book is a strategic call for leadership in the design and development of the places where Americans live, work, and play. All sustainability is local. The leaders who shape the built environment in the United States are decentralized and number in the millions of people. They include, among others; governors, mayors, city councils, municipal staff, government regulators, businesses, financiers, architects, planners, engineers, developers, builders, green builders, urbanists, environmentalists, farmers, utilities, voters, neighbors, and NIMBY groups. This book is designed to be a comprehensive how-to manual and implementation playbook to overcome the organizational challenges created by this broad decentralized leadership.

This book seeks to create a brand, agenda, and standards for an emerging and growing design reform movement: sustainable urbanism. Sustainable urbanism is an integration of walkable and transit-served urbanism with high-performance buildings and high performance infrastructure. It is related to the LEED for Neighborhood Development (LEED-ND) initiative, which the principal author of this book has chaired for several years. The book complements LEED-ND by trying to accelerate the parallel reforms needed to create a tipping point in support of widespread adoption of this approach.

This book provides a historical perspective on the standards and regulations that are often barriers to reform. Hundreds of separate national standards, and likely millions of local regulations, interact to increase resistance to change and make it difficult or even illegal to create sustainable urbanism. A working knowledge of when and why a given regulation was first adopted is essential to making a persuasive argument to change it.

This book is an urgent call to action concerning the design of the places where Americans live, work, and play. We are just coming to understand some terrible truths about the lifestyle choices made by the average American. After centuries of increasing longevity, U.S. life expectancy may be dropping due in large part to a sedentary and indoor lifestyle. Our affluence allows us to accumulate massive amounts of stuff, and we build increasingly larger dwellings to store it. Given the well-known environmental harms that result from our lifestyle, our failure to change amounts to a de facto plan to burden our children and grandchildren with the enormous costs of adapting to a changed global climate. Timelines communicate, at a glance, the key events leading up to the development of emerging thresholds of sustainable urbanism.

This book embraces the precautionary principle, a cornerstone of intergenerational courtesy. The precautionary principle states that any action or policy that might cause severe or irreversible public harm needs to be subjected to the highest scrutiny. The advocates of such untested actions or policies are burdened with proving that harm will not result. The design of land use and infrastructure—the crucial support structures for how we live, work, and play—should be subject to this kind of scrutiny because thoughtless design is already linked to adverse impacts on human health as well as climate change. While land use and infrastructure are arguably the most long-lasting and deterministic attributes of human settlements, the current debate on climate change tends to skip over them in favor of quicker fixes. Time is of the essence in adopting the reforms of sustainable urbanism. The precautionary principle demands the reform of land use and infrastructure as part of a comprehensive reform agenda targeting critical health and climate issues.

How to Use This Book

The purpose of this book is to help catalyze the adoption of Sustainable Urbanism to become the dominant pattern of human settlement by the year 2030. The book is organized to fulfill this ambitious goal in a comprehensive step-by-step manner.

Part One: The Case for Sustainable Urbanism

The task of implementing sustainable urbanism will require the participation of the next several generations of development professionals. The first part of this book functions essentially as an outline for courses in planning, architecture, engineering, environmental studies, and interdisciplinary sustainable development that could be used to train development professionals, public officials, and municipal staff on the emerging practice of sustainable urbanism. It posits that the American lifestyle puts society and the planet on the wrong course, and it proposes sustainable urbanism, a comprehensive reform of the built environment, as an achievable remedy. This first part of the book narrates and quantifies the magnitude of the problem, provides a history of pioneering reforms, makes the compelling case for sustainable urbanism, and outlines an agenda of strategic reforms leading to the dominance of sustainable urbanism.

Part Two: Implementing Sustainable Urbanism: Turning a Swarm into a Movement

Sustainable urbanism represents a generational shift in how human settlements are designed and developed. Its adoption as a societal norm requires all of the many participants in the process of planning and developing the built environment to work as a single organism toward a shared purpose. Part II of this book is designed to serve as an operating system to coordinate the work of discrete individuals to achieve magnified benefits. The leadership section details specific steps for mayors, municipal planners, banks, realtors, state governments, transit agencies, utilities, think tanks, Congress, municipal bond rating agencies, architects, developers, and others to implement sustainable urbanism one action at a time. The process section describes the detailed steps needed to implement sustainable urbanism through individual planning and development projects. It also provides templates for selecting qualified design professionals, project types, and development teams. Finally, it provides a communications and marketing framework for communicating the concept, benefits, and synergies of sustainable urbanism. This section also introduces the transect—a powerful communication tool for illustrating the spectrum of human place types and their capacity for sustainability.

Part Three: Emerging Thresholds of Sustainable Urbanism: Design Benchmarks and Rules of Thumb

In order to facilitate the widespread adoption of sustainable urbanism, benchmarks for design and development are essential. Part III features nearly thirty emerging thresholds of sustainable urbanism. Each is a distillation of the professional judgment of national experts regarding the performance that is likely or possible across a broad spectrum of human and natural systems. The thresholds can be used as benchmarks for designers to use as performance targets on projects, particularly useful in conjunction with the LEED for Neighborhood Development standard, or to provide the foundation for developing even more robust standards. The standards span five comprehensive areas of concern: density, corridors, neighborhoods, biophilla, and high-performance buildings and infrastructure. Together these constitute some of the most challenging opportunities for design integration in sustainable urbanism.

Part Four: Case Studies: Lessons Learned and State-of-the-Art Sustainable Urbanism

This case study portfolio captures a moment in time at the genesis of a revolutionary and powerful design movement. Part IV of this book documents a diverse and mature worldwide movement of visionary neighborhood-scale projects, both those already built and those yet to be built, that take a sustainable urbanist approach. Intriguing case studies from the United States, Canada, Mexico, Europe, Australia, and China integrate walkable urbanism, natural habitats, and high-performance infrastructure and building. The redevelopment and greenfield projects integrate infrastructure, building, and natural systems to varying degrees and levels of visibility. The sustainable leadership behind each project is described in narrative form to serve as a model for future projects. The project metrics, including key benchmarks, and a summary of sustainability systems also provide design guidance and goals.

Like so many projects that snowball, this book started as a modest pamphlet. The initial goal was to establish standards to coordinate the work of the planners and architects at Farr Associates. That initial idea grew in scope, complexity, and personnel and came to involve more than fifteen people in our office and more than fifty experts and case study practitioners worldwide. A project of this magnitude takes a village. I regret that I cannot hope to extend thanks to every one of the many, many people whose contributions and hard work were essential for this project to succeed.

This book would not have happened without Kevin Pierce, former Principal at Farr Associates; I thank him profusely for making the connections and seeing the opportunity herein. And I thank John Czarnecki, our editor at Wiley, for his patience during our many distractions through the long course of this project.

This book would not have been possible without the help of many talented and hardworking current and former staff members at Farr Associates. Joyce Coffee, Elizabeth Lindau, Elena Disabato and Renee McGurk oversaw the project through its long gestation. Leslie Oberholtzer, Christina Anderson, James Gwinner, April Hughes, Carolee Kokola, Adam Lund, Jamie Simone, and Christian Schaller all brought their talents to shaping the content. Book interns Meghan Bogaerts, Genevieve Borich, Erica Burt, and Ben Smith carried this project to the finish line, and I further credit Genevieve with the clarity of the book's thesis. Annalise Raziq, Jonathan Boyer, and Leslie Oberholtzer each deserve extra-special thanks both for their critical inputs to the book and for helping to sail the ship during this odyssey.

While the concept for sustainable urbanism was born in our office, a significant share of the content of this book is the work of others outside our firm, I am humbled by the stature of both the threshold contributors, all leaders in the respective fields. and the case study teams who participated in this project. I am indebted to these people and thankful for their generosity in sharing their work and wisdom for this book.

The roots of my interest in sustainable urbanism and in the benefits of working in interdisciplinary teams sprang from Project Clear, a land use and water quality study conducted at the University of Michigan Biological Station. I owe lifelong thanks to my incredibly smart team members and friends: project director Dr. Art Gold, administrator Mark Paddock, biologists Linda Greer and Marion Secrest, geologist Michael Tilchin, attorney Stanley Pollack, and Dr. Seth Ammerman.

Scott Bernstein, Director of the Center for Neighborhood Technology (CNT), has been a mentor, collaborator, and friend for more than twenty-five years. While no formal contribution of his appears here, his ideas and those of his many colleagues at CNT, including friends Michael Freedberg and Jackie Grimshaw, permeate this book.

Thanks to the early Chicago members of the American Institute of Architects' Committee on the Environment, including Steve Blonz, Pat Dolan, Mike Iverson, Helen Kessler, and Carol McLaughlin, who together learned and debated the principles of green building and urban sustainability years before LEED. Thanks to Scot Horst and the members of the LEED Steering Committee, whose sustained debate of these issues sharpened many arguments herein.

Through the course of more than fifteen congresses, the board, staff, and membership of the Congress for New Urbanism (CNU) contributed content to this book. David Hudson, Heather Smith, Steve Filmanowicz, Payton Chung, Nora June Beck, and Lee Crandell all helped out generously. Four board members merit special thanks: Dan Solomon, my architecture professor at Columbia University, for his mentorship, for his design excellence, and for introducing me to

CNU; John Norquist, for his insights on the inherent value of urbanism; Susan Mudd, for her committed environmental leadership within CNU; and Andrés Duany, for his intelligence, generosity, and tireless advocacy of urbanism, and especially for conceiving the urban-rural transect.

This book would not exist had I not served as Chair of the LEED for Neighborhood Development project. While success has many parents, I credit the troika of Kaid Benfield, Christine Irvin, and Shelley Poticha with getting this important initiative off the ground and Nigel Howard, Peter Templeton and Bill Browning for early support at the U.S. Green Building Council (USGBC). Over the last four years, I have earned the equivalent of a Ph.D. by serving as chair to the immensely talented members of the Core Committee who developed the draft LEED for Neighborhood Development standard: Dana Beech, Kaid Benfield, Victor Dover, Sharon Feigon, Rebecca Flora, Daniel Hernandez, Bert Gregory, Jessica Cogan Millman, Michael Pawlukiewicz, Tom Richman, Susan Mudd, John Norquist, Elizabeth Schilling, Laura Watchman, and Sandy Wiggins. I thank each and every one of them for sharing their wisdom in what I hope is not a once-in-a-lifetime process of interdisciplinary collaboration, the fruits of which appear both in LEED-ND and in this book.

Kaid Benfield, my co-chair, deserves credit for patiently schooling me in the history, values, and accomplishments of the smart growth movement, and helping me to tell the story of this pioneering reform. Rob Watson—Kaid's colleague at the Natural Resources Defense Council and "father of LEED"—filled in the history of USGBC and LEED.

Thanks to Tim Beatley for his pioneering book on European green urbanism and to the German Marshall Fund for allowing me to see "green" Europe first hand. Thanks to Joe Van Belleghem, developer of Dockside Green, for making sustainable urbanist development look easy, and to John Knott for his faith and courage in taking on the full agenda at Noisette. I also credit the work of Eliot Allen, a brilliant planner and analyst, for first showing me how to elegantly map and quantify the seemingly unknowable attributes and benefits of sustainable urbanism, and Hillary Brown for pioneering the field of high-performance infrastructure.

Numerous friends deserve thanks for their generosity as sounding boards and critical listeners: Ellen Dunham-Jones, Ellen Greenberg, Jen Henry, Rick Mosher, Knute Nadelhoffer, David Pott, Annalise Raziq, Jill Riddell, Janette Sadik-Kahn, Jeff Speck, Susie Spivey, and Alison True. Thanks, too, to Dr. Howard Frumpkin and Dr. Andrew Dannenberg of the Centers for Disease Control.

Finally, this book could not have happened without support from Chicago and Illinois. Thanks to my dear wife, Gail Niemann, for her tireless support, tough editing, and sincere interest in the topic of this book. Thanks to my son, Will, whose "How far did you get on the book today, Dad?" kept me going. Thanks to my sister, Anne Farr, for her generous help, and to Jonathan Black, whose eleventh-hour editorial input greatly strengthened the power of the essay. Thanks to the Chicago Green Brain Trust: Jim Patchett, David Yocca, Howard Learner, Jim Slama, and Craig Sieben. Thanks to Chris Koos, mayor of Normal, Illinois, and the citizens of McLean County, Illinois, for allowing us to first test many of the sustainable urbanist ideas in this book. Thanks to David Reynolds and Commissioners Bill Aboldt and Sadhu Johnston of the Chicago Department of the Environment for their patronage and support in implementing sustainable urbanism on the ground in Chicago. Finally, thanks to Chicago's mayor, Richard M. Daley, who, by adopting sustainable urbanism as the hallmark of his tenure, has tasked his administration with implementing the book's thesis.

PART ONE: THE CASE FOR SUSTAINABLE URBANISM

Chapter 1
The Built Environment:
Where We Are Today

The American Lifestyle on the Wrong Course

"We have seen the enemy and he is us."
Pogo, by Walt Kelly

It's the American way to celebrate our robust range of life choices. We pride ourselves on being able to pick where we work, whom we live with, where we shop, and how we play. We decide on our government. We treasure the right to vote. For centuries we've believed that the sum total of these highly personal decisions will lead to an optimal society, that community can best evolve through every individual pursuing his or her own "rational," enlightened self-interest. That presumption is now being put to a severe test—and many of us would argue it has failed us badly. Our lifestyle, to put it simply, is on the wrong course.

The evidence is all around us. The lifestyle we, the American middle class, have selected has led to a serious deterioration in public health. We have become a sedentary population, deprived of exercise, and the result is a rising incidence of obesity. In 1991 the four states with the highest levels of adult obesity had rates between 15 percent and 19 percent.[1] A mere fifteen years later, the proportion of all adults *nationally* over age twenty who are obese has reached a shocking 30 percent, dramatized in Figure 1-1.[2] To provide another perspective, weight-related health problems account for 9.1 percent of all health care expenditures in the United States.[3] But according to a study by the National Institutes of Health, over the next few decades the greatest price that obesity may exact from society, if we fail to change course, is a life expectancy that is up to five years lower.[4]

Why have we grown obese? Several reasons can be found in the spatial environment we've designed for ourselves. While four-, five-, and even six-story residential walk-up buildings were commonplace in most large American cities during the nineteenth century, the use of stairs has been actively discouraged by the fire stair enclosure requirements of twentieth- and twenty-first-century U.S. building codes. At one time, most Americans got to their destinations by foot; many never ventured far from home their entire lives. People lived locally; they settled in one place and stayed there. They did not require mechanical means to get them across town to Costco. Children walked to school. Abraham Lincoln famously walked six miles each way to reach the library; today we walk as little as an average of four minutes a day.[5]

Not only are we sedentary, but we've chosen a life that is increasingly lived indoors. A baby born in the United States will spend close to 87 percent of his or her lifetime indoors and another 4 percent in enclosed transit (see Figures 1-4 A & B and Chart 1-1).[6] The reason? We've become experts at creating shelter with ever-increasing levels of indoor comfort. The possibility of cooling a room with an air conditioner became a reality in the 1960s. Soon entire buildings sealed themselves off from the outside with grid-powered mechanical ventilation. Open windows were a thing of the past. The welcome frigid blast of an air conditioner in summer has obscured the price we pay in health costs; the U.S. Environmental Protection Agency estimates that indoor air is two

Figure 1-1
On average 30 percent of adult Americans are obese. Adapted from "U.S. Obesity Trends 1985–2005," based on the Centers for Disease Control's Behavioral Risk Factor Surveillance System. Available at http://www.cdc.gov/nccdphp/dnpa/obesity/trend/maps.

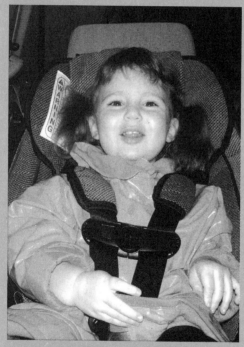

Your SUV Makes You Look Fat™

to five times more polluted than outdoor air because of smoking, indoor combustion, material off-gassing, and mold.[7] Children are at an even greater risk than adults due to their faster breathing rates, greater activity levels, and still-developing lungs and other tissues.

There is an economic cost, too. In substituting mechanical means for what was otherwise free in nature, a significant amount of the energy consumed by the average building is used to circulate oxygenated air, formerly the work of open windows.

We pay a psychic price as well. In choosing to become an indoor species, we have cut ourselves off from the natural world, making us increasingly oblivious to what we are doing to our immediate outdoor surroundings. Private yards and public streets alike are asphalted, floodlit (Figure 1-5), and filled with hot, noisemaking mechanical devices (Figure 1-6). While air conditioning condensers provide comfort and security to people indoors, they amount to a de facto plan to keep people indoors. The unpleasant characteristics of today's outdoor spaces are especially harmful in close urban settings, actually deterring people from spending time outdoors and reinforcing the tendency to stay indoors and close the windows. This neglect is hardly surprising given that adult Americans spend five times more hours driving a car than exercising and playing sports.[8] In other words, we spend more time traveling, typically by car, to the next building than we do enjoying outdoor spaces between them.

"We found that an average white male living in a compact community with nearby shops and services is expected to weigh 10 pounds less than his counterpart in a low-density residential-only subdivision." —Lawrence Frank, associate professor at the University of British Columbia's School of Community and Regional Planning

Not surprisingly, perhaps, the more time we spend indoors, the more indoor space we have come to demand. Not only are Americans themselves getting bigger, their homes are getting bigger. From 1970 to 2000, the average household size in the United States shrank from 3.14 to 2.62 people,[9] while the size of the typical new American house increased from 1,385 square feet to 2,140 square feet, a rise of 54 percent (see Figure 1-7).[10]

All of this time spent indoors deprives humans of the physical and mental benefits of walking, outdoor exercise, and time immersed in nature. Much new development is designed to discourage outdoor living. New streetscapes are hostile to pedestrians and discourage travel by foot. New buildings are designed with air-conditioning for indoor living rather than with open windows and doors that draw people outdoors. These design choices contribute directly to our obesity epidemic and likely impact our mental acuity. According to the *Wall Street Journal*, a recent gerontology study concludes that "as little as three hours a week of aerobic exercise increased the brain's volume of gray matter (actual neurons) and white matter (connections between neurons). . .to that of people three years younger."[11]

The lack of human contact with nature has inured and possibly blinded us to the terrible damage we do to our planet. Modern consumer society, for instance, exploits natural resources at a rate that the Earth cannot sustain. Our appetite for petroleum, electricity, mobility, indoor living space, and material goods is enormous and unrelenting. An unequivocal international scientific consensus backs the fact that, after only a few generations of the petroleum age, the resulting increase in human population and the increasing per capita impact from human activities have changed the Earth's climate.[12] This, the worst of all problems

Figure 1-5
Overlighting contributes to sleep disorders and severs ties to nature. Image © Clanton & Associates.

Figure 1-6
These hot, buzzing air conditioning condensers encourage people to go indoors and close windows.

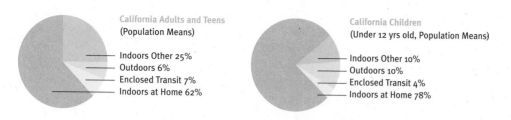

Where Californians Spend Time
(Jenkins et al., 1992a; Phillips et al., 1991)

California Adults and Teens
(Population Means)

Indoors Other 25%
Outdoors 6%
Enclosed Transit 7%
Indoors at Home 62%

California Children
(Under 12 yrs old, Population Means)

Indoors Other 10%
Outdoors 10%
Enclosed Transit 4%
Indoors at Home 78%

Chart 1-1
These charts confirm that humans are an indoor species. From *Indoor Air Pollution in California*, page 2, California Air Resources Board, July 2005. Images © California Air Resources Board.

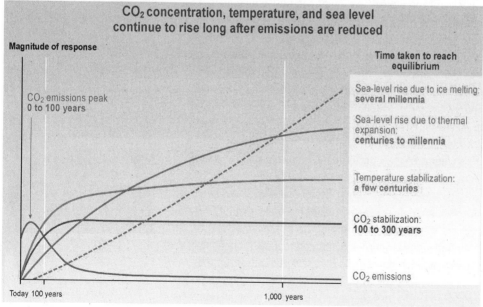

Figure 1-7
The "obese" American home.

CO$_2$ concentration, temperature, and sea level continue to rise long after emissions are reduced

Magnitude of response

CO$_2$ emissions peak
0 to 100 years

Time taken to reach equilibrium

Sea-level rise due to ice melting:
several millennia

Sea-level rise due to thermal expansion:
centuries to millennia

Temperature stabilization:
a few centuries

CO$_2$ stabilization:
100 to 300 years

CO$_2$ emissions

Today 100 years   1,000 years

Figure 1-8
Our current lifestyle will result in long-term climate change. Image © Intergovernmental Panel on Climate Change.

resulting from our lifestyle, is also the most difficult to overcome, as the harm is slow to materialize (Figure 1-8) and does not present the sort of imminant external threat against which history confirms humanity can unite.[13]

The metaphor of the "ecological footprint" approximates and visually illustrates the capacity of nature's systems to support the demands placed on it by contemporary lifestyle. It categorizes human demands on land into food, goods and services, transportation, housing, energy use, location, green practices, and income. According to research prepared by WWF, and displayed in Figure 1-9, starting around 1977 human resource demands exceeded the planet's capacity to provide them.[14] By far the most surprising and provocative finding concerns the energy-intensiveness of providing food to Americans. According to Michael Pollan, author of *The Omnivore's Dilemma,* America's food is "drenched in fossil fuel,"[15] reflecting both the energy-intensiveness of agribusiness and the 1,494-mile average that a plate of food is transported in the United States.[16]

A prime villain in all this, and a lifestyle choice made early and rarely questioned, is our love affair with the automobile. We have become addicted to driving. Most Americans rely on cars to meet the most basic needs of life. We cherish the "freedom of the road" and safeguard it with a zealousness that suggests it was written into the Constitution. Americans drive more than any other society on Earth and are locked into doing so by choosing to live, work, and shop in out-of-the-way places that demand driving. A family chooses to buy a large house in a new subdivision at the edge of town because they understand they can get there by car. A job across town, remote from where they live and not served by public transit, is just as good as a job nearby. Whoever shops drives miles to a big-box store, bypassing numerous local stores that carry the same merchandise, in order to save a few cents per item.

People making these lifestyle choices are automobile dependent. As a result, roughly two-thirds of all oil consumed in the United States is processed into fuel for transportation.[17] While Americans might acknowledge our country's oil and auto dependence, indeed, even George W. Bush has declared the United States to be "addicted to oil,"[18] most are too immersed in it to see it as an addiction (see Figure 1-10).

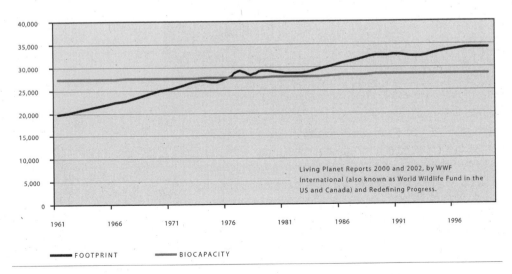

Figure 1-9
We exceeded the Earth's capacity to sustain our lifestyle around 1977. Image © Redefining Progress, www.rprogress.org

Living Planet Reports 2000 and 2002, by WWF International (also known as World Wildlife Fund in the US and Canada) and Redefining Progress.

FOOTPRINT   BIOCAPACITY

The joint addiction to driving and oil comes at an extremely high cost to individuals and families. The average cost of owning, operating, and maintaining a new car is now estimated to be $7,000 per year.[19] The average vehicle is driven more than 12,000 miles per year, equivalent to halfway around the Earth.[20] The average American household has 2.6 members and drives 21,500 miles per year.[21] This translates to every family in America driving its cars a distance equivalent to 90 percent of the Earth's circumference every year.

These averages conceal the varied rates of family car ownership across a metropolitan region. The cost burden of car ownership falls disproportionately on suburban and exurban residents, where some families own one or even more cars per adult. These metropolitan differences are dramatized in Figure 1-11, showing that the average rural or exurban Atlanta area resident drives nearly eight times more each day (forty miles versus five miles) than the average central-city Atlantan.[22]

Parking exacts its own toll on business, government, and the environment. Street networks and parking spaces are expensive to build. In 1973, Planner Victor Gruen estimated that every car in America is provided with four parking spaces, equivalent to a 25 percent occupancy rate for America's roughly one billion parking spaces.[23] This alarming statistic is still cited by today's acknowledged parking expert, Donald Shoup, a professor of urban planning at UCLA. If this were all surface parking, it would cover roughly the entire state of Maryland.[24] The cost of constructing parking spaces is high, anywhere from $2,500 to $5,000 for a surface spot to between $30,000 and $50,000 for underground spaces—a national capital investment of between $5 trillion and $10 trillion. Despite this enormous investment in parking, it is generally offered free to users (see Figure 1-12), paid for by the private sector through increased prices and by the public sector in taxes. Donald Shoup singles out free parking as possibly the most powerful inducement to own and drive cars in the built environment, an unlikely but essential link in our addiction to driving and oil (see Figure 1-13).[25]

Figure 1-10
Societal addictions are easier to spot in cultures other than one's own. Image © Frank and Frances Carpenter Collection, Library of Congress.

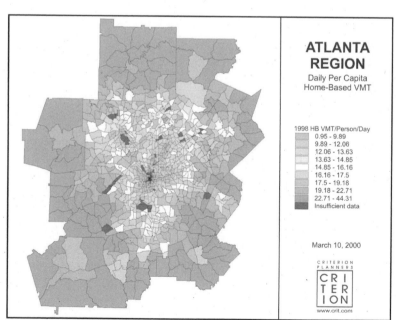

Figure 1-11
You are where you live: exurban Atlantans drive an average of eight times more than urban Atlantans. Criterion Planners, Impact Analysis of Smart Growth Land-Use Planning, Georgia Regional Transportation Authority, Atlanta, GA, April 2000. Image © 2000 Eliot Allen, Criterion Planners.

Our subsidies and inducements to drive do not end there. There are 8,271,117 lane-miles of highways, roads, and streets in the United States, nearly all of which are free to the motorist.[26] Less than 1 percent of these roadways charge tolls,[27] with gas taxes paying most of the cost of highway construction and maintenance, while the vast majority of local roads are paid for with local taxes.[28] Ready for more bad news? America's investment in automobiles and roads has resulted in an unprecedented rate of land consumption. During the past generation Americans have chosen to develop land at up to ten times the rate of population growth.[29] The external harm from this pattern of development is its consumption of undeveloped land that would otherwise provide natural habitat or land for agriculture. Internally this low-density development increases the travel distance between any two destinations (see Figure 1-14), making it ever more likely that people will drive.

This low-density development results in the highest per capita demands on natural systems and habitats. In a comparative analysis of two projects in Sacramento, California (Figure 1-15), the lower-density development resulted in across-the-board per capita increases in impervious land cover, miles driven, water use, energy use, air pollution, and greenhouse gas production.[30] At one extreme of the sustainable lifestyle spectrum is the Manhattan family who lives in a compact apartment, has no excess space to amass consumer goods, chooses to walk or use public transit, and has no lawn to water or fertilize. Unfortunately, the American lifestyle norm has gone in exactly the opposite direction.

It is troubling how the modest progress we are making in energy efficiency cannot keep up with our appetite for bigger houses and cars. While energy codes adopted by states and municipalities over the last few years have increased building energy efficiency per square foot, the size of the average American house appears to be increasing more quickly, canceling out any efficiency savings.

Even worse, since 1988 the United States has experienced a steady 2.5 percent annual increase in miles driven that are not being offset by any energy efficiency gains.[31] The Corporate Average Fuel Economy (CAFE) standards have been flat since 1972, a fact made worse by a loophole allowing SUVs (Figure 1-16) an exemption from the standards.

In addition to these adverse environmental impacts, the public infrastructure necessary to support this low-density development is expensive to build and maintain. Infrastructure is made up of the public facilities and services that are necessary—to support living in a community, including facilities—roads, pipes, and wires—as well as services education, police, and fire protection. The cost of building and maintaining infrastructure is divided among the number of people it serves, described as the cost per capita. National studies show that low-density development increases the cost of hard infrastructure, and with it the tax burden, in developed areas by an average of 11 percent.[32]

It should be clear now that the lifestyle choices we've made, our "rational" decisions to live in comfort and access jobs and stores by mechanical means, have inexorably altered our built environment. We are paying a terribly high price in individual health, a general sense of well-being, and happiness. We have alienated ourselves from nature, which we need to sustain us. Perhaps worst of all, we are jeopardizing our global climate and are confused as to the causes.

The conventional view in America is to think of cities as the source of the pollution that is causing climate change. Indeed, per unit of land area, cities generate a great deal of pollution (see the traditional view in Figure 1-17). However, on a per capita basis, city dwellers

Figure 1-12
Abundant *free* parking creates demand for driving.

Figure 1-13
Paving itself is made of oil or coal byproducts and creates toxic runoff.

Figure 1-14
Far-flung, autodependent suburbs will require complete redevelopment to support a sustainable urbanist lifestyle.

generate the least CO_2 (see the emerging view in Figure 1-17). The American dream of a large house on a large lot in the suburbs is what's most responsible for cooking the planet.

To rectify these wrongs we need to take a cold, hard look at some of our most cherished assumptions and pet comforts. We need the courage to challenge the course we have chosen, whose symptoms have been so long in the making and may seem so resistant to change. But it is not an optional effort. Too much is at stake. And if we approach it right, if we allow ourselves to explore and confront this resistance to change, then the rewards can be incalculable. Our plan is not to focus on the wrongs of the past; it is to chart a compelling future.

Comparison of Environmental Transect Performance in Sacramento, California

Design Context	Suburban	Antelope	Metro Square	Urban
Residential Density (net DU/ac)	0.20	7.00	20.00	35.00
Open Space (% total land area)	20.00	0.00	10.00	5.00
Employment Proximity (jobs w/i 1 mi.)	10.00	35.00	29,266.00	30,000.00
Street Density (centerline mi./sq.mi)	1.00	10.00	20.00	25.00
Transit Proximity (avg. ft. DU-closest stop)	25,000.00	23,500.00	665.00	400.00
Auto Use (total VMT/capita/day)	35.00	22.00	11.20	10.00
Environmental Performance				
Land Consumption (gross ac/capita)	10.00	0.06	0.02	0.01
Water Use (gal/capita/day)	200.00	160.00	102.00	50.00
Energy Use (MMBtu/capita/yr)	200.00	176.00	110.00	100.00
Imperviousness (impervious ac/DU)	0.20	0.04	0.03	0.03
Nonpoint Source Pollutants (kg/capita/yr)	0.04	0.03	0.02	0.01
Criteria Air Pollutants (lbs/capita/yr)	800.00	753.00	195.00	200.00
Greenhouse Gases (tons/capita/yr)	12.00	10.00	5.50	4.00

Figure 1-15
Per capita environmental impacts, across the board, decrease with increasing density. From E. Allen, "Measuring the Environmental Footprint of the New Urbanism," *New Urban News* 4, 6 (1999). Image © Criterion Planners.

Figure 1-16
This "light truck" gets less than 10 miles per gallon.

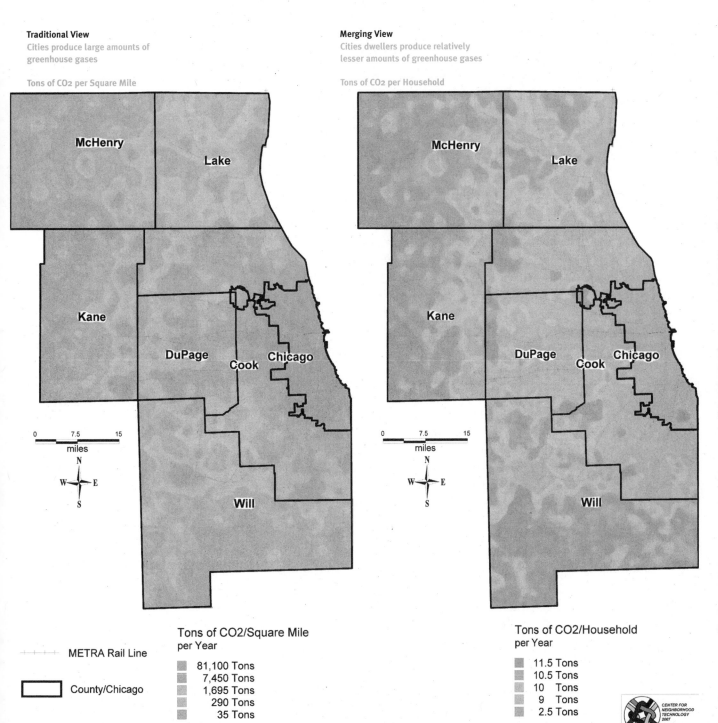

Two Views of Cities and CO2

CO2 Generated by Automobiles in the Chicago Region per Year

Figure 1-17
The emerging view of cities and CO2.
Image © Center for Neighborhood
Technology 2007.

Traditional View
Cities produce large amounts of
greenhouse gases

Tons of CO2 per Square Mile

Merging View
Cities dwellers produce relatively
lesser amounts of greenhouse gases

Tons of CO2 per Household

McHenry

Lake

Kane

DuPage

Cook

Chicago

Will

McHenry

Lake

Kane

DuPage

Cook

Chicago

Will

0   7.5   15
miles
N
W — E
S

0   7.5   15
miles
N
W — E
S

┼┼┼┼┼ METRA Rail Line

▭ County/Chicago

Tons of CO2/Square Mile
per Year

- 81,100 Tons
- 7,450 Tons
- 1,695 Tons
- 290 Tons
- 35 Tons

Tons of CO2/Household
per Year

- 11.5 Tons
- 10.5 Tons
- 10   Tons
- 9   Tons
- 2.5 Tons

CENTER FOR
NEIGHBORHOOD
TECHNOLOGY
2007

Pioneering Reforms: Setting the Stage for Sustainable Urbanism

"America is ready to turn the page. American is ready for a new set of challenges." Illinois Senator Barack Obama[33]

Sustainable urbanism draws attention to the enormous opportunity to redesign the built environment in a manner that supports a higher quality of life and promotes a healthy and sustainable American lifestyle. The basis for this transformation of the built environment is a synthesis of urbanism—the millennia-old tradition of human settlements—with late 20th Century environmentalism that started with Rachel Carson's *Silent Spring*. The synthesis of these two intellectual and practical histories requires a new consensus on the role of humans in nature. The best place to start this discussion is with the influential 1969 book *Design with Nature* [34] by Scottish landscape architect Ian McHarg.

While unknown to many today, this influential book was the first to explain to a relatively wide audience geographic information systems (GIS), the natural transect (Figure 1-18), and other ecological principles. *Design with Nature* also tells the story of McHarg's harsh reaction as a young man against the pollution, ugliness, and lack of vegetation in his native Glascow, which instilled in him, and many of his generation, a lifelong link between cities and pathology. The subtitle of this book *Urban Design with Nature* was chosen both to credit McHarg for his influential work, but also to rebut his bias against cities, his distaste for human systems, and his focus on wilderness free of humans.

Given how critical McHarg was of the design of cities, it is ironic that *Design with Nature* ignored the task of trying to improve cities by better integrating their design with natural systems. When asked why his book failed to address cities and "social systems," McHarg replied: "I had experienced four graduate years at Harvard, dominantly in social science, and concluded that much of it, conspicuously economics, was antithetical to ecology, while the remainder, including sociology, history, government, and laws, was oblivious to the environment. As I could not reconcile social science with ecology, I had simply excluded the subject." While not unique, McHarg's self-imposed blinders are indicative of the long-running divide between nature-focused environmentalists and human-focused urbanists. This obliviousness to human systems carried over to McHarg's built work—essentially well landscaped, auto-dependent suburbs—which are still mistakenly seen as sustainable development.

Sustainable urbanism grows out of three late 20th Century reform movements that have transcended McHarg's antisocial environmentalism to highlight the benefits of integrating human and natural systems. The smart growth, new urbanism and green building movements provide the philosophical and practical bones of sustainable urbanism. While all three share an interest in comprehensive economic, social and environmental reform, they differ greatly in their history, constituencies, approach, and focus.

Ocean	Beach	Primary Dune	Trough	Secondary Dune	Backdune	Bayshore	Bay
Tolerant	Tolerant	Intolerant	Relatively Tolerant	Intolerant	Tolerant	Intolerant	Tolerant
Intensive recreation	Intensive recreation	No passage, breaching	Limited recreation	No passage, breaching	Most suitable for	No filling	Intensive
Subject to	No building	or building	Limited structures	or building	development		recreation
pollution controls							

Each of these movements, highly worthy in and of itself, has suffered from a certain insularity, that has resulted in a myopia when it comes to searching for long-term solutions. Further, there has been an understandable but unfortunate tendency toward self-validation, resulting in an unwillingness to engage a larger, comprehensive agenda. For instance, a certified green building isn't really a positive for the environment when it turns out to be surrounded by a massive paved parking lot; a walkable neighborhood is hard to sustain when its houses are wastefully constructed and energy inefficient.

Sustainable urbanism attempts to bring these three important movements together and knit them into a design philosophy to allow and create truly sustainable human environments.

Smart Growth: The Environmental Conscience of Sustainable Urbanism

Smart Growth has its roots in the environmental movement of the 1970s which was strengthened by President Richard Nixon's environmentally focused legislative agenda. With bipartisan support, Nixon signed into law what serves as the backbone of United States environmental policy to this day (Figure 1-20). This includes the Clean Water Act, the Clean Air Act, the Endangered Species Act, the National Environmental Protection Act (NEPA), the Coastal Zone Management Act, as well as the creation of the Environmental Protection Agency.

Amidst this unique burst of federal environmentalism, Senator Henry "Scoop" Jackson introduced the National Land Use Policy Act in 1970.[35] Designed as a bookend to NEPA, it was intended to encourage states to develop coordinated state land use plans and proposed a new federal agency and land-planning database. The legislation passed twice in the Senate but failed in the House, and was then dropped amidst the turbulence of Nixon's second term. But while the proposed act failed, its proposal for state-by-state land use planning was adopted by several pioneering governors in the intervening years.

In Oregon, Governor Tom McCall proposed legislation to manage the state's population growth and land development, responding to Oregon's long tradition of land conservation and interest in preserving its scenic beauty. In 1973 Oregon's legislature passed a law requiring all the state's municipalities to designate Urban Growth Boundaries (UGBs), rings beyond which land development was not permitted.[36] These boundaries were designed to expand in an orderly fashion as each ring of land was developed. However, they remain the subject of serious debate. UGB succeeded in controlling the scope of land development, thus preserving the state's scenic treasures, but it did little to ensure the quality of development within the UGB, leading to well-located bad development, or what could be called "smart sprawl."

Figure 1-18
Natural Transect drawing by the office of Wallace, Roberts, McHarg & Todd, circa 1970. Image © Wallace Roberts & Todd, LLC.

Figure 1-19
A New Urbanist custom home builder throws away the material equivalent of one house for every five built.

Figure 1-20
Our nation's most environmental president, Richard M. Nixon. Image courtesy of the National Archives and Records Administration.

Other states took different approaches to regulating land use. Judy Corbett of the Local Government Commission has explained that Colorado Governor Roy Romer first used the term in 1995 when, concerned about sprawl in the State of Colorado, he put forward a new vision for what he called 'Smart Growth.' Former Maryland Governor Parris Glendening subsequently picked up and popularized the term. Maryland's state land use law was rooted in good governance—the extension of state-financed infrastructure to those areas with the lowest cost of delivering municipal services. Maryland's legislation, the Smart Growth and Neighborhood Conservation Program, was enacted in 1997 and designated urban growth areas that were eligible for state infrastructure. While the law remained in effect only until shortly after Glendening stepped down in January 2003, this strategy influenced other states, notably New Jersey, to follow suit. These development location criteria helped to inform similar criteria in LEED for Neighborhood Development (see Chapter 2).

The smart growth movement embraced a broader agenda in 1996 with the development of ten principles of smart growth (see sidebar), initiated by Harriet Tregoning, then Director of Development, Community, and Environment at the U.S. Environmental Protection Agency. At the time, many environmentalists were simply anti-growth and viewed all development, largely without distinction, as hostile to the environment. The principles were successful in uniting a decentralized grassroots movement of local and regional citizen activists and municipal leaders under the Smart Growth banner. However, the vagueness of the standards and the Smart Growth movement's decision to lend its name to development projects of sometimes minimal incremental improvement worked to devalue the smart growth "brand." Nonetheless, this national coalition of regional, not-for-profit organizations has a dedicated membership, promoting urban redevelopment and sound land conservation policies. The local, on-the-ground leaders who form the broad membership base of the smart growth movement are the foot soldiers of sustainable urbanism, and are essential to its success.

Congress for the New Urbanism: Sustainability's Urban Design Movement

The Congress for the New Urbanism (CNU) was founded by six architects—Peter Calthorpe, Andrés Duany, Elizabeth Moule, Elizabeth Plater-Zyberk, Stephanos Polyzoides, and Daniel Solomon—and first met as an organization in Alexandria, Virginia, in 1993. Many of the six founders had ties to Princeton University and collaborated on the design of Playa Vista, a large mixed-use development in California, and participated in the writing of the Ahwahnee Principles for Resource-Efficient Communities in 1991. They united around a shared vision of promoting traditional urbanism as an antidote to conventional sprawl and created an ad hoc organization to convene four annual congresses.

To best understand CNU, it helps to go back seventy-five years to the founding of the Congrès Internationale d'Architecture Moderne, or International Congress of Modern Architecture (CIAM), in 1928. Like CNU, CIAM was a design reform movement with a stated focus of bettering public health and design by improving cities and housing. At its core the CIAM movement was a humane and essential attempt to improve human health and sanitation; at the time large sections of the older cities of Europe were dangerous and unhealthy places to live, especially for the lower classes. CIAM's analysis accurately captured the gravity of the problem, citing "a mortality rate reaching as high as twenty percent" in some city quarters.[37]

The Ten Principles of Smart Growth

1. Create a range of housing opportunities and choices.
2. Create walkable neighborhoods.
3. Encourage community and stakeholder collaboration.
4. Foster distinctive, attractive places with a strong sense of place.
5. Make development decisions predictable, fair, and cost-effective.
6. Mix land uses.
7. Preserve open space, farmland, natural beauty, and critical environmental areas.
8. Provide a variety of transportation choices.
9. Strengthen and direct development toward existing communities.
10. Take advantage of compact building design.

"You never change things by fighting the existing reality. To change something, build a new model that makes the existing model obsolete." R. Buckminster Fuller

The CIAM reform movement brought together many of Europe's leading modernist architects including Gropius, Le Corbusier, Sert, and Aalto. Over nearly 30 years they conducted an ambitious program of annual retreats, design studies, and declarations, with the goal of establishing a comprehensive agenda for the reform of the built urban environment. The philosophy of CIAM combined three dissimilar intellectual strains: (1) humanistic reforms concerning the provision of dignified shelter, enhanced sanitation and health; (2) an enthusiastic embrace of the use of cars, the use of which required a redesign of the built environment; and (3) a preoccupation with modernist architectural styles and rational ("one size fits all") solutions.

CIAM's analysis of thirty-three cities became the basis for its Athens Charter published in 1943, "by which the destiny of cities will be set right."[38] A typical declaration reflecting the problems with cities read: "The nuclei of the old cities were generally filled with close-set structures and deprived of open space. But, in compensation, verdant spaces were directly accessible, just outside the city gates, making air of good quality available nearby."[39]

This idea that cities lacked "lungs" would come to shape the CIAM approach to the design and site planning of individual buildings. In a pivotal turn in the history of CIAM at its third congress, held in Brussels in 1930, the participants prepared design studies of housing alternatives, concluding that high-rise dwellings solved almost all of the cities' problems: "High structures respond to this purpose [the aeration of the city] since they permit a considerable increase in open spaces which can become reserves of trees and verdure. . ." These reserves closely encircling the dwelling-places will turn the joys of nature into a daily occurrence and not merely an optional Sunday pleasure."[40]

Indeed, this single CIAM congress served as the source for the "towers in the park" pattern of public housing development widely built in the United States following World War II (Figure 1-21), which, outside of New York City, has since been largely dismantled.

Particularly notable in the Athens Charter is the confident voice given to the needs—one might say rights—of drivers to travel at high speeds unimpeded by constraints. At the expense of pedestrians and a fine-grained street grid, this passage elevates the poor acceleration and braking of early cars as a fundamental basis for street design: "Before reaching their normal cruising speed, mechanized vehicles have to start up and gradually accelerate. Sudden braking can only cause rapid wear and tear on major parts. A reasonable unit of length between the starting up point and the point at which it becomes necessary to break must therefore be gauged. Street intersections today... are not suited to the proper operation of mechanized vehicles. They should be separated by intervals of from 200 to 400 yards."[41]

The CNU founders found direct ties between CIAM's vision of a so-called rational city and the postwar American suburbs' automobile dependence and segregated land uses. High speed street designs, land use segregation, and stand-alone buildings were all required in standard municipal regulations that still shape today's sprawling land uses. Furthermore, the ascendancy of modernist architectural training essentially erased all knowledge of pre-CIAM town planning techniques.[42] So when the CNU began to promote traditional town planning as an alternative to sprawl, it was largely forced to start from scratch.

A founding goal of the CNU was to write a charter that would rebut CIAM and its Athens Charter, and serve as the governing document for this reform movement. The final draft of the CNU Charter was developed through an intense collaboration among the founders over most of a year. It was debated, revised, and adopted by more than three hundred people at the fourth congress, in Charleston, South Carolina, in 1996. The Charter (see sidebar) has a preamble and three sections of nine articles each, organized by scale, starting with the region, city, town, and proceeding to cover the neighborhood, street, block, and building.

Auspicious for the CNU at that time, Henry Cisneros, then secretary of the U.S. Department of Housing and Urban Development, was among the charter signatories. The CNU principles were adopted as the centerpiece for the HOPE VI program of public housing revitalization, which aimed, fittingly, to dismantle and rebuild CIAM-inspired postwar public housing developments. This robust housing and community rebuilding program proved vital, introducing new urbanist principles to the real estate industry nationally and creating a market for new urbanist development.

Throughout the 1990s new urbanism became an increasingly large part of mainstream development practice, despite being dismissed by some as artificial instant urbanism. Its stature was reinforced by the impressive coffee table book *The New Urbanism* (1994),[43] which featured expensive, suburban greenfield and resort development, and was further promoted by Disney's decision to develop the town of Celebration, Florida, using new urbanist principles. The development industry embraced the look and feel of New Urbanism through the Urban Land Institute's repackaging of new urbanist work as "master planned communities" or "lifestyle centers."

The greatest strength of the CNU has been its design excellence and rhetorical mastery in communicating the vocabulary of urbanism as it related to clients' projects. It has excelled at creating mixed-use neighborhood developments and transit villages, featuring town centers, fine-grained walkable street grids, and a highly diverse ensemble of traditional buildings and architectural styles. Because the projects are routinely deemed illegal under local zoning laws and go against most conventional development practices, the new urbanists have pioneered new approval techniques (notably the town planning charrette).[44] The desire to control the long-term placement and design of buildings led to the development of form-based coding, a high-performance alternative to conventional Euclidean zoning (Figure 1-22).

The new urbanism has also developed significant new approaches to, and tools for, regional planning, a particularly challenging area due to our country's lack of regional government and planning authority. Among its accomplishments is Peter Calthorpe's innovative strategy as exemplified by the Envision Utah process, which his firm has used successfully to plan a large number of major metropolitan regions. The most successful of these plans have proven effective at influencing large regional investment decisions, such as transit system funding, road and highway alignments, and overall land use development patterns.

Figure 1-21
CIAM reforms inspired this Soviet-style public housing, now largely dismantled.
Image © 2002 Carolee Kokola.

Two other new urbanist innovations, the urban-rural transect and the Smart Code, both developed by Andrés Duany, principal of Duany Plater-Zyberk, also have the capacity to shape regions. The natural transect (Figure 1-23), developed in nineteenth-century Germany and mentioned earlier in this chapter in connection with Ian McHarg, is a longitudinal drawing used in ecology to describe the unique ecological niches found across a landscape. The urban-rural transect (Figure 1-24) applies this ecological framework to describe human settlements or place types across a spectrum of intensity ranging from wilderness to dense urban centers.

The Smart Code is a transect-based, form-based code which seeks to replace existing zoning codes with new codes of breathtaking clarity and simplicity. It combines aspects of conventional zoning codes, subdivision codes, and overlay districts into one integrated document. The Smart Code is an open framework that establishes code criteria to be "calibrated" locally. After only a few years, the Smart Code has been adopted by numerous cities and counties as the basis for their land development controls.

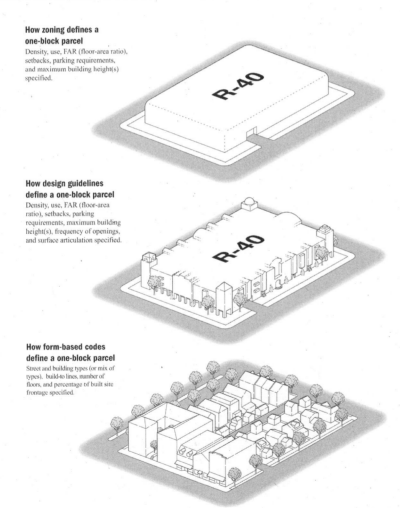

How zoning defines a one-block parcel
Density, use, FAR (floor-area ratio), setbacks, parking requirements, and maximum building height(s) specified.

How design guidelines define a one-block parcel
Density, use, FAR (floor-area ratio), setbacks, parking requirements, maximum building height(s), frequency of openings, and surface articulation specified.

How form-based codes define a one-block parcel
Street and building types (or mix of types), build-to lines, number of floors, and percentage of built site frontage specified.

Figure 1-22
Three forms of development regulation: conventional zoning, design guidelines, and form-based codes. Image © Peter Katz and Steve Price.

Figure 1-23
This ecological transect records soil, terrain, and vegetation. Used with permission from B. V. Barnes, University of Michigan, and with the permission of John Wiley & Sons, Inc.

Figure 1-24
The Urban-Rural Transect arrays a spectrum of place types. Image courtesy of Duany Plater-Zyberk.

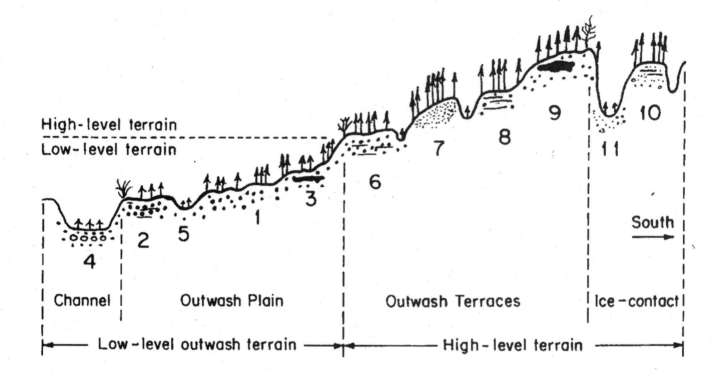

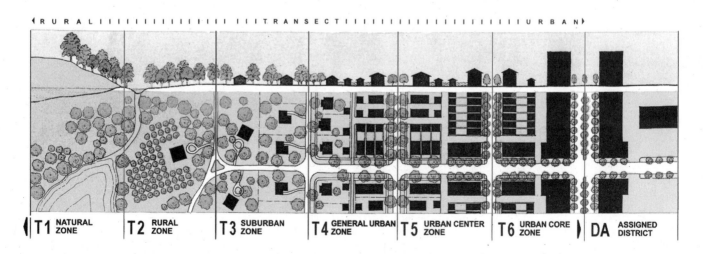

Despite its many achievements, however, the CNU has proved only somewhat successful in reforming state or national practices. In large part this is because the CNU has focused on convincing local regulators to create exceptions to conventional practice and to allow the approval of individual projects. While effective on a case-by-case basis, this pragmatic approach has left intact a foundation of hostile single-issue standards as well as a built environment that remains dominated by climate-changing sprawl.

A larger perspective is needed, one that goes beyond reviewing and debating the dozens of exemplary projects that members design each year. At this time, no national organization has taken on the call to systematically dismantle the regulations and subsidies, known best to CNU members working on the front lines, that generate sprawl. Nor has the CNU gone beyond its self-identification as an "elite" organization of creatives, declining to agree on standards of any sort so as not to limit the creative process. However, because of its effectiveness at design, persuasion, and selling, the CNU membership will play a leading role in implementing sustainable urbanism.

USGBC: Sustainability's Building Performance and Certification Movement

The oil shocks of the 1970s jump-started a movement for building energy efficiency and solar heated and powered buildings. Unfortunately these movements were unable to attract much governmental policy support throughout the 1980s and gained little traction. In 1993, however, the American Institute of Architect's Committee on the Environment, inspired by the 1992 Rio Earth Summit, published *The Environmental Resource Guide*. This comprehensive catalogue on the theory, practice, and technology of "environmental" buildings drew heavily on the pioneering work that preceded it.

This same confluence inspired the creation of the third founding reform of sustainable urbanism, the United States Green Building Council (USGBC). The USGBC was founded in Washington D.C., in 1993 by three development industry professionals: David Gottfried, Richard Fedrizzi, and Michael Italiano.[45] They too were inspired by the Rio Earth Summit and were largely concerned with the same intellectual ground explored in The Environmental Resource Guide. The USGBC made two very smart moves to accelerate the adoption of environmental or green building practices: it expanded its audience outside the architecture profession, and it sought to mobilize the private sector.

Shortly after its founding the USGBC drafted pioneering standards for green building, completing a "final" version in 1995. The name Leadership in Energy and Environmental Design (LEED) was adopted in 1996.[46] USGBC launched the pilot version in 1998 and its rating system in 2000. The LEED standard combines prerequisites, with optional credits that earn points toward an overall score. As a project's point score goes up it earns LEED certification at increasing levels of performance from Certified on the low end to Platinum on the high end. This flexibility works well in the marketplace, allowing a project to incorporate only well-suited green building strategies.

USGBC set an initial target of certifying 5 percent of the U.S. market for new construction buildings as green buildings under its LEED program. A helpful early breakthrough was the decision by the U.S. General Services Administration to adopt LEED standards as a requirement for all government-owned and -developed buildings. This single administrative act created a market for LEED-rated buildings and continues to deliver large square footages of LEED-certified projects every year. As a result, LEED has become an increasingly mainstream force that has refocused the entire building industry toward more sustainable practices.

By the end of 2006 there were more than forty thousand LEED Accredited Professionals—almost a baseball stadium (see Figure 1-26)—and increasing numbers of municipalities, universities, and private developers adopting LEED as a standard for their building portfolios.

The backbone of the success of LEED has been the ability of the U.S. Green Building Council to increase its staff and certification operations at a geometric pace while maintaining quality and integrity. This success is based on USGBC's ability to mobilize and harness a huge amount of volunteer effort from hundreds of professionals. So far LEED has found a middle ground between competing arguments that LEED documentation was too rigorous on one hand and no longer cutting edge on the other.

A second engine driving green building practice is the concept of integrated design: working in interdisciplinary teams to optimize overall building performance without adding construction cost. Integrated design teams have succeeded by reallocating existing budget monies to achieve a higher-performing building, largely by stressing the performance of systems over components. The classic illustration of design integration is increasing the energy performance of a building's envelope, which in turn enables the installation of a smaller and more efficient mechanical system.

The LEED system currently has two significant unrelated drawbacks. The first relates to the number of buildings that have actually achieved certification under the LEED system. In 2006, six years after LEED was launched, fewer than a thousand buildings have reached any level of certification (see Figure 1-27). This falls far short of any of the USGBC's ambitious market penetration goals and represents an insignificant number compared to the estimated 150,000 new buildings built each year in the United States. The low level of LEED certification poses a challenge for the USGBC, which wants to increase the number of certified projects while also raising the criteria for carbon reduction. USGBC will likely need to embrace municipal adoptions of LEED as code to yield a significant number of highly energy-efficient buildings necessary to achieve its goal.

The second shortcoming is LEED's building-centric focus and the low value it places on a project's location and context, particularly concerning auto-dependency. The dominant unit of reform within the LEED system remains the stand-alone building. The prerequisites and credit weightings from the original draft of LEED, heavily weighted toward the building itself, are nearly unchanged since 2000. In the flagship LEED-NC (LEED for New Construction), there are no prerequisites for location or context, and only about 6 percent of all credits address these issues.[47] This greatly limits the power of LEED certifications for individual buildings to have any effect on their surrounding context (see Figure 1-25). The original drafters of LEED can be forgiven for failing to adopt more rigorous land use and location criteria, since none existed at the time. Subsequent initiatives suggest a shift toward a more comprehensive view. In 2002, the USGBC Board of Directors inaugurated the LEED for Neighborhood Development rating system in partnership with the Congress for New Urbanism and the National Resource Defense Council. It is expected that this will begin to inform the remainder of LEED, presumably by increasing the weighting given to land use and transportation concerns. In 2005, in a significant signal of its intention to move beyond the stand-alone building, the USGBC board modified its mission to address both buildings and community. Because of its entrepreneurial outlook and enormous base of LEED Accredited Professionals, the USGBC is well positioned to be a virtual green army of sustainable urbanists

Figure 1-25
A green building project on this site could achieve LEED Platinum—the highest level of certification—despite its auto-dependent location.
Image © William T. Cook, Mauser Harmony with Nature Foundation.

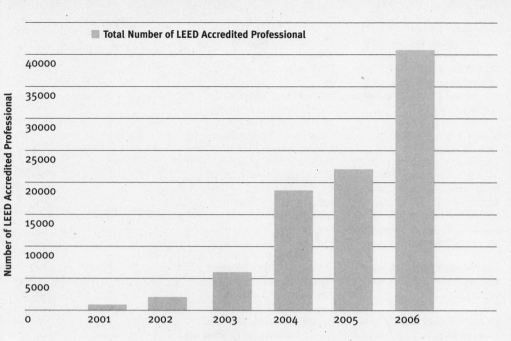

Figure 1-26
At current rates of growth, LEED
Accredited Professionals would fill
every seat of the Rose Bowl by 2015.
Data courtesy of the U.S. Green
Building Council.

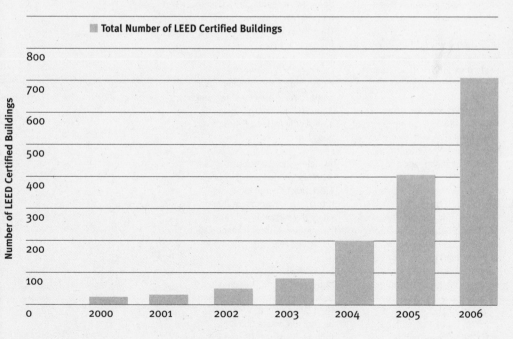

Figure 1-27
After roughly 7 years, the USGBC
has certified fewer than 1000 LEED
buildings. Data courtesy of the
U.S. Green Building Council.

Notes

1. Centers for Disease Control and Prevention, "Overweight and Obesity: Obesity Trends: U.S. Obesity Trends 1985–2005," http://www.cdc.gov/nccdphp/dnpa/obesity/trend/maps/index.htm (accessed September 29, 2006).

2. Centers for Disease Control and Prevention, "Overweight and Obesity: Home," http://www.cdc.gov/nccdphp/dnpa/obesity (accessed February 2, 2007).

3. Centers for Disease Control and Prevention, "Overweight and Obesity: Economic Consequences," http://www.cdc.gov/nccdphp/dnpa/obesity/economic_consequences.htm (accessed September 29, 2006).

4. "Obesity Threatens to Cut U.S. Life Expectancy, New Analysis Suggests," NIH News, http://www.nih.gov/news/pr/mar2005/nia-16.htm (accessed February 5, 2007).

5. T. Keith Lawton, "The Urban Structure and Personal Travel: An Analysis of Portland, or Data and Some National and International Data," Rand Corporation, http://www.rand.org/scitech/stpi/Evision/Supplement/lawton.pdf (accessed February 2, 2007).

6. James A. Wiley, John P. Robinson, Yu-Teh Cheng, Tom Piazza, Linda Stork, and Karen Pladsen, "Study of Children's Activity Patterns," California EPA Air Resources Board, #94-6, April 1994, summarized as "California's Children: How and Where They Can Be Exposed to Air Pollution, http://www.arb.ca.gov/research/resnotes/notes/94-6.htm (accessed February 2, 2007).

7. Consumer Product Safety Commission and Environmental Protection Agency, "The Inside Story: A Guide to Indoor Air Quality," http://www.cpsc.gov/cpscpub/pubs/450.html (accessed February 13, 2007).

8. Alisa Tanphanich, "U.S. TV Time Far Exceeds Time Spent on Exercise," Daily Californian, March 31, 2004, summarizing report by the National Human Activity Pattern Survey (NHAPS) study published in the International Journal of Behavioral Nutrition and Physical Activity, 2004.

9. U.S. Census Bureau, Current Population Survey, March: 1970 to 2000.

10. National Association of Home Builders, NAHB Public Affairs and NAHB Economics, "Housing Facts, Figures and Trends," March 2006, http://www.nahb.org/fileUpload_details.aspx?contentTypeID=7&contentID=2028 (accessed February 2, 2007), p. 14.

11. Sharon Begley, "How to Keep Your Aging Brain Fit: Aerobics," Wall Street Journal, November 16, 2006.

12. Elisabeth Rosenthal and Andrew C. Revkin, "Science Panel Says Global Warming Is 'Unequivocal,'" The New York Times, February 3, 2007.

13. Intergovernmental Panel on Climate Change, "CO2 Concentration, Temperature, and Sea Level Continue to Rise Long After Emissions Are Reduced," Climate Change 2001 Synthesis Report (SYR), Figure 5-2, http://www.ipcc.ch/present/graphics.htm (accessed February 19, 2007).

14. WWF, Living Planet Report 2002, http://www.panda.org/news_facts/publications/living_planet_report/lpr02 (accessed February 5, 2007).

15. Michael Pollan, The Omnivore's Dilemma: A Natural History of Four Meals (New York: Penguin, 2006), p. 182.

16. Rich Pirog, "Checking the Food Odometer: Comparing Food Miles for Local Versus Conventional Produce Sales to Iowa Institutions," Leopold Center for Sustainable Agriculture, Iowa State University, July 2003, http://www.leopold.iastate.edu/pubs/staff/files/food_travel072103.pdf (accessed February 19, 2007).

17. "U.S. Oil Demand by Sector, 1950–2004," Annual Energy Review, Tables 5.12a and 5.12b, U.S. Department of Energy, http://www.eia.doe.gov/pub/oil_gas/petroleum/analysis_publications/oil_market_basics/dem_image_us_cons_sector.htm (accessed February 3, 2007).

18. George W. Bush, State of the Union Address, January 31, 2006, http://www.whitehouse.gov/stateoftheunion/2006 (accessed February 5, 2007).

19. American Automobile Association, "Your Driving Costs 2005," http://aaanewsroom.net/Assets/Files/Driving_Costs_2005.pdf (accessed February 5, 2007), p. 4.

20. Energy Information Administration, "Energy Efficiency," Energy Kid's Page, http://www.eia.doe.gov/kids/energyfacts/saving/efficiency/savingenergy.html#Transportation (accessed February 5, 2007).

21. Marilyn A. Brown, Frank Southworth, and Therese K. Stovall, Towards a Climate-Friendly Built Environment, Pew Center on Global Climate Change, June 2005, p. 39, http://www.pewclimate.org/docUploads/Buildings%5FFINAL%2Epdf (accessed February 5, 2007).

22. Criterion Planners, "Impact Analysis of Smart Growth Land-Use Planning," report prepared for the Georgia Regional Transportation Authority, Atlanta, April 2000.

23. Victor Gruen, *Centers for the Urban Environment: Survival of the Cities* (New York: Van Nostrand Reinhold, 1973), p. 89.

24. Author's calculation: 1,000,000,000 spaces @ 350 square feet per space (including aisles) = 12,554 square miles.

25. Donald C. Shoup, *The High Cost of Free Parking* (Chicago: Planners Press, 2005).

26. U.S. Department of Transportation, Federal Highway Administration, Conditions and Performance Report, Exhibit 2-7, 2002. http://www.fhwa.dot.gov/policy/2002cpr/Ch2b.htm.

27. World Bank Group, "Toll Roads and Concessions," http://www. worldbank. org/transport/roads/ toll_rds.htm (accessed February 5, 2007).

28. Todd Litman, "Whose Roads? Defining Bicyclists' and Pedestrians' Right to Use Public Roadways," Victoria Transport Policy Institute, November 30, 2004, http://www.vtpi.org/whoserd.pdf (accessed February 5, 2007), p. 6.

29. Henry Diamond and Patrick Noonan, "Change in Metropolitan Population and Developed Land Area, 1970-1990," *Land Use in America,* Washington D.C.: Island Press, 1996.

30. E. Allen, "Measuring the Environmental Footprint of the New Urbanism," *New Urban News,* December 1999.

31. U.S. Department of Transportation, Federal Highway Administration, "Air Quality Trends Analysis," http://www.fhwa.dot. gov/environment/vmt_grwt.htm (accessed February 5, 2007).

32. *Costs of Sprawl—2000,* TCRP Report 74, Transit Cooperative Research Program, Transportation Research Board, National Research Council, 2002, http:// onlinepubs. trb.org/onlinepubs/tcrp/tcrp_rpt_74-a.pdf (accessed February 5, 2007). Calculations done by author from data on pp. 222, 249.

33. Barack Obama, broadcast of Manchester, New Hampshire, book signing, National Public Radio, December 10, 2006.

34. Ian L. McHarg, *Design with Nature* (New York: John Wiley and Sons, 1992 [1969]), p. v.

35. Government Law Center, Albany Law School, "Smart Growth and Sustainable Development: Threads of a National Land Use Policy," spring 2002, http://www.governmentlaw.org/files/VLR-Smart_growth.pdf (accessed February 13, 2007), p. 4.

36. Oregon State Senate, Oregon Land Use Act (SB 100), enacted 1973, http://www.oregon.gov/LCD/docs/bills/sb100.pdf (accessed February 5, 2007).

37. Le Corbusier, *The Athens Charter* (New York: Viking, 1973 [1943]), p. 54.

38. Ibid., p. 25.

39. Ibid., p. 54.

40. Ibid., p. 20.

41. Ibid., p. 81.

42. John Norquist, president, Congress for the New Urbanism, speech, January 2004, McLean County, Illinois.

43. Peter Katz, *The New Urbanism: Toward an Architecture of Community* (New York: McGraw-Hill, 1994).

44. Bill Lennertz and Aarin Lutzenhiser, *The Charrette Handbook: The Essential Guide for Accelerated, Collaborative Community Planning* (Chicago: American Planning Association, 2006).

45. David Gottfried, *Greed to Green: The Transformation of an Industry and a Life* (Berkeley, CA: WorldBuild, 2004).

46. Rob Watson, "What a Long Strange Trip It's Been," PowerPoint presentation, Greenbuild Conference, Atlanta, 2005.

47. LEED for New Construction, Version 2.2, October 2005, U.S. Green Building Council, https://www.usgbc.org/ShowFile.aspx?DocumentID=1095 (accessed February 24, 2007).

Chapter 2
Sustainable Urbanism:
Where We Need to Go

Sustainable Urbanism:
The Grand Unification

Our times offer an historic opportunity for society to rethink where and how we live, work, play, and shop. The path to a sustainable lifestyle builds on the principles of smart growth, new urbanism, and green buildings. If successful, it will not only vastly reduce environmental harm but also offer stunning enhancements to the current quality of life. The setting for this lifestyle is sustainable urbanism, the creation and support of communities that are so well designed for a high quality of life that people will eagerly opt to meet their daily needs on foot and transit. Compared to the American lifestyle as we now know it, the quality of a life lived in sustainable urbanism is healthier, happier, more independent and not least of all longer. What's not to like? (See Figure 2-1.)

Figure 2-1
Vibrant streets accommodate diverse land uses and mobility choices.

Our choice of lifestyle, that stubborn adherence to the wrong course, remains a significant barrier to the improved health and prosperity of individuals and families as well as to the viable future of our communities and country. Beyond that is the truly frightening prospect of planetary climactic change. The work and principles of the aforementioned groups and movements—smart growth, new urbanism, and green buildings as represented by USGBC and LEED—are heartening developments. They are essential stepping-stones. Individually, however, none can solve the challenges that face us. Only with a concerted effort, only by fusing their various initiatives into a cooperative whole, can we forge a new framework that supports a truly sustainable lifestyle.

In other words, the rules of what constitutes sustainable development are hereby changed, or more accurately, established for the first time. It is no longer acceptable to build a high-performance building in a greenfield, automobile-dependent context and have it certified as "green." It is no longer good enough to develop in a responsible location and build an admirable, walkable, mixed-use neighborhood while ignoring the level of resources required to build and maintain the buildings there. The time for half measures has passed.

It is not that any of these sustainability achievements is insignificant or not praise-worthy; it is just that they are optimizing the components of a dead-end, automobile-dependent or resource squandering pattern of development. Cognizant of the benefits of design integration, leaders committed to sustainable urbanism now can and will choose not to build in a bad location at all, or without a walkable, mixed-use context, or without integrating high-performance buildings and infrastructure. The times demand that the design and development of human settlements both pursue a big vision *and* sweat the details.

Reduced to its most basic tenets, sustainable urbanism is *walkable and transit-served urbanism integrated with high-performance buildings and high-performance infrastructure.* Compactness (density) and biophilia (human access to nature) are core values of sustainable urbanism. The structure of traditional urbanism is synonymous with the framework of urbanism described in the charter of the Congress for the New Urbanism. It comprises three essential elements: neighborhoods, districts, and corridors. According to the CNU charter, neighbor-hoods are "compact, pedestrian-friendly, and mixed-use."[1] Districts, like neighborhoods, should be compact and pedestrian-friendly, but typically have a single use—think college campus or industrial park. Corridors, ranging from "boulevards and rail lines to rivers and parkways, connect neighborhoods and districts."[2]

To the American public the most appealing aspect of sustainable urbanism is certain to be the sustainable neighborhood. Built on the American tradition of Main Street and neigh-borhood planning advanced by the new urbanists, this book rigorously defines the sustain-able neighborhood to enable its understanding and design and to support the establishment of performance expectations. Sustainable urbanism emphasizes that the personal appeal and societal benefits of neighborhood living—meeting daily needs on foot—are greatest in neighborhoods that integrate five attributes: definition, compactness, completeness, connectedness, and biophilia. Compactness and biophilia, also core attributes of the sustain-able corridor, will be discussed later in this essay, as will high performance buildings and infrastructure. Part 3 of this book, "Emerging Thresholds of Sustainable Urbanism," provides potential benchmarks and rules of thumb for designing sustainable neighborhoods and corridors. Let's examine the neighborhood attributes one by one.

Defined Center and Edge

Since ancient times, neighborhoods have been the basic unit of human settlements. The earliest citation for *neighborhood* in the *Oxford English Dictionary* predates Columbus's arrival in America. It defines neighborhood in social, spatial, and character terms, including "community," "the people living near to a certain place," and a "portion of a town or county frequently considered in reference to the character or circumstances of its inhabitants." A more perform-ance-based definition of neighborhood used by new urbanists is a settlement that has a defined center and edges, is walkable, and is diverse in terms of building types, people, and uses. The classic illustration defining the neighborhood for the modern era is Clarence Perry's neighborhood unit, first developed in 1924 and later published in the *Regional Plan of New York and Its Environs.*[3] It called for an ideal neighborhood size of 160 acres bounded by major streets, a mix of retail, office, civic, and park uses connected by a street network, and a population large enough to support a walk-to elementary school (see Figure 7-1). Perry's neighborhood diagram was highly influential with the new urbanists in the 1990s, serving as an ideal unit for planning and phasing large-scale new urbanist projects. However, the ideal did not always correspond to development reality, with many self-declared "neighborhoods" either too small to support any land use variety or too large to be considered walkable. Victor Dover addresses this problem by proposing a minimum neighborhood size threshold of 40 acres and a maximum of 200 acres, with a neighborhood center comprising between 6 and 10 percent of the total land (see Chapter 7).

Among the many benefits of defined neighborhoods is a finite social network. The sidewalks and close quarters typical of urban neighborhoods encourage sociability. The limited size of a neighborhood increases the chances of being recognized or met by an acquaintance or friend—of being known. People enlarge their circles of acquaintances and friends by daily contact on the street, on porches, in third places, and through local organizations and activities. This enlarged network of friends and acquaintances can increase well-being and social capital—the advantage created by a person's location in a structure of relationships.

So many Americans are transients—moving to attend school, get a better job, or find housing better suited to their needs—that on average we move eleven times in a lifetime.[4] While moving to a new place can expand social networks, moving also increases the difficulty of maintaining relationships with people who are no longer close by. Neighborhoods that offer a full range of housing types at least allow individuals and families to "age in place" by offering housing suited to every phase of life. The lifelong relationships and deep social connections that go along with aging in place, according to the emerging field of happiness research, have been correlated with increased health, happiness, and longevity (see Figure 2-2).[5]

The limited size of a neighborhood also serves to increase the convenience and value of relationships and the transactions that occur *inside* it, encouraging a change in behavior. For instance, nowadays people balance cost, convenience, and quality in deciding where or how they want to shop. A focus on cost may lead them to Wal-Mart, convenience to the Internet, and quality to a smaller shop offering personalized service. However, many people shop only on the basis of cost, not realizing or caring that their purchasing decisions undermine the viability of local businesses. Ideally, a bounded neighborhood increases the potential for residents to develop personal relationships with the local merchants and vice versa, building customer loyalty, creating value and convenience, and changing how people decide where to shop.

As described in the CNU charter, bounded neighborhoods "form identifiable areas that encourage citizens to take responsibility for their maintenance and evolution."[6] Sustainable urbanism holds that a bounded neighborhood should play a key role in girdling the distance beyond which key social and environmental concerns cannot be shifted.

Sustainable urbanism expands the role of the neighborhood to address its proportionate share of society's social and environmental needs. As an example, most everyone agrees that the United States needs to house its poorest, eldest, and most infirm citizens, but many otherwise reasonable citizens band together into not-in-my-backyard (NIMBY) groups to exclude certain demographic populations from living nearby or to prevent any new development. While less an act of willful neglect than the prior examples, the "out of sight, out of mind" attitude of many Americans toward stormwater and wastewater merits comment. People are concerned mostly that stormwater and wastewater leave their building or site and not so much about where they go. Sustainable urbanism's commitment to filter all its stormwater within the neighborhood and its surrounding open space assigns clear responsibility to a neighborhood (see Figure 2-3). The bounded sustainable neighborhood is the physical manifestation of the phrase popularized by environmentalist David Brower: "Think globally, act locally."

Figure 2-2
A defined, complete neighborhood encourages strong social networks.

Figure 2-3
Green boulevards can define neighborhoods, grow food, and process waste.

Sustainable urbanism is simply not achievable at low densities, below an average of seven or eight dwelling units per acre.[7] Christopher Leinberger of the Brookings Institution echoes this: FARs (floor area ratios—the percentage of land covered by the equivalent of one story buildings) between 0.05 and 0.30, typical of current drivable suburban development, "do not efficiently support transit" and result in neighborhoods where "there are generally no destinations that are walkable on a day-in, day-out basis" (see Figure 2-4).[8] For these reasons, sustainable urbanism requires minimum development densities roughly four times higher than the average new U.S. development density of two dwelling units per acre.

While the real estate market ultimately determines development density, these density thresholds are achievable in neighborhood-scale projects across the country. This is done by offering a spectrum of housing types, ranging from multifamily dwellings to large-lot detached single-family homes, all in the same neighborhood. Within a neighborhood it makes sense to concentrate density in the neighborhood center with the upper-floor dwellings and lower-floor businesses adding vitality and pedestrian buying power.

Increasing neighborhood population density also supports improved public transit service. The frequency of service and number of types of transit (bus, trolley, etc.) increase as the market of people willing and able to walk to the station increases. Concentrating development density in and around transit stops and adjacent to transit corridors maximizes this population. Increasing density reduces the length of walk trips, can reduce car ownership and use (miles driven per family), and can shift car trips to walking trips, sometimes dramatically. According to researcher John Holtzclaw, "San Francisco's higher density and better transit service shortened trip lengths sufficiently to allow one mile [ridden] on transit to replace eight miles of driving," as compared to outlying suburbs (see Figure 2-5).[9]

Increased population within a reasonable walking distance of a neighborhood center also increases the primary market area for those goods and services. A larger neighborhood population increases purchasing power for goods and services and enhances the sustainability of those business enterprises.

Sustainable urbanism seeks to create sustainable neighborhood businesses by integrating them with a permanent market of surrounding residential density. This is contrary to current development practices for neighborhood retail which rely overwhelmingly on the automobile traffic passing by the neighborhood rather than customers on foot.[10] This conventional practice can isolate neighborhood retail from its walk-to neighborhood customers. This, along with commercial overzoning, discourages neighborhood retail. Neighborhoods that combine a critical mass of uses with high residential density create viable long-term neighborhood commercial opportunities.

Sustainable urbanism also recognizes that the opportunities to integrate infrastructure design increase with density. At high enough densities, concentrated mixed-use development can support district energy systems, reducing carbon generation by 30 percent and energy consumption by as much as 50 percent.[11] The per capita pipe and trench lengths required for district systems shorten as density rises, increasing their viability. Compared with detached single-family housing, the reduced building envelope of attached multifamily housing can reduce the energy required to heat and cool by 30–35 percent.[12]

Figure 2-4
Sprawl's low development densities and segregated land uses preclude walk-to destinations.

Figure 2-5
The density of this lovely street supports robust walk-to destinations.

Compact development is also good for the natural world. Adding population to an already developed place helps protect undeveloped and sensitive lands by concentrating development in one part of a watershed and works to maintain viable habitat in the remainder. It can also decrease the paved area per person, further improving water quality. Compactness, as compared to conventional development, is essential to achieving sustainable urbanism's potential benefits for communities, regions, and the planet.

Completeness: Daily and Lifelong Utility

Neighborhoods exist to meet both one's daily needs and one's needs over a lifetime. To meet these short- and long-term needs and to support robust life choices, neighborhoods need to include a wide variety of land uses, building types, and dwelling types (see Figure 2-6).

Neighborhoods are places where all daily needs can be met on foot. Sustainable urbanism turns this capability into an expectation that, with great design, people will *prefer* to meet their daily needs on foot. Ideally, from the time people get out of bed in the morning until they go to sleep at night, they will be able to live a high-quality life without needing a car to achieve it. The enticement to walk to a neighborhood center is the presence of a corner store, a day care center, a newsstand, a coffee shop, a deli, a food market, a transit stop, offices, and workshops. An increasing number and variety of commercial uses in a neighborhood center increases its completeness and its power to draw walkers to it. Add a neighborhood plaza, a post office, a school, or a place of worship and this becomes the go-to civic place for community events. This ability to meet daily needs on foot creates universal independence at opposite ends of the age spectrum—it benefits the youngster who is not yet licensed to drive as well as the elder who can no longer drive. With thoughtful detailing, this same environment can also provide independence to people with mobility impairments.

Completeness also refers to the diversity of dwelling types needed to accommodate the varied needs for housing over a lifetime. Young adults moving out of the family home often start by renting a small, low-cost apartment. As their economic circumstances improve, they move up by renting a better apartment and perhaps eventually by purchasing an condominium. If they get married and start a family, they may buy a modest starter home. As their income and family grow, they trade up to a larger home. Once they are "empty nesters," parents may move to a smaller home requiring less maintenance or stair climbing. Finally, in old age people may need to move into an assisted-living facility or a nursing home. Maintaining lifelong relationships with family and friends has been shown to increase health and longevity.[13] Aging in place allows relationships to be foot-powered, avoiding the expense and energy use of cars or airplanes. A neighborhood that provides a full range of housing types allows people and families to remain in the neighborhood even as their housing needs change.

Connectedness: Integrating Transportation and Land Use

Sustainable urbanism means that people have abundant opportunities to walk, ride, bike, and even use a wheelchair around the neighborhood, as well as having access to good transit service to adjacent neighborhoods and regional destinations (see Figure 2-7). To achieve internal connectedness, the entire neighborhood needs sidewalks on both sides of the street, and the distance between intersections needs to be relatively short, ideally no longer than 300–400 feet. The majority of the street network should be designed for a

Figure 2-6
A complete neighborhood includes retail and commercial uses and a range of housing types.

Figure 2-7
Connectedness, the antidote for auto dependence, gives people mobility choices within their neighborhood and corridor.

Figure 2-8
Bikes can share traffic lanes on low-speed streets.

maximum automobile speed of 25–30 miles per hour, and the widest street should have no more than two travel lanes between curbs (see Figure 2-8). These low-speed streets have many benefits and are vitally important—not only are they safer for pedestrians and able to accommodate sharing the street network, but they also have the greatest capacity to move vehicles (see Figure 2-9).

Starting at an early age, kids can get daily exercise and gain some independence by walking to school on a grid of safe, narrow streets. The percentage of school-aged children walking or bicycling to school in the United States has reached an all-time low of just 31 percent of those who live less than one mile from school and only 15 percent for all students.[14] To reverse that trend, elementary schools either should be located in the center of a neighborhood with enough population to support them or should straddle adjacent neighborhoods.

Sustainable Corridors

Transit corridors are the backbone of sustainable urbanism, linking neighborhoods together with districts and other regional destinations (see Figure 6-1). Sustainable urbanist developments need to be located in existing or proposed transit corridors and with sufficient properly-distributed density to support a robust level of bus, bus rapid transit, streetcar, trolley, or light rail service. A core tenet of sustainable urbanism is its commitment to tightly integrating transportation technology—subway, trolley, bus—with the density and distribution of adjacent land uses, a pattern essential to an automobile-independent lifestyle.

Sustainable urbanism also recognizes that Americans require dependable transit to make the lifestyle-altering decision to live in a sustainable corridor and rely on fewer or no cars. They need to be certain that the transit route cannot be realigned or the transit service abandoned, an assurance provided only by strong transit funding, high-density corridors and/or fixed-route transit. Sustainable corridors also support all kinds of utility infrastructure and can also provide wildlife corridors linking habitats within and across a region.

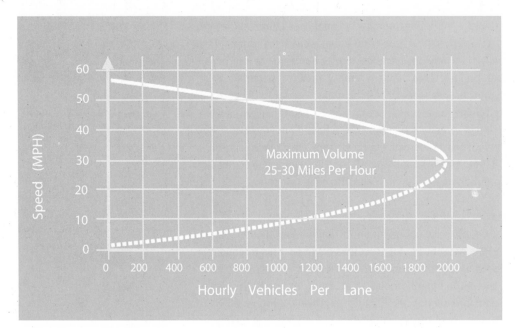

Figure 2-9
Narrow two-lane street networks have the greatest capacity to convey pedestrians and automobiles. From *Special Report 209: Highway Capacity Manual,* © 1985 by the Transportation Research Board, National Research Council, Washington, D.C., Figure 7-2. Reprinted with permission of TRB.

Shelley Poticha, a national expert on transit-oriented development, stresses the dominant role that corridors play in viable transit systems nationwide. More than three decades of retrospective research on existing transit-served areas by Jeffrey Zupan, John Holtzclaw, and Reid Ewing, among others, documents the key correlation between development density and levels of transit service. The received wisdom from this body of research is that a minimum corridor development density of seven dwelling units per gross or net acre is necessary to support basic bus service and a minimum of somewhere between fifteen and twenty dwelling units per acre is necessary to support streetcar or trolley service.[15] Sustainable urbanism embraces these thresholds as the integrating link between land use patterns and viable transportation.

Land use patterns routinely co-evolved with transit through the 1920s and 1930s, exemplified by the linear density generated by the continuous boardings possible in a streetcar corridor.[16] These legacy transit corridors have tended to retain their adjacent land use configuration even when the transit was later removed. Many of the most successful new light rails starts built in the last few years occupy parts of former streetcar corridors. However, most new American suburbs developed when land use was no longer integrated with transit corridors, resulting in an automobile-dependent dystopia. Consequently, contemporary transit planning focuses on stringing together the significant destinations within a region—for example, Denver's light rail—with widely spaced stops occurring at nodes of concentrated development.

Sustainable urbanism pragmatically, and of necessity, embraces both of these approaches. Over the next generation the demand for transit-served development sites will far outstrip the supply.[17] If sustainable urbanism is to become the dominant pattern of American development by 2030, a large number of sustainable urbanist projects will have to be developed as "transit-ready". Transit-readiness cannot be done after the fact by stand-alone developments. Transit-readiness requires development to be located in corridors that link to employment centers and satisfy transit warrants—the development density and configuration that will entice the public transit agency to extend transit service. Noted regional planner Peter Calthorpe believes that corridors, rather than neighborhoods or municipalities, are the urban scale in which to balance jobs and housing.[18] Sustainable urbanism embraces this approach as well.

Utility integration is another function of corridors. Conventional electrical, gas, and sewer systems should be located in corridors and coordinated with the adjacent land uses. The same is true for piping for district heating, cooling, and graywater systems.

Transit-readiness includes:

1. Locating the project in an approved public transit corridor with a planned balance of residences and employment

2. Entering into a transit warrant program with the regional transit agency

3. Satisfying the transit agency's transit warrant, which likely requires a minimum corridor density of seven dwelling units per acre, with provisions to allow as-of-right density to increase to fifteen dwellings per acre or greater

4. Clustering density along proposed alignments and around transit stops

Human life is not viable and human health is not possible without manifold free services provided by the Earth. The Earth receives sunlight, cleanses water, makes oxygen, and grows plants that feed humans and other animals. Humans evolved outdoors, immersed in natural vegetated habitats and exposed to sunlight, fresh air, and water. *Biophilia* is the name given to the human love of nature based on this intrinsic interdependence between humans and other living systems (see Figure 2-10).

Although there is no definitive estimate of the size of the native human population of North America at the time of Christopher Columbus's arrival, most historians have estimated that there were between 1 million and 12 million people.[19] Considering the enormous landmass of North America, these first peoples were spread sparsely over a vast wilderness. Humans were an integral part of the cycles of nature, a relationship that could be sustained indefinitely with sparse human populations. While some portion of the population was migratory, moving seasonally between camps located near growing plots or hunting grounds, others were settled in semipermanent villages. The largest precolonial settlement north of the Rio Grande River was thought to be Cahokia, located in what is now Illinois, just northeast of modern-day St. Louis, with an estimated population of between 8,000 and 40,000 at its zenith, just before Columbus sailed to America.[20] Even in this largest settlement, life was largely lived outdoors and in direct contact with nature.

Privately owned land, a concept introduced to North America by Europeans, favored the creation of permanent fixed colonies and settlements. During the industrializing decades before and after the turn of the twentieth century, private developers expanded towns into cities at an amazing clip. Land was cleared, swamps were drained, streams and rivers were put into pipes, and the profit motive discouraged the use of land for parks. Coal heat and smoke-stack industries polluted city air. Runoff and untreated sewage contaminated surface water bodies. Public lighting blocked views of the heavens.

Unlike the earlier life lived largely outdoors and in direct contact with nature, nature in the industrial city consisted of lawns, street trees, and public parks. Despite the many benefits urbanism bestows on the Earth, conventional urbanism obliterates virtually all the systems of nature it comes into contact with.

Automobile-dependent suburbs do the same, but without the benefits of urbanism. Conventional postwar suburbs approached land development and infrastructure similar to the industrial city, though at much lower densities, well below those necessary to support walk-to destinations or transit. While these lower densities allowed a higher percentage of the land area to consist of vegetation, much of it is residual and fenced into small private parcels, devaluing the utility of this unbuilt land for both human delight and nonhuman habitat.

As a consequence of this tendency of all types of human settlement to suppress nature, most people live out of daily contact with natural systems. They have no idea where their water or food or energy comes from or where their liquid or solid wastes go. As they get no feedback regarding the enormous stress that their lifestyle places on nature, they conduct their daily lives largely unconstrained by concerns about it.

This disconnect from nature is increasingly thought to contribute to a number of psychological harms, such as increased stress and attention deficit hyperactivity disorder (ADHD).[21] Rather than reconnecting with nature, we more and more frequently try to patch over these unmet psychological needs with pharmaceuticals. A sedentary lifestyle—one with little built-in daily physical activity—is also a big factor in our well-documented obesity epidemic.

Sustainable urbanism seeks to connect people to nature and natural systems, even in dense urban environments. The passive benefits to humans of introducing daylight and fresh air *indoors* are potentially dwarfed by implementing active-living strategies *outdoors*. People are three times more likely to walk along landscaped pedestrian routes.[22] Mature tree cover can further encourage daily outdoor activity by cooling outdoor summer temperatures between five and ten degrees Fahrenheit.[23] It can also increase the value of adjacent real estate by 3–6 percent.[24] Regular walking can reverse age-related brain deterioration.[25] Dense vegetation provides viable habitat for songbirds, adding an aural benefit. Taken together, the human benefits of living proximate to vegetation and habitats are immense, and are captured by studies that document the willingness of homebuyers to pay up to a 24 percent premium for a house lot facing a park or natural area.[26]

While people can derive immediate benefit and pleasure from seeing landscaping and natural areas, most other aspects of human interdependence with nature are neither visible nor immediately recognizable. With the resource flows that support our lifestyles hidden from view, should we be surprised if our lifestyle is unsustainable? In order to strengthen human interdependence with natural systems, sustainable urbanism believes that human settlements need to be designed to make resource flows visible and experiential. For example, a wastewater system that extracts nutrients to grow food in one's neighborhood creates an incentive not to dump toxic chemicals down the drain. The ability to see and experience where resources are produced and where they go after they are used promotes a human lifestyle better integrated with natural systems.

Finally, sustainable urbanism is committed to the ongoing livelihood of nonhuman species located in habitats close to human settlements. While sustainable urbanism recognizes the harm caused by human encroachment on natural habitats, it also recognizes the greater benefit of providing immersive nature within a reasonable walking distance of human settlements. Sustainable urbanism embraces the interweaving of riparian and wildlife corridors between and through neighborhoods (see Figure 2-11). Weaving habitat corridors through human settlements requires the creation of "critter crossings" (see Figure 2-12). Roads, the human intervention most lethal to animals, must bridge over or tunnel under habitat corridors to create connectivity for nonhuman species. As a basic interspecies courtesy, the edges of the corridors must be landscaped, fenced, or even grade-separated to deter animals from wandering freely in a neighborhood.

Two Further Concerns: High-Performance Infrastructure and Integrated Design

In addition to the five essential attributes of sustainable neighborhoods above, there are two related areas that merit attention: high-performance infrastructure and integrated design.

High-performance infrastructure is an emerging field that combines many strains of reform: the smart-growth concern about the financial burden imposed by new infrastructure needed to support greenfield development, the new urbanist's desire for humane, pedestrian-scaled infrastructure design, and the green building movement's focus on resource "greening" and consumption efficiencies (see Chapter 9). More than fifteen years of smart-growth studies have documented that low-density, automobile-dependent development results in higher

Figure 2-10
People benefit immensely from daily contact with nature.

Figure 2-11
This conceptual campus plan is organized around a biodiversity ring including critter crossings. Image © 2007 Loebl Schlossman & Hackl.

Figure 2-12
Grade separated critter crossings are essential when habitat corridors intersect roads.

per capita municipal infrastructure and service costs than does more compact development.[27] A compact pattern of infrastructure conserves the physical materials necessary to construct them as well as the fiscal resources necessary to finance and maintain them.

New urbanism has demonstrated the benefits of infrastructure effectiveness over simple efficiency. A cul-de-sac street system can efficiently access the most building lots per unit of street length, and omitting alleys reduces per capita paving. However, dead-end cul-de-sacs increase vehicle miles traveled (VMTs) by reducing connectivity, and the absence of alleys drives the need for front-yard driveways and garbage collection, compromising walkability.

Government-owned infrastructure—streets, parks, schools, sewers, buses, trees, wetlands, and the like—often represents the most valuable assets of a municipality. Until recently there were no requirements to account for these assets in audited financial statements. In 1999, the Government Accounting Standards Board (GASB) published Standard 34, which for the first time require municipalities to account for the cost of constructing and maintaining their infrastructure.[28] This accounting change is expected to begin to drive reform in the design and ongoing maintenance of government infrastructure and to introduce life cycle analysis into infrastructure accounting.

The green building concern with urban heat islands, stormwater filtration, recycled and local content, and life cycle costs is also starting to alter conventional infrastructure practices. Impervious surfaces, an unavoidable aspect of human urbanization, are environmentally destructive because they alter native hydrology, cause erosion, and concentrate flooding and water pollution. These paved surfaces are often dark and absorb heat, contributing to the urban heat island phenomenon. The U.S. Environmental Protection Agency has estimated that the heat island effect raises ambient neighborhood temperatures between two and ten degrees Fahrenheit.[29] Emerging practice addresses this through new approaches to the design and maintenance of the surface and subsurface of public rights-of-way (ROWs), including stormwater-filtering streets and fifty-year paving. Other significant ROW innovations include trenchless utilities and dark urban skies. The pioneering *High Performance Infrastructure Guidelines,* recently published by the New York City Department of Design and Construction, is the first documentation of this emerging field (see Figure 2-13).[30]

Figure 2-13
A high-performance stormwater street. Image © Mathews Nielsen Landscape Architects PC, New York, NY; High Performance Infrastructure Guidelines, October 2005, Design Trust for Public Space, www.designtrust.org., and New York City Department of Design and Construction.

High Performance Buildings

The US Green Building Council's LEED green building standard is one of a number of voluntary leadership standards for enhancing the environmental performance of buildings. In order to gain market acceptance, most all green building programs in the U.S. combine minimal fixed performance requirements with an optional menu of sustainable building practices. This means that a building might be certified as "green" even though it fails to perform well in any given category, including energy efficiency. A 2003 study of LEED-certified buildings concluded they were on average 25 to 30% more energy-efficient than conventional buildings, but acknowledged that there is great variability in performance.[31] Sustainable urbanism promotes voluntary leadership standards such as LEED as an essential transitional step to develop expertise and support for the concept of future mandatory high performance requirements.

Sustainable urbanism concludes that society will inevitably move to require high performance building (HPB). HPB is defined as per-capita-based mandatory performance standards set by public or private codes, that is covenants and restrictions, at levels well above conventional codes. California's Title 24 and ASHRAE Standard 189, a first-ever national high-performance building code now under development, both establish requirements above conventional codes. Like virtually all codes across the country, these two energy codes measure energy use on a square foot basis, allowing for easy comparisons between buildings of similar type and size.

However, the global goal of reducing the production of carbon dioxide requires a focus on per-capita reductions. The ever increasing size of the American house, not to mention the increasing number of dwellings owned by Americans, appears to more than cancel out all the gains of increasing energy efficiency per square foot. Measuring energy efficiency per square foot also creates the anomalous and indefensible situation in which Bill Gate's 66,000-square-foot, earth-bermed house may be considered more energy efficient than a modest single-family home that houses the same number of people.

Sustainable urbanism is uniquely conceived to achieve per capita building energy efficiencies through both square foot energy efficiencies and per capita space efficiencies. The shared exteriors walls and floors characteristic of multi-family dwellings found in urban settings reduce energy use on a per square foot basis (see Figures 9-2 and 9-3). Moreover, the higher real estate costs and smaller lot sizes typical of urbanism constrain per capita dwelling size and encourage the use of community facilities. The reduced building envelopes and smaller floor areas of sustainable urbanism will likely emerge as affordable, integrated design strategies for meeting the high performance building codes of the future.

Figure 2-14
Sustainable urbanism brings together professionals from a variety of disciplines to efficiently integrate human and natural systems at a large scale.

Integrated Design

Integrated design is a hallmark of the green building movement. By optimizing the performance of a building as an entire system, this design approach can improve a building's performance at little or no added cost simply by shifting money within the project. This requires a high level of interdisciplinary teamwork and budgetary discipline. A classic illustration is to reallocate a building's construction budget to specify more insulation and better windows and recoup some or most of those costs by buying a smaller, less expensive mechanical system. The resulting building will incur a small construction premium but will produce an acceptable return of investment on that premium, using far less energy and costing far less to operate.

Sustainable urbanism is really a call for integration of all of the human and natural systems that make up a neighborhood or corridor (see Figure 2-14). As with an integrated building design, the magnified benefits come at little or no additional cost. The difference between optimizing the systems of a single building versus those of an entire neighborhood or corridor is the number, complexity, and general lack of understanding of many human systems. The thresholds described in this book are an attempt to compile, for purposes of integrated design, many of the social, economic, and ecological systems that support complete neighborhoods and corridors.

A precondition for design integration is a critical mass of people living within the confines of a complete neighborhood. Neighborhood density can increase the available choices: a walk-to elementary school becomes supportable within the neighborhood; higher-efficiency district heating, cooling, and power systems become viable; the multifamily buildings typical of higher-density development are themselves more energy-efficient; the higher land values associated with more intense development encourage smaller dwellings and more efficient uses of indoor space; more and better transit service can be supported. Each added increment in development density can be credited with protecting undeveloped and sensitive lands from development.

The locations with the greatest potential for cross-system integration are dense, mixed-use and served by transit. In traditional urbanism, such places were densely developed with no off-street parking, because the uses were integral to their locations. These locations and developments attract people who rely on walking or riding transit and who own or use fewer or no cars. Today it is common for new development located within steps of a transit station to be required to provide off-street parking at the same ratio as if the transit service were not there. This failure of integration contributes to the oversupply of parking, reduces development density and affordability, and reduces walking and transit ridership while increasing driving and air pollution. The integration of transit and land use will create a profitable development niche to rent or sell car-free dwellings or office space at lower cost to the segment of the population willing to rely on walking, transit, and shared cars.

Rights-of-way offer significant potential for better integration. (See Figure 2-15.) Historically, human settlements were established with little or no infrastructure. Today's highly complex ROW and utility systems are an accretion of centuries of after-the-fact infrastructure patches. The holy grail of design integration is when efficiencies allow entire systems to be eliminated. Potentially immense economic and environmental benefits may result from integrating high-performance transport, water, sewer, lighting, and power systems with high-performance buildings that consume few to no resources and produce little to no waste.

Figure 2-15
Rights-of-way, even lovely ones, are complex systems both above and below ground.

The Three Steps of Sustainable Urbanism

While it is far from the mainstream today, sustainable urbanism is an achievable norm for the entire United States. Over the next decade two generations of Americans—baby boomers and their progeny called Generation X—will both seek out urban lifestyles, creating an irresistible demographic demand for urban living. In addition, Generation X—also called the Millenials, the 77 million Americans born between roughly 1977 and 1988—have been raised with recycling and other environmental values. Over the next generation, they will become a powerful societal force—voting and buying real estate. Having both sustainability and pragmatism among their core values, they are certain to expect sustainability to be part of their consumer and lifestyle choices. Their buying power is already driving the market to provide sustainable urbanism with increasing numbers of projects combining new urbanism with green homes and buildings.

As taxpaying voters presented with a bill for the full cost of the gloomy consequences of the prior generation's wrong course on the built environment, they are also likely to embrace urbanism. Take, for example, the country's oil policy. The United States is "addicted to oil,"[32] 66 percent of which is used for driving.[33] Given that this same pattern of land use that is cooking the planet is also contributing to the obesity epidemic, land-wasting low-density development, social isolation, heightened levels of pollution, higher taxes, and a shortened lifespan, it is hard to imagine that sustainable urbanism will not come to occupy the center of Gen X policy and governance.

As evidenced by the growing number of projects that appear to embrace sustainable urbanism, including nearly two hundred reviewed for this book, the movement has developed considerable momentum. The twenty case studies in this book (see Chapters 10 and 11), culled from this much larger pool of projects, indicate a robust inventiveness and heterogeneity of size, location, and approach. Worldwide, thousands of projects likely aspire to integrate walkable and transit-served urbanism with high performance buildings and infrastructure. On the broadest level, sustainable urbanist reforms are underway in many, many communities in America.

Despite this momentum, sustainable urbanism will grow far too slowly to become the United States norm in a generation without a twenty year strategic plan. It took over two generations to create climate-changing sprawl and the interlocking system of finance, land use, transportation, and infrastructure necessary to perpetuate it. Implementing sustainable urbanism should by all expectations take at least that long. The urgency of climate change does not allow us this much time to react, and the United States is playing catch up, being more than ten years behind the leading European countries in addressing this issue. The climate changing aspects of the American lifestyle result more from auto-dominated sprawl than do those of Europe, making the tenets of sustainable urbanism even more imperative here. To address this need, the next sections outline three distinct reform steps to accelerate the adoption of sustainable urbanism as the United States norm in a generation.

"Tributary, west of Atlanta, is a 1,600-acre master-planned development built on many of the principles of Sustainable Urbanism. Focus groups identified community design, architectural quality, and EarthCraft (green) homes as three of the top five reasons for buying there. Aimed at the primary market of GenX buyers and their sense of "doing it my way," the positioning tag line at Tributary is "Reshaping the Possibilities," that is, choosing a lifestyle suited to the young buyer's values and desires. It is a similar story at Vickery, a 214-acre Traditional Neighborhood Development in Atlanta where buyers want to live where they can walk to the YMCA, their kids can walk to school, they can have the amenities of a town center, and they can live in an energy-efficient home. Sales associates say that buyers chose Vickery because "it's the right thing to do" and are willing to pay a 25 percent price premium to do so."

Jackie Benson, TND marketing guru and Managing Director of Milesbrand Atlanta.

Economic history shows the important role that agreed-on weights and measures play in making a market for goods and services. Over time the pent-up demand for a good or service can take off with the introduction of recognizable standards with an appropriate seal of approval. In *The Tipping Point,* Malcolm Gladwell explains that there is "a maxim in the advertising business that an advertisement has to be seen at least six times before anyone will remember it."[34] In the green building sector, the LEED standard has built up such a recognizable brand identity that it has helped to accelerate interest in the concept of green buildings and the adoption of specific technologies and practices.

There is a pent-up demand for communities and developments that integrate the features and benefits of urbanism with those of environmentalism. The ability to develop consensus standards has been retarded by urbanists who resist environmental performance and by environmentalists who oppose urbanist development. The urgency with which we need to move on needed reforms means we do not have time to indulge this old spat. Weights and measures of sustainable urbanism that strike a proper balance have the potential to produce something extraordinarily positive from the seemingly impossible integration of opposites. The development industry senses the pent-up demand for sustainable communities while society senses it is now time to confront the sustainability challenges created by our lifestyle. Both are hungry for a branded standard of sustainable urbanism.

LEED for Neighborhood Development may be just that branded standard. It builds on the recognition of the LEED brand for green buildings, but expands the focus beyond the scale of the individual building to address multiple buildings, infrastructure, and entire neighborhood-scale developments. Closely related to the themes of this book, LEED for Neighborhood Development is a voluntary leadership standard to define what constitutes smart, sustainable land development. LEED for Neighborhood Development was developed through a unique partnership between the Congress for New Urbanism, the Natural Resources Defense Council (representing the Smart Growth movement), and the United States Green Building Council (see Figure 2-16). Having started in development in the year 2003, the standard likely will be fully piloted and operational sometime in 2009. This three-way partnership accounts both for the richness of the standard as well as for the long development cycle. It will create a brand for sustainable urbanism that will prove central to its widespread adoption.

The standards are organized into three divisions. While there are many overlaps, the three divisions correspond roughly to each constituency's core concerns. The location of a project in a region—*where* it is—is a principal concern of the Smart Growth movement and is addressed in the Smart Location and Linkage division of LEED for Neighborhood Development. Walkability, land uses, urban design, and architecture of place—*what* goes on there—is a primary focus of the Congress for New Urbanism and is addressed in the Neighborhood Pattern and Design division. Finally, the greenness of the construction and the operation of a development—*how* it is built and managed—are principal concerns of the U.S. Green Building Council and are addressed in the Green Construction and Technology division.

More than half of the topic areas covered in the LEED for Neighborhood Development pilot draft are new to the LEED family, greatly expanding the agenda of the green building movement. For the first time, social issues such as housing diversity, affordable housing, ungated communities, visitability for all including the handicapped, and community

Figure 2-16
LEED for Neighborhood Development was able to blend the agendas of three sustainability movements through close collaboration.

participation are now part of LEED. The LEED for Neighborhood Development standards also pioneer performance thresholds for urban design attributes such as walkability, connectivity, and a mix of uses. The standard applies design strategies long associated with green building, such as stormwater filtration, energy efficiency, and local and recycled content, to the design of infrastructure and entire neighborhood-scale developments.

Probably the most demanding aspects of the LEED for Neighborhood Development draft concern two particular prerequisites (requirements for any project seeking LEED for Neighborhood Development certification): Smart Location and Compact Development. The Smart Location requirement demands that projects be located on infill or redevelopment sites or sites adjacent to existing developed areas. While it provides for some flexibility, it generally prevents leapfrog or discontinuous greenfield developments from gaining certification. These same criteria also exclude what new urbanists call "new towns"—master planned developments in nonurban areas—even though many are planned to become full neighborhoods over time complete with jobs, schools, and services.

The Compact Development prerequisite requires that projects develop to a minimum residential or commercial density, both to decrease the rate at which development consumes land and to concentrate population to create markets. The LEED for Neighborhood Development Core Committee set the minimum level of compactness at seven dwelling units per acre of buildable land or the equivalent commercial density, which is the minimum development density required to support basic public transit and walk-to retail services. This prerequisite requiring density is a radical departure from contemporary development norms; new greenfield development in the United States averages less than two dwelling units per acre.[35]

The development of LEED for Neighborhood Development is a major achievement in the campaign to make sustainable urbanism the national norm. It is an open-source tool available for free to everyone, and it will have many applications—serving as the duct tape of sustainable urbanism. It also has three national organizations behind it that have all pledged to maintain its integrity and operation for the foreseeable future. This is a precious and irreplaceable investment that will have taken more than six years to complete. While LEED for Neighborhood Development no doubt has room for improvement, it is a new and powerful tool with advantages not easily replicated.

If the development of LEED for buildings is any guide, LEED for Neighborhood Development will generate a market for designers and developers who can deliver projects that will satisfy the required level of certification. Few practitioners currently have a command of the many specialized areas of design addressed by sustainable urbanism. We need a wave of interdisciplinary design and development professionals who can quickly master the intricacies of the LEED for Neighborhood Development system.

By combining three critical areas of concern—traditional urbanism, high-performance building, and high-performance infrastructure—sustainable urbanism and LEED for Neighborhood Development represent a potentially immense market. The goal of this book, and the challenge our country is poised to address, is to make sustainable urbanism the norm across the country in a generation. In order to do this, the entire development industry needs to agree on this one standard of excellence. All people interested in sustainability and especially those affiliated with smart growth, new urbanism, and green building should push this standard as far as possible. The coordinated efforts of large numbers of people striving for the same goal can create immense benefits.

"The components of sprawl do not announce themselves as such."
John Norquist, President and CEO, Congress for the New Urbanism

Step Two: Dismantling Petroleum-Era Barriers to Sustainable Urbanism

Climate-changing sprawl has been foisted on us by a comprehensive, but largely invisible, system of self-reinforcing standards, regulations, and subsidies. Take, for instance, today's zoning and land use regulations, which often segregate residential, retail, and commercial land uses, forcing people to drive between them. Roadway design standards are focused almost exclusively on conveying cars long distances at high speeds. The construction of new wide arterial streets that enable sprawl is justified by self-fulfilling forecasts of future traffic demand and congestion prepared by traffic planners who, because of professional specialization, have no authority to regulate land use patterns. Or consider that virtually all sprawl in the United States was developed under legally adopted land use plans, many prepared by members of the American Institute of Certified Planners (AICP).

Neighborhood-scale institutions have been in decline across society for decades. Walk-to elementary schools, the traditional heart of a neighborhood, have been replaced with supersized schools, inevitably located on the far side of a wide, busy street. Most states contribute to this problem by requiring a high minimum acreage for building new schools—as much as fifty acres for a high school—ensuring that new schools will be built outside of neighborhoods on either former industrial sites or on the edge of town. Neighborhood and Main Street retail have been driven out of business from competition with national retailers, who offer free parking lots that draw shoppers in cars from a large area. Not only do they undermine efforts to build complete neighborhoods, these big stores on large streets are a key driver of ever-increasing vehicle miles traveled. Even the neighborhood post office, a traditional anchor on Main Street in many neighborhoods, has been rethought as a trucking depot and moved to the edge of town. With American consumers spending most of their retail dollars in big-box, anti-neighborhood stores, putting the neighborhood back together again requires a shift in shopping patterns.

These standards and patterns hardwire the country's automobile dependence and oil addiction, undermining Americans' ability to meet their daily needs without reliance on a car. To an individual the system is nearly unstoppable. However, a recent initiative led by the Congress for New Urbanism can serve as a model for how to dismantle the invisible apparatus of sprawl. State departments of transportations (DOTs) have been particularly destructive to urbanism by constructing wide, high-speed roads between, around, and through cities nationwide (see Figure 2-17). The CNU joined with the Institute for Traffic Engineers (ITE), an independent trade organization founded in 1930 that develops consensus standards for the design of roadway facilities. They jointly produced a draft design manual entitled

Context Sensitive Solutions in Designing Major Urban Thoroughfares for Walkable Communities.[36] This design manual provides guidance for the design of pedestrian-friendly street networks and is part of an effort to resuscitate the boulevard as a viable street type worthy of public funding. This half-complete, ten-year project to dismantle this particular part of the apparatus of sprawl has been laborious and slow, but it is an important milestone and should serve as a model for a host of other sorely needed reforms.

Understandably missing from the complex negotiation on roadway reform were any of the emerging ideas about high-performance infrastructure, such as life cycle costing, stormwater filtration, or dark sky standards. Many of the barriers to implementing sustainable urbanism result from disintegrated regulations that fail to engage a more complete menu of concerns. For this reason the CNU-ITE project should be considered a first-generation sustainable urbanism reform, destined for future tweaking. Indeed, it is now the time to reexamine the exemptions granted in the Clean Water Act for filtering runoff from public streets and agricultural land. This free right to pollute is decidedly old thinking in light of emerging practices on stormwater, streets and alleys, an increasingly routine part of sustainable urbanist projects (see Figure 2-18).

It is shocking to realize that while we bemoan sprawl—as well as the role it plays in wars that involve petroleum resources and how it is helping to accelerate climate change—it is no one's job to prevent or undo it. That the CNU, an organization with only three thousand members, should play David to sprawl's Goliath is a symptom of how little our society has cared about taking on this challenge. On the other hand, the CNU-ITE project demonstrates how, with patient and persistent leadership, it is possible to systematically turn things around.

Step Three: A National Campaign to Implement Sustainable Urbanism

In order for sustainable urbanism to move forward and gain traction, it is essential that it be seen as playing an integral role in addressing the key issues of our times. The opposite is currently true. The biggest development policy debate in our generation, that of climate change, has mysteriously skipped over the idea of a change in the built environment. Even *An Inconvenient Truth*, the 2006 documentary that seems to be our country's bellwether message on climate change, avoided any mention of our country's transportation and land use calamity. Besides suggesting two actions a person could undertake with cars—pooling or sharing—the closest it came was this recommendation: "Reduce the number of miles you drive by walking, biking, carpooling or taking mass transit wherever possible."[37] This feeble guidance seems to reveal a sense of resignation and powerlessness when it comes to taking on the built environment where we live, work, and play.

Maybe the makers of *An Inconvenient Truth* were just being realistic by not listing any big ideas and instead focusing on things that are easy to do right here and now. Unfortunately this point of view is tragically shortsighted. The climate change dialogue to date has been all about technical fixes—better light bulbs, appliances, cars, buildings—an essential but still insufficient response to climate change. According to credible scientists working on climate change, human caused climate change is well under way and will play out over decades and centuries. These same scientists say we have up to a generation to turn things around drastically before increasingly catastrophic results appear.[38] America is still in denial that our lifestyle has to change, instead betting heavily that a silver-bullet such as better fuel or a technological fix—hydrogen-

ROAD
HIERARCHY

Figure 2-17
Pedestrians are an afterthought in conventional traffic engineering. Image © Wisconsin Department of Transportation.

Figure 2-18
Stormwater streets filter their own stormwater within the right-of-way.

and ethanol-fueled cars, to name two—will pay off. If the United States continues to refuse to confront the root causes of climate change, it is unlikely to respond to the threat of climate change with enough urgency to meet the called-for schedule. Instead of betting on long shots, precaution requires that all viable strategies to address change be pursued.

We need to begin to demand both better widgets *and* sustainable urbanism now, and here's why. Installing more energy-efficient lighting is essential and can occur in as soon as a year or less. By investing in caulking and better windows, existing buildings can improve energy efficiency in just a few years. Following a national energy crisis in the 1970s and 1980s swapping out the national vehicle fleet for more fuel-efficient makes and models took roughly ten years. Substituting more energy-efficient appliances can occur over a decade or two as inventory is naturally replaced. Major building renovations that upgrade power-consuming systems to increase energy efficiency and reduce carbon emissions occur once in a generation. By contrast, land developments are highly persistent with public infrastructure and land parcelization patterns lasting generations, even centuries. Consider that the mandate of climate change may require the retrofitting of auto-dependent sprawl into walkable places, a decades long task. It is alarming to think that the United States might allow five or ten or twenty more years of new sprawl development to occur, knowing it may need to be abandoned or torn out in the relatively near future. The widespread adoption of sustainable urbanism, with its potential to voluntarily change the course of the American lifestyle, emerges as a powerful central tool in the urgent campaign against climate change.

The question then becomes how to sell something so complex, so resistant to sound bites, to a change-resistant, materially comfortable American society that asks, "What are the benefits? What is in it for me?" It is even possible to communicate to a comfort-demanding-country, past the low-hanging fruit of better widgets—light bulbs, appliances, cars, and buildings—to focus on the neighborhood or corridor?

Remarkably, the sustainable neighborhood is a convenient truth and an easier sell than the energy-efficient light bulb. An efficient light bulb saves a household a few dollars a year in electricity but offers little other benefit to the individual. Sustainable urbanism supports a compelling quality of life with economic, health, and environmental benefits tangible to individuals and families. It promotes a way of life that people are choosing voluntarily out of self-interest.

Sustainable urbanism overcomes the palpable disconnect felt in the United States today between the life people actually lead and the one called for by the issues of the day. America's next moon shot will be the opposite of extraterrestrial—it will be a rediscovery of the joys and benefits of a life lived locally.

To accelerate the rate of change of the American lifestyle, this book introduces a proposal to mount a national campaign to adopt sustainable urbanism. Modeled on the recently launched 2030 Architecture Challenge—a schedule for increasing building energy efficiency resulting in carbon neutral buildings by 2030—the 2030 Community Challenge proposes a flexible framework of stepped performance targets for implementing sustainable urbanism (see Chapter 9). While the narrow, quantifiable issue of building energy use has proven to be especially suited to such a campaign format, this same approach can also benchmark the complexity of sustainable urbanism.

This campaign will expedite the uptake of sustainable urbanism over the next generation by employing a bottom-to-top implementation strategy. The primary focus will be on building an informed and persuasive leadership in support of sustainable urbanism. This in turn is meant to reinvigorate and add rigor to local planning and zoning practice and to build support for the adoption of needed state and federal enabling legislation. If done strategically, the 2030 Community Challenge will organize the citizenry—from block association leaders to developers to governors—into a vast army to implement the three "hooks" of sustainable urbanism: training; model projects, and plans and codes.[39]

Let's start with training. Many of the decision makers determining the pattern of development in the United States are volunteers untrained in development practice. These potential troops of sustainable urbanism, especially those on the front lines of fast-moving sprawl, are routinely sent ill-equipped into battle with the embedded apparatus of sprawl , and so it is no surprise that they lose. There is an enormous opportunity to change this outcome by educating these decision makers about the benefits of, and barriers to, sustainable urbanism.

There are few more powerful tools of local reform than excellent model projects. An enormous opportunity exists in most municipalities for the best and most capable local developers, working in concert with municipal officials and leaders, to bring forward a model of sustainable urbanist development. Indeed, most case studies in this book were the result of a municipally supported vision implemented by an equally dedicated developer team. The implementation section of this book (Chapters 3 and 4) spells out exactly how to approach this task both for the municipality and the development team. The case studies included in this book (Chapters 10 and 11) illustrate the range of scale and ambition evident in such projects. The case study benchmarks add specificity to the process of raising the bar on the quality of development.

As noted previously, virtually all the climate-changing, pedestrian-hostile sprawl in the United States was developed legally under existing comprehensive plans and zoning. By contrast, the life-lengthening, tax-reducing, planet-saving approach of sustainable urbanism, as expressed by LEED for Neighborhood Development, is illegal across the country. Often, the development density required to support transit exceeds the maximum allowed under zoning, codes call for minimum levels of parking, and regulations require dangerously wide streets. This is destined to change, possibly very quickly. The state statutes that empower local municipalities to prepare and update comprehensive plans routinely call for the protection of the health, safety, and welfare of residents as one of the goals of the plan.[40] In light of the well-documented links between sprawl and the potential for shortened life spans, obesity, and accelerated threats to the Earth, a comprehensive plan that enables sprawl should, in the near future, run afoul of the law. With a growing awareness of how auto-dependent land use can be hostile to human well-being, in just a few years sustainable urbanist plans may be the law of the land.

Notes

1. Charter of the Congress for the New Urbanism, 2001.

2. Ibid.

3. Guide to the Clarence Arthur Perry Lantern Slides, Collection Number 3442, Division of Rare and Manuscript Collections, Cornell University Library, http://rmc.library.cornell.edu/EAD/htmldocs/RMM03442.html (accessed February 24, 2007).

4. Factoid Central, Casale Media, http://www.factoidcentral.com/facts/people.html (accessed February 5, 2007).

5. Reid Ewing and Richard Kreutzer, "Understanding the Relationship between Public Health and the Built Environment: A Report Prepared for the LEED-ND Core Committee," May 2006, https://www.usgbc.org/ShowFile.aspx?DocumentID=1480 (accessed April 6, 2007), p. 92.

6. Ibid.

7. LEED for Neighborhood Development requires a minimum of seven dwelling units per acre. U.S. Green Building Council, LEED for Neighborhood Development Rating System (Pilot Version), Neighborhood Pattern and Design Prerequisite 2: Compact Development, http://usgbc.org/ShowFile.aspx?DocumentID=2310 (accessed February 24, 2007).

8. Christopher B. Leinberger, "Back to the Future: The Need for Patient Equity in Real Estate," Brookings Institution, January 2007, http://www.brookings.edu/metro/pubs/200701226_patientequity.htm (accessed February 24, 2007), p. 3.

9. John Holtzclaw, "Using Residential Patterns and Transit to Decrease Auto Dependence and Costs," National Resources Defense Council, 1994, http://www.smartgrowth.org/library/cheers.html (accessed February 24, 2007), p. 8.

10. Steven Lagerfeld, "What Main Street Can Learn from the Mall" (interview with Robert Gibbs), Atlantic Monthly, November 1995, p. 8.

11. Federal Energy Management Program, Combined Heat and Power Program Overview, U.S. Department of Energy, 2004, http://www1.eere.energy.gov/femp/pdfs/chp_prog_overvw.pdf (accessed February 24, 2007), p. 1.

12. Alan Chalifoux, "The Impact of Site Design and Planning on Building Energy Usage: Building Energy Usage: A Primer Threshold on Energy Efficiency," in Chapter 9 of this volume.

13. Ewing and Kreutzer, "Understanding the Relationship Between Public Health and the Built Environment," p. 92.

14. U.S. Department of Health and Human Services, Centers for Disease Control and Prevention, "Kids Walk-to-School: Resource Materials," http://www.cdc.gov/nccdphp/dnpa/kidswalk/resources.htm#presentation (accessed February 24, 2007).

15. Jeffrey Zupan, "Where Transit Works in 2006," Exhibit 6.4, http://www.reconnectingamerica.org/pdfs/BriefingbookPDF/Zupan%20Where%20Transit%20Works.pdf (accessed February 24, 2007), p. 5.

16. Scott Bernstein, "How Streetcars Helped Build America's Cities," in Gloria Ohland and Shelley Poticha, Street Smart: Streetcars and Cities in the Twenty-first Century (Oakland, CA: Reconnecting America, 2006), pp. 13–19.

17. Center for Transit Oriented Development, "Hidden in Plain Sight: Capturing the Demand for Housing Near Transit," Oakland, California, September 2004, p. 7.

18. Peter Calthorpe, interview by author at Greenbuild conference, Denver, Colorado, November 15–17, 2006.

19. John D. Daniels, "The Indian Population of North America in 1492," William and Mary Quarterly 49, 2 (1992): 298–320.

20. Calculation of density by author based on http://en.wikipedia.org/wiki/Cahokia (accessed February 25, 2007).

21. Richard Louv, The Last Child in the Woods: Saving Our Children from Nature-Deficit Disorder (Chapel Hill, NC: Algonquin Books, 2005), pp. 104–5.

22. See Melanie Simmons, Kathy Baughman McLeod, and Jason Hight, "Healthy Neighborhoods," Chapter 7 of this volume.

23. Center for Urban Horticulture, University of Washington, College of Forest Resources, "Urban Forest Values: Economic Benefits of Trees in Cities," November 1998, http://www.cfr.washington.edu/research.envmind/Policy/EconBens-FS3.pdf (accessed February 25, 2007).

24. Ibid.

25. News Bureau, University of Illinois at Urbana-Champaign, "Exercise Shown to Reverse Brain Deterioration Brought on by Aging," November 20, 2006, http://www.news.uiuc.edu/news/06/1120exercise.html (accessed February 25, 2007).

26. Andrew Ross Miller, "Valuing Open Space: Land Economics and Neighborhood Parks," master's thesis, Department of Architecture, Massachusetts Institute of Technology, http://dspace.mit.edu/handle/1721.1/8754 (accessed February 26, 2007).

27. Costs of Sprawl—2000, TCRP Report 74, Transit Cooperative Research Program, Transportation Research Board, National Research Council, 2002, http://onlinepubs.trb.org/onlinepubs/tcrp/tcrp_rpt_74-a.pdf (accessed February 5, 2007), Tables 7.8 and 8.4.

28. Government Accounting Standards Board, "GASB Releases New Standard that Will Significantly Change Financial Reporting by State and Local Governments," June 30, 1999, http://www.gasb.org/news/nr63099.html (accessed February 25, 2007).

29. U.S. Environmental Protection Agency, "Heat Island Effect," http://yosemite.epa.gov/oar/globalwarming.nsf/content/ActionsLocalHeatIslandEffect.html (accessed February 25, 2007).

30. Transportation Research Board, "High-Performance Infrastructure Guidelines: Best Practices for the Public Right-of-Way," October 2005, http://trb.org/news/blurb_detail.asp?id=5549 (accessed February 25, 2007).

31. Greg Kats, "The Costs and Financial Benefits of Green Buildings: A Report to California's Sustainable Building Task Force," October 2003, http://www.cape.com/ewebeditpro/items/O59F3259.pdf (accessed February 25, 2007), p. 19.

32. George W. Bush, State of the Union Address, January 31, 2006, http://www.whitehouse.gov/stateoftheunion/2006 (accessed February 25, 2007).

33. Energy Information Administration, U.S. Department of Energy, "Oil Market Basics: U.S. Consumption by Sector," http://www.eia.doe.gov/pub/oil_gas/petroleum/analysis_publications/oil_market_basics/demand_text.htm#U.S.%20Consumption%20by%20sector (accessed February 25, 2007).

34. Malcolm Gladwell, The Tipping Point (Boston: Little, Brown, 2000), p. 92.

35. U.S. Environmental Protection Agency, "Protecting Water Resources with Higher-Density Development," December 15, 2005, http://www.epa.gov/smart-growth/pdf/protect_water_higher_density.pdf (accessed February 25, 2007), p. 2.

36. Institute of Transportation Engineers, Context Sensitive Solutions in Designing Major Urban Thoroughfares for Walkable Communities, 2006, http://ite.org/bookstore/RP036.pdf (accessed February 25, 2007).

37. "What Can You Do An Inconvenient Truth website, http://www.climatecrisis.net/takeaction/whatyoucando/index5.html (accessed January 12, 2007).

38. Edward Mazia, Architecture 2030, "The 2030 °Challenge," http://www.architecture2030.org/open_letter/index.html (accessed February 27, 2007).

39. Pew Center on Global Climate Change, "Toward a Climate Friendly Built Environment," June 2005, p. vi.

40. Excerpt from the introduction to the Comprehensive Plan, Ramsey, Minnesota, 2002.

PART TWO: IMPLEMENTING SUSTAINABLE URBANISM

A Step-by-Step Method for Turning a Swarm into a Movement

Sustainable urbanism represents a generational shift in how human settlements are designed and developed. Its adoption as a societal norm requires all of the many parties to the process of planning and developing urbanism to perform highly specific tasks in tight coordination. These include city administrators, developers, design professionals, and the public at large. This book proposes that sustainable urbanism be implemented continuously, by interdisciplinary terms, working at all scales, on each and every project, one project at a time. To make this easy to do, this section introduces benchmarking, the basis of incremental improvement, and the charrette, sustainability's model of interdisciplinary work. They provide form templates for selecting qualified design professionals, initiating sustainable urbanist projects, and soliciting sustainable urbanist development proposals. In order to ensure that the resulting development will perform as intended, Chapter 4 summarizes emerging trends in sustainable-urbanist-related development controls—codes, covenants, and restrictions (CC&Rs).

Sustainable urbanism is a powerful but invisible reform movement. The movement has a potential army of reformers, likely now identified with and active in pioneering reforms such as smart growth, new urbanism, and green building. The goal of the following chapters is to provide an easy means for these committed parties, who do not now identify with sustainable urbanism, to play a coordinated role in implementing its reforms. To accomplish this goal, each contribution details specific steps for senators, governors, mayors, city councils, regulators, developers, bankers, planners, engineers, architects, bond rating agencies, and others to implement sustainable urbanism one action at a time. This strategy holds the potential to create immense value simply by coordinating work that people have to do anyway to implement a larger vision. By studying the entire list, individuals will see how their actions fit together with other reforms. The hope is that after a generation of coordinated effort, sustainable urbanism will become the norm.

Outside the pages of this book, "sustainable urbanism" is a highly ambiguous term with neither name recognition nor momentum as a reform movement. As defined by this book, *sustainable urbanism uses a knowledge of human and natural systems to integrate walkable and transit-served urbanism with high-performance buildings and high-performance infrastructure.* While this all-encompassing definition describes the right thing to do, its complexity can act as a barrier to understanding and action. The goal is to jump-start this reform movement of the built environment and to position sustainable urbanism as the means to shift the American lifestyle toward sustainability over time. This section of the book focuses on implementation of this ambitious goal by offering several practical aids, they include tools to facilitate communications and leadership, and a "cookbook" process outlining the first steps of implementation.

An essential strategy in implementing sustainable urbanism is developing a clear and simple message to describe this complex undertaking. For a policy agenda to become widely adopted, it needs to be shaped into a number of written formats to complement this book-length document: a tag line, a fifteen-second "elevator message," and bulleted talking points describing the strategies and benefits of sustainable urbanism. Because its focus is the nexus of the American lifestyle and the built environment, sustainable urbanism is highly visual. The urban-rural transect introduced in this chapter is a powerful communications tool for illustrating the spectrum of human place types and their respective sustainability. To communicate the viability of creating value through offering sustainable urbanist choices, this section includes a menu of urban versus sprawl development choices.

Chapter 3
Leadership and Communications

Leadership Talking Points for Sustainable Urbanism

Jim Hackler, former head of the USGBC's LEED for Homes and Atlanta's EarthCraft House program, and Irina Woelfle, IWPR Group

Complex ideas, such as sustainable urbanism, are particularly challenging to convey in this age of sound bites and short attention spans. However, insights from the communications industry can be used to get a clear message across. The challenges and the opportunities are many. Sustainable urbanism is relevant to many different trends and current events: climate change, quality of life, the environment, building community, lowering taxes, and the like.

Communications professionals have developed methods to address these challenges:

- *Define your mission.* Decide who you are and what your goals are.
- *Define the audience.* Influencers? Partners? Potential partners? Customers?
- *Lose the jargon.* The phrase "sustainable urbanism" is suited only to a technical audience. For the general public, consider a layman's definition: neighborhoods where you prefer to walk to everything—to see people, to enjoy the parks, tree-lined streets, and environmentally friendly buildings.
- *Collect statistics in your support.* This book is a good resource; just don't overwhelm your audience with too many facts and figures.
- *Define your message for each audience.* For example:
  - Planning board members need to know that high-performance infrastructure means lower taxes.
  - Potential residents need to know your buildings use a small amount energy and help slow global warming.
  - NIMBY groups need to know that a mix of uses reduces traffic.
- *Use a positive message.* Have fun! Emphasizing the positive may attract more people than gloom and doom.
- *Use synonyms.* To connect with your audience, you may want to use related terms that may be more familiar than Sustainable Urbanism: "smart growth," "green urbanism," "eco-cities," "LEED-ND," "healthy neighborhoods," "walkable communities."

The table below lists talking points that address the three steps toward sustainable urbanism.

Table 3-1

The Three Steps of Sustainable Urbanism	Citizen/ Resident/Voter	Planner/Developer	Elected Official
1 Agreeing to weights and measures: making a market for sustainable urbanism	Having a standard for a certified walkable, healthy neighborhood adds value, like a seal of approval.	I can use LEED-ND to build, develop, and market the best possible projects for my customers.	Creating incentives such as expedited permitting or reducing impact fees can encourage more sustainable developments that embrace rating systems such as LEED-ND.
2 Dismantling petroleum–era barriers to sustainable urbanism	Subsidies and zoning laws are benefiting special interests and are not in the best interest of my community.	Density is no longer a dirty word, but in fact provides opportunities for mass transit that can liberate people from their cars.	Current codes are outdated and isolate America's communities, forcing people to drive.
3 A national campaign to implement sustainable urbanism	Getting involved in a national campaign such as the 2030 Community Challenge makes me feel like I am contributing to something bigger.	The 2030 Community Challenge is good for business and good for the planet.	The 2030 Community Challenge can conserve scarce public money and help the environment. It's just good government.

Four Principal Challenges/Opportunities in Communicating Sustainable Urbanism

1. The public's lack of recognition of the term and its complexity
2. The public's lack of focus on how the built environment affects health and quality of life
3. The need to distinguish sustainable urban developments early and often from climate-changing sprawl
4. Getting people to realize that our current American lifestyle reduces harmony in our households, our lives, and our world

The Power of Paired Choices

One of the best ways to communicate the desirability of choosing a sustainable urbanist approach, is to juxtapose it with conventional development practice. When a sustainable urbanist alternative visibly differs from conventional practice, photographs or renderings are an effective way to communicate choices. However, since not all benefits in sustainable urbanism are visible, there is a need to provide the viewer with information regarding differences in performance.

The images below illustrate how to communicate information in a sustainable urbanist manner. Images demonstrate the look and feel of spaces, while the captions can communicate the metrics. Ideally the metrics should address economic, social, and environmental benefits.

Choices in Public Transportation Investments

The United States invested hundreds of billions of dollars over the last two generations to create the interstate highway system, which helped cause today's climate-changing sprawl. In this generation the country needs to redirect its transportation dollars to reduce the amount that Americans drive. For example, a medium-sized town could have a four-mile streetcar system for the same cost as two bypass interchanges.

Which public investment in transportation provides the greater benefit?

Figure 3-1 A
A freeway interchange like this one can cost $10 to $30 million. They support unattractive, drive-to, big-box development.

Figure 3-1 B
This streetcar line supports high-quality, walkable mixed-use development. Streetcar lines reduce driving and pollution and increase walking and health.

Choices in Where to Live

The most fundamental choice that Americans make is where to live. That one decision determines many of the unintended consequences of our lifestyle.

Where should I live if I want to improve my health and reduce my impact on climate change?

Figure 3-2 A
Climate-changing sprawl: an automobile-dependent community in which the average family drives 24,000 miles per year with a three-dwelling per acre density.

Figure 3-2 B
Sustainable urbanism: a connected community with a sixteen dwellings per acre density and walk-to destinations in which the average family drives only 9,000 miles per year.

How might a streetcar change the most auto-dependent corridor in our community?

Figure 3-3 A
Automobile-dominated arterials have pedestrian-hostile traffic speeds of up to 50 miles per hour. Crosstown trips dominate, resulting in little commercial activity along the road.
Image © 1998 urban-advantage.com

Figure 3-3 B
This same street, served by a streetcar, calms traffic to average speeds of 30 miles per hour. Local trips dominate, increasing sales for neighborhood businesses.
Image © 1998 urban-advantage.com

The Criteria for Condemnation of Private Property

Many states grant municipalities the authority to condemn private property to promote economic development and the public health, safety, and welfare. This authority was first granted as a part of the urban renewal movement of the 1950s and 1960s. As defined in *The American Heritage Dictionary of English Language,* blight is "something that impairs growth, withers hopes and ambitions, or impedes progress and prosperity." The original CIAM-inspired, anti-urban criteria for deciding what to condemn are still on the books in many states.

Which of the criteria below should serve as the basis for condemnation?

Figure 3-4 A
This mixed-use, urban neighborhood area could be considered blighted, as it satisfies several of today's common criteria for blight: inadequate parking facilities, excessive land coverage and overcrowding of structures, and incompatibility of adjacent land or buildings.

Figure 3-4 B
Sprawl characteristics like the following should be considered a new kind of blight: a lack of pedestrian facilities, presence of high-fatality street types (paving wider than 34 feet), excessive surface parking, and lack of land use diversity resulting in automobile dependence.

Implementation Agendas for Leaders

Making sustainable urbanism the dominant pattern of land development across the country is actually a lot easier than one might imagine. Remember, the benefits of this approach are enormous and will appeal to the general public. The trick is to view every change in the regulatory and built environment and in people's lifestyles as an opportunity to implement sustainable urbanism. We can and need to make different choices. The real power comes when actions occur in concert, magnifying the effect of any one individual's activity. The mind-set needs to be that the country is ready for a change; that this represents an enormous opportunity to advance society, the economy, and the environment; and that the reason it hasn't been done before is a lack of shared vision and coordinated leadership.

This section is a first effort to create an action agenda for the many key shapers of the development process and the built environment. Everyone has a role to play. Each catalyzing action listed below suggests a set of steps that might be taken to jump-start the sustainable urbanist movement, one project at a time. Think of it as a word-of-mouth, underground movement. Bring this book to meetings and point out the different sections to your friends, neighbors, mayors, city councilors, and real estate developers to get them to appreciate that every project undertaken in your city or town can implement sustainable urbanism.

Table 3-2 Implementation Agendas for Leaders

Catalyzing Action	Implementation Agenda
Promote a sustainable urbanist	Consult *Chapter 3: Leadership Talking Points* for ways to communicate the many benefits of sustainable urbanism. Update progress on sustainability.
	Sponsor a sustainable urbanist lecture series to increase awareness and build the capacity to integrate sustainable urbanism into each and every project. See *Chapter 4: Conducting a Charette.*
Hire sustainable urbanist professionals	Rely on *Chapter 4: RFQ for Sustainable Urbanist Professionals* for information on hiring staff and a development team with a sustainable urbanist outlook.
	Require that an experienced sustainable urbanist be included on each project team.
Select and support sustainable urbanist developers	Use *Chapter 4: RFP for a Sustainable Urbanist Developer* for selecting development teams.
	Use *Chapter 4: RFP for a Sustainable Urbanist Developer* as the criteria for evaluation the level of public support for a given project.

Catalyzing Action	Implementation Agenda
Benchmark sustainability goals	Use *Chapter 4: Benchmarking Municipal Sustainability* to develop benchmarks for a municipality's sustainability goals. Track progress towards those benchmarks regularly.
	Modify comprehensive plan law to require sustainable initiatives and benchmarking of all sustainability goals in future municipal land use plans.
Revise outdated regulations	Replace parking, lighting, and building setback minimums with maximums. *For detailed examples see Chapter 8: Public Darkness.*
	Replace building height, density, and share car maximums with minimums. Adopt standards that address multiple variables on a per capita or sliding scale.
Initiate a catalytic sustainable urbanist project	Refer to *Chapter 11: Scales of Intention* to find a model project of the appropriate size to emulate in your town.
	Initiate a car-share program. Municipal planners should perform GIS analysis of neighborhoods to determine the number that can viably support car share. Increase this area by 5% per year. See *Chapter 7: Car Sharing.*
	Develop a car-free housing project. See *Chapter 7: Car-Free Housing.*
Develop a sustainable neighborhood	Perform a SNAP (Smart Growth Analysis Protocol). See *Chapter 4: Shaping Smart Neighborhoods.*
	Assess neighborhood completeness according to standards developed by Victor Dover and Eliot Allen. See *Chapter 7: Neighborhood Definition and Neighborhood Completeness.*
	Municipal planners should map neighborhoods in terms of auto-dependent zones, pedestrian zones, and mixed zones. Aim to increase pedestrian zones by 5% per year.
Develop a sustainable corridor	Prepare a master land use plan identifying transportation, infrastructure, and wildlife corridors and the adjacent areas of influence.
	Transit agencies should adopt "corridor transit warrants" that require the provision of public transit service when corridor land development conforms to minimum densities.
	Meet demand for transit-oriented development by planning for regional corridors. See *Chapter 6: The integration of Transportation, Land Use, and Technology.*
	Integrate wildlife corridors into the regional network and protect them from development. See *Chapter 6: Biodiversity Corridors.*

Chapter 4
**The Process and Tools
for Implementing
Sustainable Urbanism**

RFQ for Sustainable Urbanist Professionals

The most important step in pursuing a sustainable urbanist approach is selecting a professional or team with the right understanding and skills. In order to overcome incredible development, legal, and political barriers, the practice of sustainable urbanism requires a unique combination of attributes. New urbanist planning practice alone requires a broad range of talents in analysis, visual communication, interpersonal persuasion, and debate. In addition, a sustainable urbanist needs to possess commitment to and expertise in both high-performance buildings and high-performance infrastructure. Below is a list of criteria for selecting qualified urban planners and planning/design firms.

Understanding and Commitment
- A demonstrated adherence to the principles outlined in the Charter of the Congress for the New Urbanism (see http://cnu.org/charter). Planning and design track record reflects an understanding that disinvestment in central cities, economic and racial segregation, the spread of placeless sprawl, loss of farmland and wilderness, environmental degradation, and erosion of our built heritage are interrelated problems that must be addressed simultaneously and urgently.
- A detailed understanding of the cost and benefits of green building, such as the ability to address issues of climate change, energy, water and resource conservation, indoor environmental quality, and solid waste reduction through integrated design.

Leadership
- An ability to effectively engage and persuade colleagues, public officials, and clients unfamiliar with or opposed to new and sustainable urbanist planning theory and practice.
- Demonstrated success as a minority voice within the broader spectrum of status quo planning and development. Experience selling new urbanist principles to the media and public.
- The ability to build bridges with other development professionals to convince them of the value of an approach that features comprehensiveness, sustainability, smart growth, and new urbanism integrated with high-performance buildings and high-performance infrastructure.

Experience
- Demonstrated participation in new urbanist projects such as transit-oriented development, mixed-use development, traditional neighborhood development, and form-based codes, which also incorporate high-performance buildings and infrastructure.

Figure 4-1
There are specific qualities to identify in New Urbanist professional candidates.

Skills

- Excellent public speaking, professional publication, and graphic design capabilities.
- Willing to work in diverse environments and communities; demonstrates abilities to provide individual and teamwork initiatives. Successful in multidisciplinary team settings where architects, engineers, public officials, planners, and community activists work together.

Expertise

- Professional expertise in one or more subtopics within sustainable urbanism— for example, sustainable development, street network design, urban infill, open space preservation, affordable housing, real estate, zoning and policy, stormwater engineering, etc., highly preferred.
- Master's degree in urban planning or design, public administration, public policy, social sciences, architecture, or engineering, with academic exposure to the full spectrum of urban planning and design theory, and practice is most desirable.
- Professional accreditation through multiple leadership organizations, including the U.S. Green Building Council's LEED program and the American Institute of Certified Planners and, as may be offered in the future, through the Congress for New Urbanism and LEED for Neighborhood Development.

Benchmarking Municipal Sustainability:
The Santa Monica Sustainable City Plan

The city of Santa Monica, California, commissioned its Sustainable City Program in 1994. Its major goal was to ensure that Santa Monica was meeting its current needs—environmental, social, and economic—without compromising the ability of future generations to do the same. It accomplished this objective by addressing root causes of problems rather than symptoms and by creating criteria for evaluating the long-term impacts of community decisions. Many of the initial targets were met or exceeded in the following years.

In 2001, the city's Task Force on the Environment began reviewing and updating the program, ultimately proposing significant changes to the initial indications and creating new ones. The resulting process, known as the Santa Monica Sustainable City Plan (SCP), was founded on ten guiding principles, including the precautionary principle, and focuses on eight goal areas. Each goal area has a set of specific goals, which in turn have a set of specific indicators. Targets for each indicator have been created for the year 2010, using 2000 as a baseline.

Santa Monica Targets

The matrix on the following page lists all of the Sustainable City Plan indicators down the left side. Performance targets are shown for every goal area.

Table 4.1 Santa Monica Municipal Sustainability Targets
(Selected Targets from the Santa Monica Sustainable City Plan Revised October 24, 2006)

Indicators – System Level	Targets
Resource Conservation	
Water use	
• Total citywide use	• Reduce overall water use by 20% by 2010. Of the total water used, non-potable water use should be maximized
• % local vs. imported	
• Potable vs. nonpotable	• Increase percentage of locally-obtained potable water to 70% of total by 2010
Greenhouse Gas Emissions	
• Total citywide emissions (also report per capita, by source and by sector)	• At least 30% below 1990 levels by 2015 for City Operations
	• At least 15% below 1990 levels by 2015 citywide
Ecological Footprint for Santa Monica	• Downward trend
"Green" Construction	
• Total number of LEED™ certified buildings in Santa Monica as a percent of new construction	• 100% of all buildings >10,000 sq. ft. and 50% of all buildings <10,000 sq. ft eligible for LEED™ certification constructed in the year 2010 shall achieve it or its equivalent. Of those >10,000 sq. ft. 20%, 10% and 2% should attain LEED™ Silver, Gold, and Platinum certification or equivalent respectively.
Transportation	
Modal split	
• Number of trips by type, citywide	• An upward trend in the use of sustainable (bus, bike, pedestrian, rail) modes of transportation
• *Average vehicle ridership* (AVR) of Santa Monica businesses with more than 50 employees	• AVR of 1.5 by 2010 for Santa Monica businesses with more than 50 employees
Bicycle lanes and paths	
• % of total miles of city arterial streets with bike lanes	• 35% by 2010
• Total miles of bike paths in Santa Monica	• No net decrease
Vehicle ownership	
Average number of vehicles per person of driving age in Santa Monica	• 10% reduction in the average number of vehicles per person by 2010
• Total number of vehicles per person	• Upward trend in % of qualified low emission / alternative fuel vehicles
• % of total qualified as *low emission/alternative fuel vehicles*	
Economic Development	
Jobs / Housing Balance	
• Ratio of the number of jobs in Santa Monica to the amount housing	• Ratio should approach 1
• % of Santa Monica residents employed in town	• Increasing trend
Community Education and Civic Participation	
Voter Participation	
• % of registered voters who vote in scheduled elections. Compare to voter participation rates at regional/national levels.	• Increase Santa Monica voter participation to 50% in off year elections by 2010
Sustainable Community Involvement	
• % of City residents aware of Santa Monica's Ecological Footprint and understand their contribution to it	• 25% by 2010
Human Dignity	
Basic Needs – Economic Opportunity	
• % of Santa Monica residents who work more than 40 hours per week in order to meet their basic needs	• Downward trend

Table adapted from the Santa Monica Sustainable City Plan available at:
http://santa-monica.org/epd/scp/pdf/SCP_2006_Adopted_Plan.pdf

Documenting Community
Preference in Form and Sustainability:
Image Preference Survey (IPS)

Christina Anderson
Farr Associates

A critical step in creating a sustainable urbanist plan and ultimately a code to implement that plan is an image preference survey. An image preference survey is a powerful tool for soliciting group preferences on community character and appearance. Because this survey method relies on participants individually registering their quantitative preferences on a test form, the results are perceived to be fair and neutral, helping to build consensus within the community. Discussing the images immediately following the survey allows participants to highlight and debate a photograph's features.

In an image preference survey, participants are shown a series of PowerPoint slides, each containing a pair of photographs in several themed categories (see Figures 4-2, 4-3, 4-4). The categories differ based on the needs of the community and can include general themes, such as first impressions, streetscape, and neighborhood centers, as well as specific geographical locations within the project study area.

The goal of this tool is to gather preferences on community character that will later guide the plan and the zoning code. The photographs must therefore be selected carefully and include both local images and those from outside the community. The collection of photographs must not only illustrate obvious examples of appropriate and inappropriate development, but also, and even more importantly, provide the participants with a range of options that can be developed throughout the community or only in specific locations within the community. Photographs clearly illustrating good and bad development examples set a baseline, while photographs illustrating choices within good or appropriate development allow the community to make the plan and code their own.

An image preference survey for a sustainable urbanist project includes such images as building forms and siting, open space types, and street types. These photographs provide a range of choices from which the community can select to create a built environment that promotes active, walkable neighborhoods. The survey would also include images of high-performance green features, such as outdoor lighting options or stormwater systems. These sustainable urbanist images expand the choices for development character and performance. The information gathered through the image preference survey shapes the activities in the charrette and influences the final plan and code.

Examples of IPS Categories

Land-Use Patterns
Figures 4-2A, 4-2B
Most communities have numerous examples of automobile-oriented, aesthetically unattractive development, such as the strip center on the left. This type of image can be contrasted in an IPS with a mixed-use building constructed to the front and corner property lines. Often it is only in viewing illustrations of better examples of development that participants realize the problems with conventional development patterns.

Building Types
Figures 4-3A, 4-3B, 4-3C
To illustrate potential building forms and siting, images such as these three can be shown to highlight options in heights, setbacks, levels of façade transparency, and roof types.

Street Types
Figures 4-4A, 4-4B, 4-4C
Depending on the size of the project study, the plan and code should allow for a variety of street types. Including these illustrations allows participants to consider that one street type may not be appropriate for all developments.

Conducting a Charrette

Bill Lennertz, National Charrette Institute
Copyright © 2006 American Planning Association

Sustainable urbanism embraces the charrette as the most effective strategy for doing neighborhood and community planning. A charrette is the catalytic event in a planning process. It is a collaborative design and planning workshop or series of workshops, the goal of which is to produce a feasible plan that benefits from the support of all stakeholders. Charrettes can be used for virtually any type of planning project, especially those that are controversial and complicated. It is held on-site and includes all affected stakeholders at critical decision-making points. Community planning charrettes have a solid track record of attracting large numbers of people, including many who normally do not participate in land planning events. (*The Charrette Handbook,* created by the National Charrette Institute and published by the American Planning Association, is the definitive resource on this topic.)

As conceived by the National Charrette Institute (NCI), a charrette occurs over four to seven consecutive days, depending on the size and scope of a project. Its goal is to bring all the decision makers together for a discrete amount of time to create a win-win solution, making it one of the most powerful techniques in the planner's tool kit. The charrette is organized as a series of feedback loops through which stakeholders are engaged at critical decision-making points. These decision-making points occur in primary stakeholder meetings, several public meetings, and possibly during an open house all of which occur during the course of the charrette. These feedback loops provide the charrette team with the information necessary to create a feasible plan. Just as important, they allow the stakeholders to become co-authors of the plan, so they are more likely to support and implement it.

All of the steps and tasks outlined in an NCI charrette still need to be performed in a sustainable urbanist project. However, in sustainable urbanism, charrettes can also be conducted as a series of shorter workshops spread out over a longer period of time. One advantage of this alternative approach is that it allows for the longer time frames and feedback cycles associated with pioneering new approaches in architecture and infrastructure. Second, a series of multiple workshops may favor local and regional consultants over national firms, a preferred direction for the future in order to build regional expertise and to reduce the multiple demands of travel.

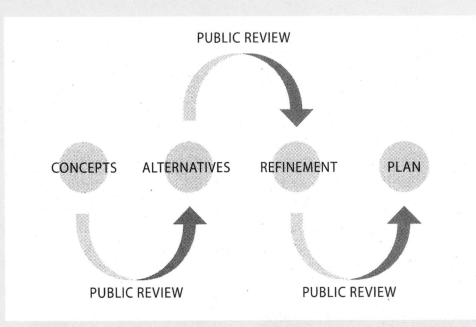

PUBLIC REVIEW

CONCEPTS   ALTERNATIVES   REFINEMENT   PLAN

PUBLIC REVIEW   PUBLIC REVIEW

Figure 4-8
Planners, architects, engineers, and social policy experts come together at a redevelopment charrette after Hurricane Katrina hit in New Orleans.

Figure 4-9
At a charrette, community members may break up into groups to discuss development possibilities.

The National Charrette Institute encourages all participants in the dynamic planning process, whether in the stages of data collection, charrette, or implementation, to internalize the following five values:

Community health. Holistic planning processes based on local values produce solutions that support healthy communities. Healthy communities improve the social, economic, and physical well-being of their people, places, and natural environments.

Collaboration. Each individual's unique contribution supports the best outcome. When project sponsors maintain this value, stakeholders are viewed as members of the larger team who have valuable input and are essential to implementation.

Transparency. Clarity in rules, process, and roles is essential to collaboration. Stakeholders know whether or not a process is genuinely collaborative, and any lack of openness will quickly erode their trust in the process. All information relevant to decision making must be made available to the stakeholders.

Shared learning. Shared learning requires the involvement of all relevant viewpoints in the decision-making process. Shared learning facilitates new understanding that can lead to a change in people's perceptions and positions.

Direct, honest, and timely communication. Collaborative work, based on shared learning, requires frequent communication and feedback between the project sponsors and the stakeholders. These feedback loops provide all parties with the reasoning behind decisions and knowledge of how their input affected the outcome.

Shaping Sustainable with the Toledo Smart Neighborhood Analysis Protocol (SNAP)

Carolee Kokola
Farr Associates

The Smart Neighborhood Analysis Protocol (SNAP) ranking criteria constitute a key strategy to plan an improved quality of life within an existing urban context. Although designed using Toledo neighborhoods as case studies, SNAP is applicable with minimal adjustment to guide redevelopment efforts in other cities. The intent of the SNAP ranking criteria is to evaluate existing neighborhoods in urban areas and proposed infill redevelopment projects in accordance with sustainable urbanist principles. SNAP includes a method for prioritizing development projects resulting in smart neighborhoods while maximizing a city's redevelopment efforts and enhancing the benefits of future investment.

SNAP will help Toledo's leaders and citizens recognize their communities' strengths and determine how to enhance their assets to result in more sustainable, value-enhancing, and attractive development options. SNAP can be used by neighborhood residents, community groups, city staff, or other stakeholders to inventory a neighborhood's assets and to target appropriate types of development. Over time, this inventory may be revisited to evaluate how a neighborhood's development efforts have progressed.

Community stakeholders called "neighborhood builders" collect information about their neighborhood, including the participants' opinions on neighborhood strengths and points of pride to be enhanced, as well as features that need improvement (see Figure 4-5 & 4-6).

SNAP encourages stakeholders to look at specific features of their neighborhoods in greater depth than they may usually do. This exercise includes a "site visit" involving the recording of data as each participant walks through the neighborhood; participants can do their site visits in small groups or by themselves. Some data may be collected in advance using the participants' knowledge of where specific features are located or even using the Internet.

Analysis of the Uptown Neighborhood Site: Key Site Characteristics

- Schools, the library, and the mixed-use area on Adams Street in the historic streetcar corridor are activity nodes.
- Several "districts" overlap: Uptown Neighborhood, Arts and Entertainment District, and Avenue of the Arts.
- Residential uses are multifamily or above retail spaces.
- Light industrial, office, and public uses are significant; several artists' studios and workshops are located north of Adams.
- Single-use, automobile-oriented commercial uses are primarily located on Monroe Street.
- The neighborhood is well served by multiple transit lines, although one-way streets restrict the flow of traffic.

Step 1: Identify Site Characteristics
Rationale
An evaluation of site characteristics and general land uses will lay the groundwork for the neighborhood analysis.

Identifying Existing Features
Locate the following features on the base map, as appropriate. This page serves as a key to Worksheet #1.

Nodes of Activity
With a black marker, circle any places that tend to be busy with pedestrian activity, such as schools, transit stations, intersections where multiple bus lines cross, community centers, etc.

Sample nodes of activity: Transit station (left) and neighborhood shopping district (right)

Edges
With a black marker, draw a jagged line along any barriers or natural features that serve as edges to the neighborhood, such as highway or a river.

Sample edges: Railroad tracks (left) and wide, busy street (right)

Landmarks
Draw a star on any prominent landmarks or monuments, such as places of worship or historic buildings with significance to the neighborhood.

Sample landmarks: Church at prominent intersection (left) and historic mansion (right)

Following is a sample site analysis worksheet.

Figure 4-5
The instructions for SNAP are intended to guide community stakeholders through what may be their first neighborhood planning exercise.

Figure 4-6
This worksheet, which shows the use of the symbols in Figure 4-5, illustrates the first of a series of exercises designed to collect data on community stakeholders' perceptions of their neighborhoods.

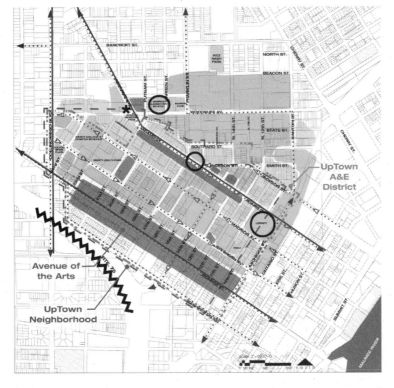

A Sustainable Urbanist Neighborhood Plan: Toledo SNAP

Carolee Kokola
Farr Associates

For an introduction to SNAP, see "Shaping Sustainable Neighborhoods with the Toledo Smart Neighborhood Analysis Protocol (SNAP)" in this chapter.

Incorporating SNAP Results into a Neighborhood Plan

The results of the Smart Neighborhood Analysis Protocol (SNAP) should be used to guide a neighborhood redevelopment plan. An example of a recommended development plan for the Uptown Neighborhood is on the facing page. It takes advantage of the identified opportunity sites, it fills retail voids and it increases density to support the recommended retail uses. Uses missing from the overall neighborhood should be proposed for the neighborhood activity center. The result is a smart neighborhood with a walkable neighborhood center and appropriate infill development, all of which enhance the quality of life.

Although some of the elements of the recommended plan may not ultimately be feasible, the overall concept and some of the specific recommendations should be used to guide redevelopment efforts. Any new civic or public buildings should be designed in accordance with the U.S. Green Building Council's LEED for New Construction standards.

Further Analysis

The existing neighborhood may also be evaluated with the applicable sections of LEED for Neighborhood Development, which may supplement SNAP by providing guidance on specific building elements and site features for a development site. The recommended site design and proposed development are in keeping with the goals of LEED-ND.

SNAP Summary: Key Recommendations for Future Development

- The boundaries of the identified neighborhood and the Arts and Entertainment District are larger than the walkable neighborhood scale (see Table 7-1); a redevelopment priority area was identified, focusing on the strongest retail node.
- The intersection of Franklin, Adams, and 17th can become a key focal point and center of activity with the construction of new mixed-use buildings to complement the existing neighborhood.
- The plan proposes approximately 20,000 square feet of neighborhood retail.
- Recommended residential unit types include apartment/condo buildings, residential units above shops and townhouses; density should be concentrated on Adams Street.
- New parks provide open space within a three-minute walk of all residences; at least one stormwater park should be located in a high-visibility area.
- Vehicles used in a car-sharing plan would ideally be placed in a visible location adjacent to new mixed-use construction.

Figure 4-10
The ideal neighborhood inventory would include a vibrant mix of uses to create a strong node of activity.

Figure 4-11
Sample development plan for the Uptown neighborhood illustrates both the current locations and the recommended future locations of various land uses.

Ideal Neighborhood Inventory

Use	Location	Voids
Convenience food store	1 a	
Family restaurant	2	
Coffee shop	3 b	
Bank	4	
Laundry/dry cleaner	5	
Drug store	c	
Medical/dental office	6 d	
Day care center	7 e	
Elementary school	8	
Library	9	
Community center	10 f	
Place of worship	11	
Post office/govt services	12 g	
Park/stormwater park	13 h	
Transit lines	– – –	
Car-share vehicles	i	

Totals: 16 of 16 key uses

Score: 100%

Key
- Existing uses
- Recommended uses

Regulating Plan and Form-Based Code

Christina Anderson
Farr Associates

Conventional zoning generally ignores building form and focuses solely on use. The result has been generic buildings that are out of character with existing development and the preferences of the community. Form-based codes focus on building form and how it affects public spaces. By relating buildings back to the street and open spaces, rather than to parking lots or private yards, public spaces are redefined from the conventional automobile-oriented scale to the human- or pedestrian-oriented scale. This focus allows form-based codes to guide the creation of active, sustainable neighborhoods. Here are some of the more important aspects of form-based code.

Focus on Form

At a minimum, each building type will detail building and parking siting, façade and use requirements, and height. The regulations frequently include acceptable ranges, such as minimum and maximum heights or a build-to zone rather than a setback. These ranges allow for flexibility in development, and there is reassurance in the level of predictability that they provide. Since each code is created based upon the preferences of the community, codes will differ among cities and among neighborhoods within cities. Based on these preferences, the façade requirements especially will vary in their level of detail. At a minimum, pedestrian-oriented characteristics such as entrance location, transparency level, base type (treatment of the ground-story front façade), and cap type (including roof type) will be regulated, and a city may choose to include additional requirements.

Figures 4-12A, 4-12B
Form-based codes can preserve
existing neighborhood character by
creating standards based on existing
development, preventing out-of-scale
development such as the single-story
ranch building on the left.

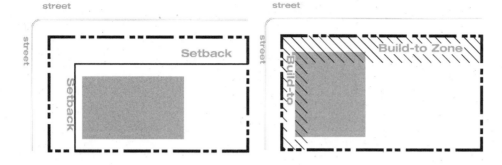

Figure 4-13
A setback establishes a line behind
which the building must be placed
and is common in conventional codes.
A build-to zone provides an
acceptable range in which a building
façade may be located.

Regulating Plan

Like a conventional code, districts are created, each allowing for the development of at least one building or open space type. Each district is mapped in the regulating plan, similar to a conventional zoning map; however, this is done by examining each parcel and block individually, and is favored in form-based codes not by establishing large swaths of one type of district. Besides mapping the building and open space types, the regulating plan also details how the street types are developed in association with the building and open space types.

Visual Representation of Form-Based Codes

One advantage of a form-based code is its reliance on clearly labeled illustrations to outline each standard. Illustrations may take several forms, depending on the standard being detailed, including plan views, sections, elevations, and 3-Ds. Besides being well illustrated, form-based codes are well organized, with most relevant information in one location, making it easy for city staff, developers, and homeowners to understand.

Landscape, Parking, Lighting, and Signage Standards

A form-based code focuses on the creation of active, sustainable neighborhoods by reconnecting buildings, streets, and open spaces. To ensure success, related zoning standards such as landscaping, parking, lighting, and signage must also be rewritten to enhance the envisioned environment. For example, parking requirements should be rewritten to better match the type of development proposed; neighborhood retail and retail on a major connector streets demand different approaches. Traditional parking standards typically ignore on-street parking and opportunities to share parking spaces between uses, not to mention proximity to transit and the growing popularity of car sharing.

Complete Set of Development Ordinances

A form-based code is one piece in the set of land development standards required for a municipality to promote sustainable development. Subdivision and administration ordinances should also be created in conjunction with a form-based zoning code. Ideally, these three pieces are brought together into one document for ease of use. Subdivision regulations detail how land should be subdivided and developed and can include block patterns, connections to existing neighborhoods, stormwater management techniques, utilities, and permitted materials for impervious surfaces. Administration of the zoning and subdivision ordinances includes

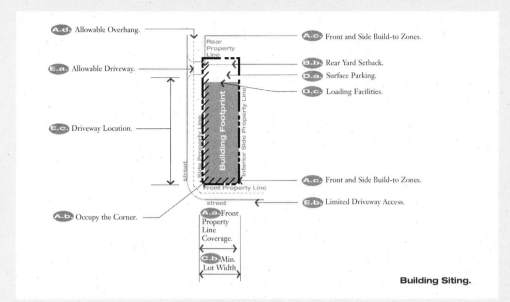

A.d. Allowable Overhang.

A.c. Front and Side Build-to Zones.

E.a. Allowable Driveway.

B.b. Rear Yard Setback.
D.a. Surface Parking.
D.c. Loading Facilities.

E.c. Driveway Location.

A.c. Front and Side Build-to Zones.

E.b. Limited Driveway Access.

A.b. Occupy the Corner.

A.a. Front Property Line Coverage.

C.b. Min. Lot Width.

Building Siting.

A.a. Building Height.

A.c. Allowable Upper Floors Height.

A.b. Allowable Ground Floor Height.

B.b. Internal Parking.

Figure 3.07-2: Height & Use Requirements.

C.a. Allowable Cap Type.

A.a. Transparency of the Upper Floors.

A.b. Maximum Area of No Transparency.

C.b. Allowable Base Type.

B.a. Primary Entrance Location.

B.b. Entrance Spacing.

Facade Requirements.

definitions, and it should also outline the processes that must be followed in order to develop land, such as rezoning, site plan approval, and special use permits. Like the other ordinances, administration should be clearly organized and outlined, to facilitate use by city staff, developers, and residents.

Incorporating Sustainability through Codes, Covenants, and Restrictions (CC&Rs)

Daniel K. Slone
McGuireWoods LLP

Stakeholders involved in master-planned communities often desire assurances that the projects will be delivered as planned and promised and that the sustainable components will not be purposely or accidentally dismantled over time. Such commitments can be difficult, if not impossible, to make or enforce in the normal regulatory process. Codes, covenants, and restrictions (CC&Rs) applied to private property can work in concert with zoning and other regulations to ensure the desired outcome. At the same time, purchasers and developers need flexibility to respond to changing market conditions, changes in technologies, and new ways of thinking about sustainability. Because of the extreme difficulty in changing them once they are hardwired, CC&Rs can become a "dead hand of time," more limiting than zoning and environmental regulations.

CC&Rs should contain the DNA for the layout of the community and its sustainability programs, explaining what they are and how they should be assembled. The CC&Rs must assist the community in understanding the desired outcome, the relative rights and obligations of stakeholders, and the mechanisms for maintaining the desired traits after they are developed. They may include detailed prescriptive elements, but in each instance there should be a statement of the intended performance standard. This allows the addition of elements not explicitly permitted, provided that they meet the performance standards.

CC&Rs are always recorded in order to apply to subsequent property owners. The "codes" referred to in CC&Rs do not have to be set out in the recorded documents; they can be detailed codes or pattern books separate from those documents provided that their enforcement mechanisms are spelled out in the recorded documents. An example of a code provision is a standard requiring that rain barrels and cisterns have appropriate safety covers. The "covenants" are promises or obligations that are detailed in the CC&Rs. An example of a covenant is a commitment to pay the costs of maintenance for a bike trail extending through a riparian buffer area. "Restrictions" are the limits on activities that are allowed within the project. An example of a restriction is the prohibition of campfires within preserved open spaces. Other important restrictions on the construction process or pertaining to the preservation of particularly important resource areas may be detailed in the deeds instead of the CC&Rs.

Timeline: The Evolution of CC&Rs	Roman Law	Early Common Law	Industrial Revolution	Present Day
	Rights to use the land of others for crossings, access to water, etc.	Added the right to use common lands	Regulation of rights-of-way, water rights, and to protect private property from undesired uses after it is conveyed	Regulation of community life, architecture, etc.

Consider the following when drafting CC&Rs. They should:

- Be written in plain English
- Use the term *shall* when guidelines are mandatory, *should* when voluntary
- Be detailed when providing instruction but not overregulate (remember that real towns typically thrive without excessive rules)
- Create resources for learning regulations rather than leaving them unexplained
- State the guiding principles or vision of the end state
- Be clear about the performance standards and flexible in the mechanisms
- Contemplate the possibility that the project will not have everything right at the beginning
- Reflect the urban-rural transect and adjust requirements according to the transect zone
- Provide conflict resolution mechanisms
- Comply with state laws that limit what CC&Rs can regulate

Following is a table outlining suggested practices for CC&Rs.

Table 4-2 The Transect: Suggested Practice in Private Sector CC&Rs

Examples	T1 Rural Preserve	T2 Rural Reserve	T3 Sub-Urban	T4 General Urban	T5 Urban Center	T6 Urban Core	DA Assigned District
Open Space Preservation							
Viewshed	●	●					
Protect historical resources (include buffers)	●	●	●	●	●	●	●
Protect ecological reserves (include buffers)	●	●	●	●	●		
Sustainable forest management	●	●					
Farmland management— protect prime farmland	●	●					
Solar shading					●	●	

continued next page

Source: Susan F. French, "Design Proposal for the New Restatement of the Law of Property Servitudes," 21 *U.C. Davis L. Rev.* 1213, 1214 (1988).

Table 4-2 cont.

Examples	T1 Rural Preserve	T2 Rural Reserve	T3 Sub-Urban	T4 General Urban	T5 Urban Center	T6 Urban Core	DA Assigned District
Restrictions							
Limits on chemical and pesticide use	●	●	●				
Limits on off-road vehicles	●	●					
Limits on forest use (avoid forest fragmentation)	●	●					
Dark sky		●	●	●	●	●	●
Standards							
Urban design			●	●	●	●	●
TND streets, correct sizes, street parking			●	●	●	●	●
Pedestrian orientation to design lots			●	●	●	●	●
Buildings							
Architecture			●	●	●	●	●
Green construction			●	●	●	●	
Green approaches to waste	●	●	●	●	●	●	●
Energy efficiency standards	●	●	●	●	●	●	●
Alternative energy opportunities	●	●	●	●	●		
Landscape							
Green common spaces	●	●	●	●	●	●	●
Green approach to yard waste disposal			●	●			
Infrastructure							
Green infrastructure	●	●	●	●	●	●	●
Green maintenance/repair standards	●	●	●	●	●	●	●
Green approaches to power generation	●	●	●				
Green approaches to stormwater management							
Rain gardens			●	●			
Rain barrels and cisterns			●	●	●		
Greenroofs				●	●	●	●
Green approaches to wastewater management			●	●	●	●	●
Green approaches to solid waste management			●	●	●	●	●
Transportation			●	●	●	●	●
Multimodal transportation opportunities			●	●	●	●	●
Easements							
Stormwater maintenance			●	●	●	●	●
Maintenance of zero-lot-line properties			●	●			
Utilities			●	●	●	●	●

RFP for a Sustainable Urbanist Developer

Sustainable Urbanism can be implemented very effectively using for-profit developers. Having the right developer selection criteria is a key initial step. Requiring a specified performance level under LEED for Neighborhood Development can serve as an effective baseline criteria. The 300-point weighted criteria excerpted below, developed by the Canadian city of Victoria, British Columbia, to initiate Dockside Green, is an effective tool for selecting sustainable urbanist developer.

Table 4-3

Criteria	Possible Points	Criteria/Questions
1. Proposed Site Remediation		
A. Consistency with development concept with regard to remediation and risk management		
Environmental	Pass/fail	Will the proposed plan meet the current requirements set out by the BC Environmental Management Act and Contained Sites Regulation?
Economic	Pass/fail	Will the costs associated with the proposed remediation plan meet the city's goal of break-even?
Economic	15	What risks for remediation are assumed by the proponent?
2. Proposed Land Use		
A. Consistency with development concept with regard to mix of uses		
Social	10	Does the development provide a mix of use (residential, commercial, light industrial, etc.) and to what extent?
Social	5	Does the residential portion provide a mix that satisfies the needs of a broad range of ages and stages of life, as well as income brackets and rental/ownership units?
Economic	5	How much postconstruction employment will be generated in the industrial, commercial, and retail uses of the lots developed?
Environmental	5	Is the mix of uses provided such that environmental concerns such as noise and air pollution are considered through design both on- and off-site?
B. Consistency with development concept with regard to density/FSR (floor space ration)		
Social	10	Does the proposed overall density of development for sites vary from the recommended density in the development concept? How does the proposed density/FSR balance revenue space and amenity/support space?

Table 4-3 cont.

Criteria	Possible Points	Criteria/Questions
Social	5	Does the proposed range of density vary from the recommended density in the development concept on a site-by-site basis?
Economic	2	Does the proposed density/FSR require increase of civic infrastructure over and above what is outlined?

3. Urban Design

A. Contextual response

Criteria	Possible Points	Criteria/Questions
Social	10	Does the building massing, form, and character coincide with that set out in the development concept? Does the proposed building massing respond to the neighborhood "texture" of development? Does it support and act as a transition/natural progression from the harbor up to the existing building skyline?
Economic	2	Is the quality of the construction proposed consistent with the development concept in terms of massing, form, and character?
Environmental	15	Does the design of massing, form, and character take into consideration wind, light and shadow, and sight lines in a positive way?

B. Environmental (LEED) Considerations

Criteria	Possible Points	Criteria/Questions
Environmental	10	Are buildings in risk-assessed portions of the site design to include soil vapor barriers or other approved engineered vapor controls?
Environmental	20	What percentage of space constructed will be LEED-certifiable and to what level?

C. Circulation

Criteria	Possible Points	Criteria/Questions
Social	10	How does the circulation encourage connectedness, a sense of place and community, both within the development area and the surrounding community?
Economic	2	Are the modes of transportation sustainable to maintain and service, both now and in the long term?
Environmental	10	To what extent does the proposal encourage alternative modes of transportation?

D. Public realm requirements

Criteria	Possible Points	Criteria/Questions
Social	10	Is the streetscape pedestrian friendly and inviting, and are building elements or spaces designed at a human scale?
Social	10	Does it meet CPTED [Crime Prevention through Environmental Design] requirements?
Economic	4	How are the operating and maintenance costs proposed to be addressed, now and in the long term? Are the operational/capital costs reasonable? Is the proposal for the developer to maintain the public realm elements in the long term at the developer's cost?
Environmental	10	What protection and/or enhancement of natural resources is proposed?

Criteria	Possible Points	Criteria/Questions
E. Negotiable/optional provisions		
Social	10	What is the proponent offering that, in his or her opinion, meets the local needs?
Economic	5	How are operating and maintenance costs proposed to be addressed, now and in the long term? Are the operational/capital costs reasonable? Is the proposal for the developer to maintain the public realm elements in the long term at the developer's cost?
Environmental	10	What are the environmental benefits of the proposed provisions?
4. Net Present Value		
A. Value of offer		
	Pass/fail	Must meet break-even of net present value of purchase. This does not include cost of remediation or amenities.
Economic	50	Formula for point calculation to be determined. Calculated based on net present value, including NPV for remediation proposal.
B. Tax revenue projections for the city		
Economic	10	Calculated based on projected tax revenue, based on build-out proposal and average value/use assessment/estimated market value. Calculated with the assistance of a subject matter expert.
Proponent Score Subtotal		
Social	100	
Environmental	100	
Economic	100	
Total	300	

PART THREE: EMERGING THRESHOLDS OF SUSTAINABLE URBANISM

Over the last 25 years, leading planners and urban designers have become sophisticated in their ability to conceive and sell attractive infill and master-planned urbanist developments. Against all odds, in the face of runaway sprawl, they have been able to convince developers and municipalities to build excellent urbanism. The projects typically include networks of narrow streets, mixes of housing and building types, a variety of walk-to parks, and address automobile parking in creative ways. The ideas expressed in these leading projects trickle down, raising the bar for the industry and offering proven, successful alternatives to sprawl. Nirvana, right?

Wrong. Urbanism provides the basis for all sustainable human settlements. However, the historic, old urbanist places that inspire the look and feel of much of today's urbanist practice were far from sustainable themselves. Both old and new urbanism dealt with many sustainability issues by putting them out of sight and mind: stormwater and sewage were and remain funneled into pipes—frequently the same pipe—buried or otherwise hidden. There are many other examples of ignored sustainability issues: energy and resource inefficient buildings, unfiltered stormwater runoff, urban heat island, waste that equals waste and a complete dependence on global supply lines for energy, food and resources. The inherent sustainability of urban form can be greatly enhanced through sustainable urbanism. But why does this matter?

Over the next 45 years, 100 million new Americans— not to mention an additional 2.6 billion people worldwide[1]— will be housed in new infill and greenfield developments.

Note

1. First figure: U.S. Census projected population growth, http://www.census.gov/population/projections/nation/summary/np-t1.txt.

Second figure: 2004 revision of the official United Nations population estimates and projections, Population Division of the Department of Economic and Social Affairs, http://www.un.org/News Press/docs/2005/pop918.doc.htm.

All of that development needs to be built to sustainable urbanist principles. But it is one thing for early-adopters to design and develop individual projects to meet LEED for Neighborhood Development and another thing altogether for every project in the country to do so. How can thousands upon thousands of mayors, councils, developers, planners, and architects across the country hope to integrate the human and natural systems of sustainable urbanism if the rules that govern those systems are unwritten?

This section, called Emerging Thresholds of Sustainable Urbanism, is devoted to teasing out those rules. More than 30 leading national experts propose thresholds, or rules of thumb, for designing and developing sustainable urbanism. These dimensional or relational metrics are based on expert judgment of what will satisfy "the 80% rule," guidance that applies most of the time and in most conditions. Every threshold is interdisciplinary and necessarily so. Take for example a single strategy, the share car. It can, and arguably should, reduce off-street parking requests and increase allowable development density. When fully integrated, this one strategy can create neighborhood wealth, reduce the cost of living, and increase the quality of life.

The organization of these thresholds into five categories is meant to focus attention on the core integration challenges of sustainable urbanism: increasing sustainability through density, sustainable corridors, sustainable neighborhoods, biophilia, and high performance buildings and infrastructure.

Through a sustained commitment to design and development, places that integrate human and natural systems with conventional development will rapidly evolve into sustainable urbanism.

Chapter 5
Increasing Sustainability
Through Density

Explaining Density

"There are two things Americans dislike: density and sprawl."
A new urbanist saying

Density is *the* hot button of sustainable urbanism. On one hand, it is a sustainability silver bullet, providing across-the-board reductions in per-capita resource use. These reductions occur in proportion to increasingly development density. Even better, this same density silver bullet provides local, regional, and global benefits. For instance, carbon dioxide, and other climate changing gases produced by human activities, respects no borders, combining each individual's contribution into one large global problem. Reducing per capita production of greenhouse gases becomes an essential strategy so much so that increasing local density has a global benefit.

On the other hand, density is a third rail, inciting local hostility to new developments in direct proportion to their density. The global benefits of reduced per capita VMT appear to be in direct conflict with local benefits. Neighbors come out of the woodwork to oppose dense development, perceiving it as a threat to their quality of life. However, tempers flare more often over traffic and parking, and occasionally blocked sunlight, than over the population density itself. Dense neighborhoods containing a broad mix of goods and services generate fewer per capita trips than auto dependent places. But project opponents do not experience per capita traffic reductions, they experience per acre traffic increases. (See Figure 5-1.) Paradoxically, the "Think Globally, Act Locally" strategy can at times seem to be hardest to achieve on the extremely important issue of density.

To overcome the emotions that arise around density, sustainable urbanism needs to strike the right balance between local impacts and global benefits. The density of new development across the United States averages roughly two dwelling units per acre—too low to support walk-to destinations. This automobile dependent land use has no future and needs to change. This chapter is devoted to development density—what it looks like, what benefits it provides, and the crucial role it plays in supporting both human and natural systems.

Population density versus travel density			
Location	Population Density (people per acre)	Person Travel (vehicle travel per person per day)	Travel Density (vehicle travel per acre per day)
Healdsburg	5 people/acre	30 miles/person	150 miles/acre
Berkeley, California	30 people/acre	10 miles/person	300 miles/acre
Downtown San Francisco	250 people/acre	4 miles/person	1,000 miles/acre

Figure 5-1
The American push-pull of higher-density living.
Image © Martin Wachs.

Illustrating Density

Illustration by John Ellis, WRT/Solomon E.T.C.

Most Americans do not think in terms of the numerical density of a place or have much understanding of what different densities look like or might cost to build. People are much more comfortable relating to the scale of development, either in person or by looking at pictures.

Developers, on the other hand, need to make money, and are acutely aware of both development density and cost. Across a spectrum of development densities, the cost of constructing a project generally increases with density. This means that for a developer to be able to build at the highest densities, rents or sales prices also have to be high to support the project. At the same time, there are lower-cost "sweet spots" along the way that strike a suitable balance between zoning and building code requirements, construction costs, and finding places to stow the parking. **Figure 5-2** illustrates a spectrum of development densities and their respective costs.

Figure 5-2
This figure illustrates and documents patterns of human settlements across a broad spectrum of densities. Image © John G. Ellis.

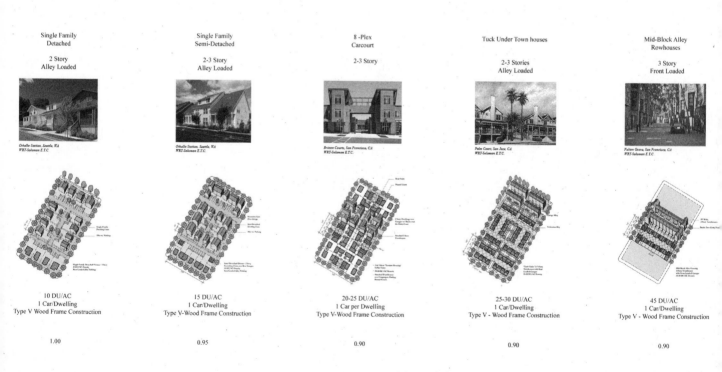

Single Family Detached	Single Family Semi-Detached	8-Plex Carcourt	Tuck Under Town houses	Mid-Block Alley Rowhouses
2 Story Alley Loaded	2-3 Story Alley Loaded	2-3 Story	2-3 Stories Alley Loaded	3 Story Front Loaded
Othello Station, Seattle, WA WRT-Solomon E.T.C.	Othello Station, Seattle, WA WRT-Solomon E.T.C.	Brinton Courts, San Francisco, CA WRT-Solomon E.T.C.	Palm Court, San Jose, CA WRT-Solomon E.T.C.	Fulton Grove, San Francisco, CA WRT-Solomon E.T.C.
10 DU/AC 1 Car/Dwelling Type V Wood Frame Construction	15 DU/AC 1 Car/Dwelling Type V-Wood Frame Construction	20-25 DU/AC 1 Car per Dwelling Type V-Wood Frame Construction	25-30 DU/AC 1 Car/Dwelling Type V - Wood Frame Construction	45 DU/AC 1 Car/Dwelling Type V - Wood Frame Construction
1.00	0.95	0.90	0.90	0.90

'4 over 1' Stacked Flats	'Texas Donut' Stacked Flats	Hybrid Building Stacked Flats over Townhouses	Below Life Safety Mid-rise Tower Stacked Flats	Above Life-Safety High Rise Tower Stacked Flats

5 Story 1 level Podium Garage	5 Story Perimeter Building Multi-level Free Standing Parking Garage	5 Story over Parking Podium	8 Stories Maximum 2 Level Podium Garage	Above 8 Stories Multi-level Podium Garage

Fine Arts Building, Berkeley, CA
WRT-Solomon E.T.C.

Addison Circle, Dallas, TX
RTKL Architects

101 San Fernando, San Jose, CA
WRT-Solomon E.T.C.

501 Bryant Street, San Francisco
LMS Architects

Perry Street Towers, New York, NY
Richard Meier

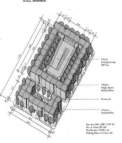

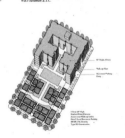

50-150 DU/AC 1 Car/Dwelling Type V - Wood Frame Construction over Concrete Podium	50-150 DU/AC 1 Car/Dwelling Type V - Wood Frame Construction Concrete Garage	100 DU/AC 1 Car/Dwelling Type III - Wood Frame over Concrete Garage	75-150 DU/AC 1 Car/Dwelling Type I - Concrete Frame Construction	150 plus DU/AC 1 Car/Dwelling Type I - Concrete Frame Construction
1.60	1.60	2.00	2.00	2.50

The Transect of the Everyday

Photos by Dhiru Thadani, Ayers/Saint/Gross Architects and Planners

The urban-rural transect describes the varied scale, density, and character of place types, from center city to wilderness. In addition to determining their impact on the Earth, the type of place where people live exerts a powerful influence on their health and well-being, and the choices available to them. Most lifestyle and consumer choices are available to anyone across the transect, but they take different forms in different places. Figures 5-3 through 5-7 were provided by architect Dhiru Thadani. They illustrate how the character of place differs across the transect and how people and businesses adjust their behavior or approach to suit each context. The differences range from the amusingly trivial, such as the kind of dog you own and the shoes you wear, to the sustainably profound, such as how much land you consume and how you get to work. One inescapable conclusion drawn from these photographs is that the denser places, having less landscape to screen or buffer development, require a greater investment in design and beauty. These images also draw attention to the sustainable dignity of the urban-dwelling family whose members walk or take transit everywhere, own no car, and live in a smaller-than-average apartment.

Figure 5-3 *(top row)*
Transect: Buildings.
Image © Dhiru A. Thadani

Figure 5-5 *(third row)*
Transect: Starbucks.
Image © Dhiru A. Thadani

Figure 5-7 *(fifth row)*
Transect: Commuters
Image © Dhiru A. Thadani

Figure 5-4 *(second row)*
Transect: McDonald's.
Image © Dhiru A. Thadani

Figure 5-6 *(fourth row)*
Transect: Washington, D.C.
Image © Dhiru A. Thadani

Natural Zone T-1	Rural Zone T-2	Suburban Zone T-3	General Urban Zone T-4	Urban Center Zone T-5	Urban Core Zone T-6

					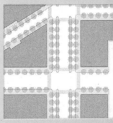

Water and the Density Debate

Lynn Richards
U.S. EPA

Material in this chapter is adapted from "Protecting Water Resources with Higher-Density Development," EPA Publication 231-R-06-001, and "Water and the Density Debate," *Planning,* June 2006.

There are a lot of components to watershed protection, such as appropriately siting development in the watershed, preserving adequate open space, and protecting critical environmental features. In addition, where and how communities choose to grow can play a critical role in watershed protection.

Across the country, most of our regions, cities, towns, and neighborhoods are growing in land area, if not also in population. Every day, new buildings and houses are proposed, planned, and built. Growth has its benefits, but communities are also grappling with related challenges— for example, the impacts on water resources. To protect those resources, local governments are adopting a wide range of land-use strategies, including low-density development.

But is that strategy misguided? Current research shows that the answer may be yes.

What the Research Shows

Virtually every metropolitan area in the United States has expanded in recent decades. According to the U.S. Department of Agriculture's National Resources Inventory, the amount of developed land area in the United States almost quadrupled between 1954 and 1997, from 18.6 million acres to about 74 million acres in the contiguous forty-eight states. From 1982 to 1997, during which period population in those states grew by about 15 percent, developed land increased by 25 million acres, or 34 percent.

Most of this growth is taking place at the edge of developed areas on greenfield sites, which can include forest, meadows, pasture, and rangeland. In one analysis of building permits issued in twenty-two metropolitan areas between 1989 and 1998, about 95 percent of the permits were for development on greenfield sites.

According to the 2000 American Housing Survey, 35 percent of new housing is built on lots between two and five acres in size, and the median lot size is just under a half acre. Some local zoning codes encourage or require relatively large lots, in part because local governments believe that approach helps protect their water quality. They get support from research showing that impervious cover can degrade water quality. Studies have shown that a watershed may start becoming impaired at 10 percent imperviousness and that impairment grows worse as imperviousness increases.

This research has prompted many communities to adopt low-density zoning and limit on site-level imperviousness, specifying a maximum percentage that can be covered by impervious surfaces such as houses, garages, and driveways. These types of zoning and development ordinances are biased against higher-density development because higher density typically produces more impervious cover at the site level.

But is that the whole story? Do low-density approaches really protect our water resources?

Check the Assumptions

A planning department typically analyzes the projected stormwater runoff impacts of a development proposal based on the acreage involved, not the number of housing units being built. Using a one-acre model, communities may conclude that lower density development minimizes runoff because runoff from one house on one acre equals roughly half the runoff from eight houses on that same acre.

However, one should consider where the other seven houses and their occupants would be located. Almost always, they are located somewhere within the same region—very often within the same watershed. Those "displaced" households still have a stormwater impact.

To better understand the stormwater runoff impacts from developing at low densities, the impacts of original and displaced houses need to be taken into account. This approach has two advantages. It acknowledges that the choice is not whether to grow by one house or twenty or ten thousand, but where and how to accommodate whatever growth the region is expected to see. It also emphasizes that total imperviousness and runoff should be minimized within a region or watershed rather than on particular sites.

To more fully explore this dynamic, the EPA modeled scenarios at three scales—one acre, development site, and watershed—and at three different time periods of build-out to examine the premise that lower-density development better protects water quality. Stormwater runoff was examined from different development densities to determine the comparative difference between scenarios (see Table 5-2).

Notably, we found that the higher-density scenarios generated less stormwater runoff per house at all scales and time periods. We found that:

- With more dense development (eight houses per acre), runoff rates per house decrease by about 74 percent from one house per acre.
- For the same number of houses, denser development produces less runoff and less impervious cover than low-density development.
- For a given amount of growth, lower-density development covers more of the watershed.

Taken together, these findings indicate that low-density development is often not the best strategy for reducing stormwater runoff. In addition, the findings indicate that higher densities may better protect water quality, especially at the lot and watershed levels (see Figure 5-8). Higher-density developments consume less land while accommodating the same number of houses as lower-density developments. Consuming less land means less impervious cover is created.

While increasing densities regionally can better protect water resources at a regional level, higher-density development can create more site-level impervious cover, which can increase water quality problems in nearby or adjacent bodies of water. Numerous site-level techniques are available to address this problem. When used in combination with regional techniques, these site-level techniques can prevent, treat, and store runoff and associated pollutants. Many of these practices incorporate low-impact development techniques such as rain gardens, bioretention areas, and bioswales (see Figure 5-9 & Chapter 8: Stormwater Systems).

Figure 5-8
Compact urbanism as pictured
here is the best tool for protecting
water quality. Image © U.S. EPA.

Figure 5-9
Street-scale bioswale.
Image © U.S. EPA.

Others go further by changing site-design practices—for example, by reducing parking spaces, narrowing streets, and eliminating cul-de-sacs.

Overall, we know that to fully protect water resources, communities must employ a wide range of land-use strategies based on local factors. Among them are building in a range of development densities, incorporating adequate open space, preserving critical ecological and buffer areas, and minimizing land disturbance.

Some site-specific strategies have spin-off effects. They can enhance a neighborhood's sense of place, increase community character, and save taxpayers money. The strategies that meet multiple community objectives are generally not the traditional engineered approaches, such as detention ponds, which are often difficult to install in urban areas or on sites where there are land constraints.

These nontraditional approaches work best in dense urban areas because they use the existing elements of a neighborhood, such as roads, roofs, abandoned shopping malls, or courtyards, and add some engineering to landscaping elements to help retain, detain, and treat stormwater on site. When done correctly, these approaches address stormwater issues and add value to a community to help to make the neighborhood a more desirable place to live.

Table 5-2

Scenario	Number of Acres Developed	Impervious Cover (%)	Total Runoff (ft³/yr)	Runoff Per Unit (ft³/yr)	Savings Over One house/ acre runoff per unit (%)
One-Acre Level: Different densities developed on one acre					
A: One house/acre	1	20	18,700	18,700	0
B: Four houses/acre	1	38	24,800	6,200	67
C: Eight houses/acre	1	65	39,600	4,950	74

Transit Supportive Densities

It is easiest to attract and retain public transit riders in densely developed corridors. Simply put, a concentrated population living or working immediately adjacent to a transit stop creates a reliable market of people within easy walking distance of transit service. Quantifying this relationship between population density in a transit corridor and its ability to support transit is both essential to sustainable urbanism and woefully under researched. Seminal research on this topic was done in the 1970s for the Regional Plan Association by Jeffrey Zupan and Boris Pushkarev. While their work covered only the New York metropolitan region and did so at a time in history when people were much less automobile reliant, their research is still resonant today. The chart below links transit modes to the minimum residential density necessary to support it (see Table 5-3).

Table 5-3 Transit Modes Related to Residential Density (Boris Pushkarev and Jeffrey M. Zupan)

Mode	Service	Minimum Necessary Residential Density (dwelling units per acre)	Remarks
Dial-a-bus	Many origins to many destinations	6	Only if labor costs are not more than twice those of taxis
Dial-a-bus	Fixed destination or subscription service	3.5 to 5	Lower figure if labor costs twice those of taxis; higher if thrice those of taxis
Local bus	"Minimum," 1/2 mile route spacing, 20 buses per day	4	Average, varies as a function of downtown size and distance from residential area to downtown
Local bus	"Intermediate," 1/2 mile route spacing, 40 buses per day	7	
Local bus	"Frequent," 1/2 mile route spacing, 120 buses per day	15	
Express bus— reached on foot	Five buses during two-hour peak period	15 Average density over 2-square-mile tributary	From 10 to 15 miles away to largest downtowns only
Express bus— reached by auto	Five to ten buses during two-hour period	3 Average density over 20 square mile tributary area	From 10 to 20 miles away to downtowns larger than 20 million square feet of nonresidential floorspace
Light rail	Five-minute headways or better during peak hour	9 Average density for a corridor of 25 to 100 square miles	To downtowns of 20 to 50 million square feet of residential floorspace
Rapid transit	Five-minute headways or better during peak hour	12 Average density for a corridor of 100 to 150 square miles	To downtowns larger than 50 million square feet of nonresidential floorspace
Commuter rail	Twenty trains per day	1 to 2	Only to largest downtowns, if rail line exists

Chapter 6
Sustainable Corridors

The Sustainable Corridor

Doug Farr, Leslie Oberholtzer, and Christian Schaller
Farr Associates

CORRIDOR DENSITY: NECESSARY TO FREE PEOPLE FROM AUTOMOBILE DEPENDENCE. MIN 7 DWELLING UNITS PER ACRE (DU/A) TO SUPPORT BASIC BUS SERVICE HIGHER PREFERRED FOR BETTER SERVICE & MODE (15 DU/A TROLLEY) 22 DU/A LIGHT RAIL

CORRIDOR LAND USE MIX: TO ACHIEVE A 1:1 JOB - HOUSING BALANCE

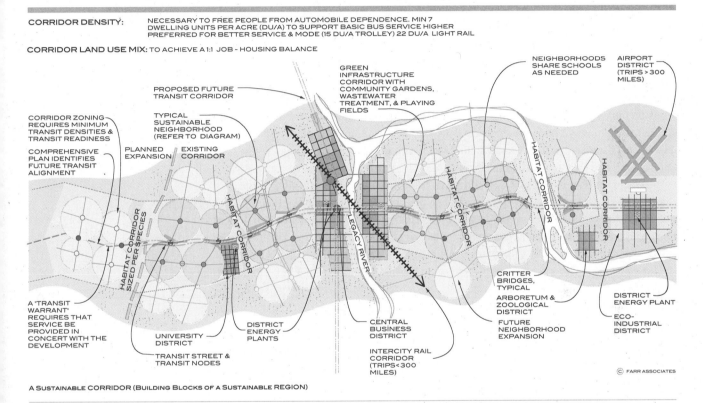

CORRIDOR ZONING REQUIRES MINIMUM TRANSIT DENSITIES & TRANSIT READINESS

COMPREHENSIVE PLAN IDENTIFIES FUTURE TRANSIT ALIGNMENT

PLANNED EXPANSION / EXISTING CORRIDOR

PROPOSED FUTURE TRANSIT CORRIDOR

TYPICAL SUSTAINABLE NEIGHBORHOOD (REFER TO DIAGRAM)

GREEN INFRASTRUCTURE CORRIDOR WITH COMMUNITY GARDENS, WASTEWATER TREATMENT, & PLAYING FIELDS

NEIGHBORHOODS SHARE SCHOOLS AS NEEDED

AIRPORT DISTRICT (TRIPS > 300 MILES)

HABITAT CORRIDOR SIZED PER SPECIES

HABITAT CORRIDOR

LEGACY RIVER

HABITAT CORRIDOR

HABITAT CORRIDOR

A "TRANSIT WARRANT" REQUIRES THAT SERVICE BE PROVIDED IN CONCERT WITH THE DEVELOPMENT

UNIVERSITY DISTRICT

TRANSIT STREET & TRANSIT NODES

DISTRICT ENERGY PLANTS

CENTRAL BUSINESS DISTRICT

INTERCITY RAIL CORRIDOR (TRIPS<300 MILES)

FUTURE NEIGHBORHOOD EXPANSION

CRITTER BRIDGES, TYPICAL

ARBORETUM & ZOOLOGICAL DISTRICT

DISTRICT ENERGY PLANT

ECO-INDUSTRIAL DISTRICT

© FARR ASSOCIATES

A SUSTAINABLE CORRIDOR (BUILDING BLOCKS OF A SUSTAINABLE REGION)

Figure 6-1
Image © Farr Associates 2007.

The Integration of Transportation, Land Use, and Technology

Shelly Poticha
Reconnecting America

For centuries, transportation modes, whether on water, in the air, or on land, have been closely correlated with the settlement patterns of our society, with each generation building new communities in areas made accessible by transportation investments. This historical interconnection was particularly profound for transit investments and housing in the late nineteenth and early twentieth centuries. Streetcar suburbs served as the mechanism for land developers to attract the growing class of new homeowners into suburban neighborhoods on the edges of crowded inner cities. The introduction of the automobile accelerated suburban development and weakened the links among mass transportation, walkable neighborhoods, mixed use, and housing that had long existed. Many of our great cities hollowed out and transit ridership declined.

How times have changed. Transit ridership is on the rebound. Since 1995, public transportation use has increased 25 percent, and in 2005 alone, riders in the United States took more than 9.7 billion trips. There are 3,349 mass transit stations in the United States today, and regions from coast to coast are building or planning to build new rail systems or expand existing systems. More than 700 new stations are currently under development.

A number of factors are driving this growth in transit use and construction. First, automobile transportation is increasingly expensive, accounting for almost 20 percent of household annual expenditures. Expenditures for personally owned vehicles drain household wealth and undercut community economic viability. Second, residents are frustrated with increasing traffic congestion and are looking for other options. Third, these motivations and new strategies for reinvesting in urban communities have combined to accelerate infill development and transit investment. People who can choose to use and live near transit are doing so.

The desire for improved accessibility and greater choice in housing and transportation has resulted in a development trend called transit-oriented development (TOD). In many ways, TOD is a return to the notion of the streetcar suburbs, where housing was provided within a comfortable walking distance of stations. While fostering new development was the original impetus for many privately funded transit lines, today TOD is often seen as an effective means of leveraging transit investments for greater transit ridership. TOD fosters greater use of a transit system by creating neighborhoods within walking distance of transit stations that offer compact development, a diversity of land uses, and pedestrian-oriented design. Where housing is built within easy walking distance of transit, residents use transit five times as often as those who drive to the station and non-automobile-mode shares are substantially higher than in neighborhoods where every trip must be made by car.

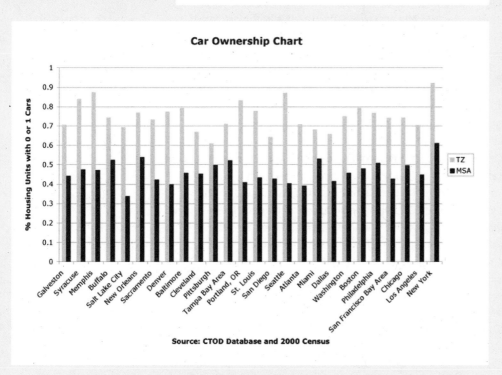

Four Transit Systems Shown at the Same Geographic Scale

Houston | Small
18 Stations

Dallas-Fort Worth | Medium
48 Stations

Washington D.C. | Large
127 Stations

Chicago | Extensive
401 Stations

0   10   20   30
Miles

— Rail Line
Urban Area

Car Ownership Chart

% Housing Units with 0 or 1 Cars

TZ
MSA

Galveston, Syracuse, Memphis, Buffalo, Salt Lake City, New Orleans, Sacramento, Denver, Baltimore, Cleveland, Pittsburgh, Tampa Bay Area, Portland, OR, St. Louis, San Diego, Seattle, Atlanta, Miami, Dallas, Washington, Boston, Philadelphia, San Francisco Bay Area, Chicago, Los Angeles, New York

Source: CTOD Database and 2000 Census

Figure 6-2
As transit systems grow and connect people to new places and activities, travel behavior and development patterns change. Image © Reconnecting America's Center for T.O.D.

Figure 6-3
In all regions, people who live near transit stations have about half as many cars as their regional neighbors. Image © Reconnecting America's Center for T.O.D.

Growing Demand for Housing Near Transit and the Role of Regional Transit Networks

The consumer market is ready for transit-oriented development. According to a study by Reconnecting America's Center for Transit-Oriented Development (CTOD), demand is strong, and as the transit system grows, demand for housing near transit will also grow. In fact, the types of households that tend to seek out TOD—singles, couples without children, the elderly, and low-income minority households—are also the types of households that are projected to grow the most over the next twenty-five years. While today there are roughly 6 million households who live within half a mile of an existing fixed-guideway transit stop, a conservative estimate is that by 2030 potential demand for housing near transit could be over 16 million households. There seems to be a growing recognition that TOD has the potential to provide important benefits to communities by sparking economic development, to transit agencies by generating additional ridership, and to developers by attracting a substantial and growing market.

Less discussed, but equally important, is the need to ensure that housing built within walking distance of transit offers opportunities to a spectrum of income levels. Almost half of the projected 16 million households with a demand for TOD will have incomes below 50 percent of the area median income (AMI). Considerable demand will also come from singles and couples without children and making $60,000 to $125,000 annually. A range of housing choices in TODs—mixed-income TOD—is crucial to realizing the full potential of the transit investments being made to provide greater transportation access and housing choice to a full array of home owners and renters.

At the same time, mixed-income TOD presents opportunities to meaningfully address the nation's growing affordability crisis by tackling housing and transportation costs together while expanding access to jobs, educational opportunities, and prosperity for the range of income groups living in our metropolitan regions. By offering (1) truly affordable housing, (2) a stable and reliable base of transit riders, (3) broader access to opportunity, and (4) protection from displacement, mixed-income TOD holds the potential to address the seemingly intractable problems of worsening congestion, rising unaffordability, and the growing gap between lower-income and wealthier residents.

As the overall housing market is starting to wake up to TOD, there is an increasing challenge to deliver TOD that can provide housing opportunities for the full range of incomes seeking housing in transit zones. Though TOD's signature qualities—pedestrian orientation, a range of services within walking distance, and access to regional jobs—make it possible for households to live with one less car and thus reduce household transportation spending, the irony is that the very factors inhibiting the TOD market are also making it hard to deliver mixed-income housing.

Defining TOD and the TOD Place Typology

Transit-oriented development is more than simply a project next to a transit station. It includes the neighborhood or district surrounding the station, comprising multiple development projects, a mix of uses, a walkable network of streets, and design that supports urban living and transportation choice.

What makes TOD different from development is its focus on improving the convenience of transit for residents. Can parents drop a child off at day care on the way to work? Can errands be done on foot? Is it possible to take a business client to lunch without having to use a car? The types of uses in a TOD must be carefully matched with the function of the station and the needs and desires of those who live and work nearby. Indeed, "place making" may be almost as important to TOD as transit service.

Development experiences demonstrate that TOD cannot be defined by a prescribed set of densities or mix of uses (see Figure 6-4). Those who live in neighborhoods near downtown, for example, use transit more often and drive less than their counterparts in suburban communities, even though they may live just as close to a transit station. The reason is that many near-in neighborhoods combine density with walkable street patterns, access to transit, neighborhood amenities, and an adequate mix of nearby retail and jobs, and also because the demographic composition of these neighborhoods is so varied. Suburban neighborhoods are more likely to be physically separated from transit by a highway right-of-way, park-and-ride lot, or wide thoroughfare filled with fast-moving traffic. Typically, in the suburbs uses are separated, with residential uses consolidated in one area and commercial, retail, and industrial uses in others. Even though densities can be comparable to the city, residents are far more likely to drive for all trips.

TOD ought to create places that integrate transit into neighborhoods and help support lively and vital communities in urban and suburban neighborhoods. The unique qualities of place should be respected and the different roles of the place within the regional context should drive the mix, density, and character of TOD. The types of questions that ought to be answered include: How much and what type of retail is needed to serve residents and employees? How can a project provide some parking but not so much that it puts a financial burden on the development and detracts from the overall pedestrian and transit orientation? What scale of development is most appropriate for different contexts—a downtown central business district or a neighborhood station?

Building Communities with Transit

Regional transit systems are made up of numerous corridors; indeed, transit systems are built corridor by corridor, gradually completing a long-range regional network (see Figure 6-5 & 6-6). To date, however, very little research has been done to distinguish the different purposes of individual transit corridors and the role they play in linking regional destinations, providing circulation, and stimulating transit-oriented development. But from a user perspective, transit corridors function very differently depending on the types of activities that are located at various stops along the line. For example, as people begin to use transit more frequently, they take trips along the corridor for regular everyday activities such as going shopping, visiting a library, or going to a park, and they connect to the region as a whole from their home or place of work. By contrast, a transit line that provides service only in the morning and evening peak hours can provide utility only to commuters, not those seeking a full range of transportation options.

Place Types

Places	Activity Mix	Housing Types	Commercial Employment Types	Proposed Scale	Connectivity	Local Examples	Color Code	Examples
Major Urban Center	Office Residential Retail Entertainment Civic Uses	Multi-Family/Loft	Employment Emphasis, with more than 250,000 sf office and 50,000 sf retail	5 Stories and above	Intermodal Facility/ Transit Hub. Major Regional Destination with quality feeder and circulator connections	Downtown Galleria District Medical Center		
Urban Center	Residential Retail Office	Multi-Family/ Townhome	Limited Office. Less than 250,000 sf office. More than 50,000 sf retail	3 Stories and above	Sub-Regional Destination. Some Park n Ride. Linked district circulator and feeder transit service	Areas of Montrose/ Museum District Allen Parkway		
Neighborhood	Residential/ Neighborhood Retail	Multi-Family/ Townhome/ Small Lot Single Family	Local-Serving Retail. No more than 50,000 sf	1-5 Stories	Walk up station. Very Small Park and Ride, if any. Local and express bus service.	Mid-Town West University Magnolia Park Montrose		
Retail Street	Residential/ Neighborhood Retail	Small Lot Single Family	Main Street Retail Infill	1-4 Stories	Bus or streetcar corridors. Feeder transit service. Walk up stops. No parking.	Rice Village 19th Street (Heights) Highland Village		
Campus/ Special Events Center	University/ Campus Sports Facilities	Limited Multi-Family	Limited Office/Retail	Varies	Large Commuter Destination	Rice University U of H TSU Reliant Park		

Figure 6-4

Fixed transit investments, such as train stations or streetcar stops, are opportunities to focus development into transit-oriented places. Loosely based on the transect, each place type describes how development around transit should be integrated into the surrounding urban fabric. High densities should be promoted, but the degree to which the station area increases its density is dependent on the planning, context, and strength of the surrounding neighborhood. Image © Reconnecting America's Center for T.O.D.

Comparing Corridors

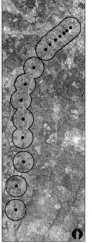

LEGEND

● Existing Or Proposed
Rail Station

Land Use
- Residential
- Commercial
- Industrial
- Civic
- Mixed Use
- Vacant/Misc.

The Circle on Each Map
Represents the Half Mile
Radius from the Station

| Portland Streetcar | Minneapolis Hiawatha Line | Boston Fairmount Line | Charlotte South Corridor |

Figure 6-5
In looking at the space in between the regional scale of transit and the place types, corridors provide another building block of transit planning. Most federal funding for transit is done at the corridor level and place types can be assigned to different stops along a corridor. Image © Reconnecting America's Center for T.O.D.

Comparing Transit Technology

Transit Technology

Technology	Heavy Rail	Commuter Rail	Light Rail	Modern Streetcar	Heritage Streetcar	Bus Rapid Transit	Express Bus
Example Cities	Washington DC New York Subway Chicago	Boston Chicago San Francisco	Denver Portland Minneapolis	Portland Tacoma Seattle	New Orleans San Francisco Kenosha	Los Angeles Pittsburg Eugene	Most Cities Served by Bus Systems
Approximate Cost Per Mile (Millions)	$50-$250	$3-$25	$20-$60	$10-$25	$2-$12	$4-$50	$1-$2
Service Type	Regional/Urban	Regional/ Interurban	Regional/ Urban	Urban Circulator	Urban Circulator	Regional/Urban	Regional/Urban
Station Spacing/Type (Miles)	Urban Core <1 Periphery 1-5 Station/Platform	2-5 Station/Platform	.25-2 Sidewalk Sign/ Station/Platform	.25 Sidewalk Sign/ Platform	.25 Sidewalk Sign/ Platform	.25-2 Sidewalk Sign/ Station/Platform	Limited Stops Along Normal Bus Routes
Peak Service Frequency (Minutes)	5-10	20-30	5-30	8-15	8-15	3-30	10-30
Operating Speed (MPH)	30-80	30-60	20-60	8-12	8-12	8-12	30-80
Alignment/ROW Width	Separate ROW 25-33 Feet	Existing Freight ROW/ 37+ Feet	Street Running or Separate ROW/11-33 Feet	Street Running 11-24 Feet	Street Running 11-24 Feet	HOV or Separated Median/28 Feet	Street Running
Typical Power Source	Electric	Diesel/Hybrid	Electric	Electric	Electric	Diesel/Hybrid	Diesel/Hybrid
Photos							

Figure 6-6
When looking specifically at corridors for transit patronage, one must examine the capacity and characteristics of specific modes. If a city is seeking to bring commuters from the suburbs, it might opt for a commuter rail format with large vehicles able to run on freight rail tracks. For circulation in and redevelopment of a downtown a streetcar is more appropriate and more cost-effective than heavy rail. Each transit type has a specific purpose and use, pointing to the need to integrate all modes instead of arguing for one over another. Image © Reconnecting America's Center for T.O.D.

Biodiversity Corridors

Rebecca L. Kihslinger, Jessica Wilkinson, and James McElfish
Environmental Law Institute

Habitat loss and fragmentation are by far the most significant threats to the conservation of native wildlife. In fact, habitat loss is among the leading causes of imperilment for 85 percent of the endangered and threatened species listed under the U.S. Endangered Species Act.[1] By influencing the amount and pattern of habitat that is fragmented, degraded, and destroyed in a landscape, land use decisions made at the local level play a significant role in the conservation of biodiversity.

Conservation biologists have made considerable progress over the past twenty years in determining how the size, shape, and connectedness of habitat affect the sustainability and persistence of species and natural processes.

A recent synthesis of scientific studies compiled by the Environmental Law Institute provides general threshold recommendations for habitat patch area, buffer size, patch connectivity, and percent of suitable habitat in a landscape to support land use, open space, and smart growth planning that will sustain species, community, and ecosystem diversity.

Land use decisions made at the local, county, and state levels have a significant and cumulative effect on the conservation of native species diversity. The types, extent, and arrangement of land uses within the landscape will influence the viability of habitat patches, the amount of suitable habitat, the severity of edge effects, and the utility of buffers and corridors. Well-planned landscapes include:

- Large, high-quality, and well-connected habitat patches capable of supporting sustainable populations of native and rare species
- Well-designed habitat corridors to connect otherwise isolated larger remnant habitat patches
- Wide and vegetated buffers to minimize edge effects on habitats and protect water quality and stream habitat

Conservation-minded landscape plans and community designs also limit development in sensitive ecosystems such as wetlands, riparian corridors, and critical habitat.

Straightforward and accessible conservation parameters, or "conservation thresholds," can provide land use planners and decision makers with concrete targets when making decisions about the amount and pattern of land to protect. Such guidelines can influence local and state land use, open space, and smart growth planning and policies, especially in situations where local, case-specific data are lacking.

1866	1969	1973	2000	2003–2004	2005	
Term *ecology* coined by the German biologist Ernst Haeckel	University of Pennsylvania landscape architect Ian L. McHarg publishes *Design with Nature*	President Richard Nixon signs the Endangered Species Act[2]	Ecological Society of America publishes guidelines for land use planning and management[3]	Environmental Law Institute publishes *Conservation Thresholds for Land Use Planners* and *Nature Friendly Ordinances*[4]	All fifty-six U.S. states and territories submit state wildlife action plans to the U.S. Fish and Wildlife Service outlining proactive,	comprehensive wildlife conservation strategies[5]

Determine the locally important and rare species and habitats in need of protection.
State wildlife action plans and natural heritage programs are good sources of local
information. These can be supplemented by consulting local biologists for additional information to tailor conservation thresholds to specific habitat types, ecological communities,
and landscapes. Land use professionals may also work with land management agencies
to identify rare species and landscapes in need of protection.

*Use local biological information and knowledge on landscape context to determine the
amount and location of land to conserve.* The quality and configuration of habitat patches
and the condition of the surrounding landscape influence the total amount of suitable habitat
that should be preserved in a given area. The proportion of suitable habitat conserved in a
plan will also vary with the local species and habitat types to be protected.

Preserve large, connected habitat patches. Land use plans should maximize habitat
patch size, minimize the degree of isolation among existing habitat patches, and optimize
the natural connectivity of the landscape using habitat corridors, stepping-stone patches,
or other specific structural components. In areas where this is not possible, land use
professionals should try to conserve the habitat that remains and identify potential areas
for habitat restoration.

*Use local biological information and knowledge on landscape context to determine
buffer size and structure.* To minimize edge effects, the area within a buffer should not be
included in the patch size measure, and roads, trails, and other development should not
occur in the buffer. Riparian buffers should include native and diverse vegetation, should be
continuous along the maximum extent of the stream, and should be free of disturbance
(see Figure 6-1).

Consider the regional context of local planning efforts. Ecological and wildlife habitat
boundaries generally do not correspond with political or planning boundaries. Landscape-
scale planning can help promote the proactive conservation of large, connected, high-quality
habitat patches while addressing the regional impacts of local land use decisions.

These standards are based on a review of a select sample of scientific papers pertinent
to species and ecosystems in the United States on critical thresholds.[6] The default recommendations are based on the goal of capturing 75 percent of the requirements found for the
species, communities, and habitats surveyed. Land use planners and land managers should
consider these results as a baseline from which to launch more tailored and in-depth
assessments based on local species and habitats.

	Percent Suitable Habitat	Habitat Patch Size	Landscape Connectivity	Riparian Buffer Size	Edge Width (Buffer Size)
Table 6-1		Conservation Thresholds for Land Use Planners			
Default	Minimum: 20–60 percent of natural habitat in a landscape. Range depends on species, taxa, and habitat quality.	Minimum: 137.5 acres. Habitat patch size is species specific. Planners should consult local biologists to determine the habitats in greatest need of protection.	Maintain connectivity among patches in the landscape. The condition of the surrounding landscape, interpatch distance, and corridor design affects species' ability to disperse through the landscape.	Minimum: 328 feet for wildlife conservation. Range: 9.8–5,249 feet. Buffer size depends on species, site and watershed conditions, adjacent land use, slope, hydrology, and management objectives.	Minimum: 755–984 feet. Edge effects on abiotic factors may extend from 26.2 to 787 feet. Measures should be taken to soften edge effects on habitat patches.
Birds	Literature range: 5–80 percent.	Literature range: 2.5–6,177 acres.	Maintain connectivity among patches in the landscape.	Literature range: 49.2–5,249 feet.	Literature range: 172.2–2,254 feet, depending on the parameter measured.
Mammals	Literature range: 6–30 percent for small mammals only. Wide-ranging or large-bodied mammals require additional habitat.	Literature range: 2.5–5.4 million acres	Maintain connectivity among patches in the landscape.	Literature range: 98.4–600 feet.	Literature range: 147.6–2,952.8 feet, for only three species.
Reptiles/ Amphibians	Consult local biologists for site-specific information.	Consult local biologists for site-specific information.	Maintain connectivity among patches in the landscape.	Literature range: 98.4–1,473 feet.	Consult local biologists for site-specific information.
Plants	Consult local biologists for site-specific information.	Literature range: 5–247 acres for tree communities.	Maintain connectivity among patches in the landscape.	Consult local biologists for site-specific information.	Consult local biologists for site-specific information.

Notes

1. B. A. Stein, L. S. Kutner, and J. S. Adams, eds., *Precious Heritage: The Status of Biodiversity in the United States* (New York: Oxford University Press, 2000).

2. See U.S. Fish and Wildlife Service, "History of Evolution of the Endangered Species Act of 1973, Including Its Relationship to CITES," http://www.fws.gov/endangered/esasum.html (accessed September 10, 2006).

3. See V. H. Dale et al., "Ecological Principles and Guidelines for Managing the Use of Land," *Ecological Applications* 10, 3 (2000): 639–70, http://www.esa.org/pao/policyStatements/pdfDocuments/LandUsePositionPaper.pdf (accessed September 10, 2006).

4. See "Resources—Environmental Law Institute," http://www.naturefriendlytools.org/tools/resources/environmental/index.html

5. See Teaming with Wildlife, "State Wildlife Action Plans," http://www.teaming.com/state_wildlife_strategies.htm (accessed November 3, 2006).

6. These standards were adapted from the Environmental Law Institute Conservation Thresholds Land Use Planners, 2003, available at http://www.elistore.org/reports_detail.asp?ID=10839 (accessed November 3, 2006).

Chapter 7
Sustainable Neighborhoods

Neighborhood Diagrams

Illustrations by Regional Plan Association, Duany Plater-Zyberk & Company
and Farr Associates

Neighborhood Unit: Clarence Perry

Clarence Perry's diagram of the neighborhood unit, published as part of the 1929 Regional
Plan of New York and Environs, has influenced generations of plans. The enduring parts of the
diagram include its quarter-mile "pedestrian shed," its ideal size of 160 acres, a neighborhood
center surrounded by civic buildings, clearly delimited edges, commercial uses at the edge,
a network of narrow streets, small walk-to parks throughout, and the population needed to
support an elementary school. From the point of view of sustainable urbanism, the plan has a
number of shortcomings. For instance, it includes no reference to public transit or varied
housing types, neglects the river asset, misaligns streets with those in adjacent neighborhoods, and is silent on buildings and infrastructure.

An Urban Neighborhood (Part of a Town): DPZ

The Duany Plater-Zyberk (DPZ) urban neighborhood diagram, based on Clarence Perry's
neighborhood unit, is an update that resolves most of the earlier plan's shortcomings.
The diagram sensibly substitutes boulevards for highways, aligns local streets, proposes
a bus stop in the neighborhood center, adds parking, and sites the school to allow it to

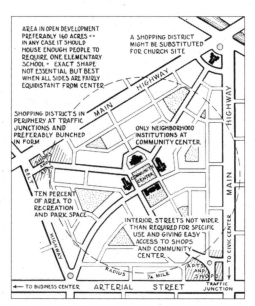

Neighborhood Unit

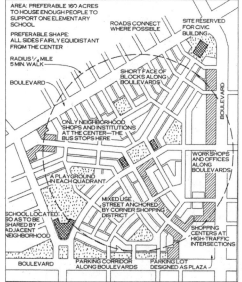

An Urban Neighborhood (Part of a Town)

Figure 7-1
Neighborhood unit for the Regional
Plan of New York by Clarence Perry,
1929. Image © Regional Plan
Association.

Figure 7-2
Updated neighborhood unit.
Image © Duany Plater-Zyberk
& Company.

serve multiple neighborhoods. The DPZ diagram also establishes a rule of thumb for establishing neighborhood parks—one per quadrant. From the point of view of sustainable urbanism, the DPZ diagram, like Perry's before it, remained silent on buildings and infrastructure and sees no role for nearby nonhuman habitat, going so far as to eliminate Perry's hypothetical river altogether.

Sustainable Urbanist Neighborhood

The sustainable neighborhood diagram below builds on the previous two, adapting them to meet current needs. Five distinctions result: (1) the neighborhood is a building block of a transit corridor; (2) the central DPZ bus stop is replaced with a higher intensity transit mode (BRT, trolley, light rail); (3) it is fitted out with high-performance infrastructure: district power, dimmable streetlights, and a share car per block; (4) the mix and density support car-free housing and a third place; and (5) habitat and infrastructure greenways give the neighborhood distinct edges.

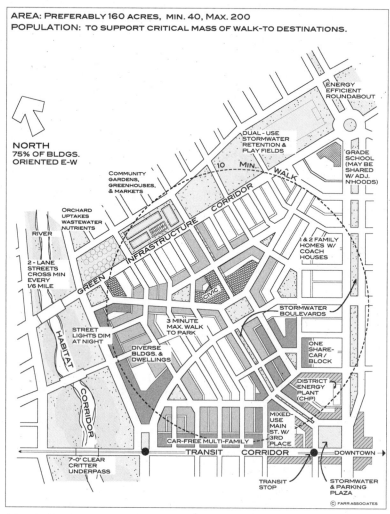

Figure 7-3
Sustainable Neighborhood Diagram.
Doug Farr, Leslie Oberholtzer
and Christian Schaller.
Image © Farr Associates.

A Sustainable Neighborhood Unit (Building Blocks of a Sustainable Corridor)

Neighborhood Definition

Victor Dover and Jason King
Dover Kohl & Partners

The traditional *neighborhood* is the basic increment of town planning. One neighborhood alone in the countryside is a *village*. Two or more neighborhoods grouped together sharing a specialized hub or main street is a town. The neighborhood concept remains in force even as the size increases to city scale; Paris, for example, is assembled from a series of many high-quality neighborhoods. Coupled with special districts and corridors, neighborhoods are the building blocks from which enduring settlements are formed. The dynamism and diversity that characterize attractive cities rely upon a solid foundation of vital and coherent neighborhoods.

In our time it's become necessary to reassert the definition of the term. We don't use the word *neighborhood* to refer to the disconnected, single-use developments that characterize sprawl, such as stand-alone apartment complexes, subdivision tracts, office parks, or shopping centers. Real traditional neighborhoods meet all those same needs—for housing, workplaces, shopping, civic functions, and more—but in formats that are compact, complete, and connected, and ultimately more sustainable and satisfying.

A genuine neighborhood is "compact, pedestrian-friendly, and mixed-use," according to the charter of the Congress for the New Urbanism. That said, we are often pressed to specify the exact parameters of the ideal neighborhood—minimum and maximum acreages, dimensions, densities, populations, commercial components, mix of dwelling types, and so on—but the metrics of neighborhoods should range widely to reflect regional customs, climates, and site conditions.

Although the numbers vary, there are five basic design conventions that provide a common thread linking great neighborhoods.

Identifiable Center and Edge to the Neighborhood

One should be able to tell when one has arrived in the neighborhood and when one has reached its heart.

There must be places where the public feels welcome and encouraged to congregate, recognizable as the heart of the community. A proper center has at least one outdoor public environment for this purpose, designed with pedestrians in mind; this is spatially the most well-defined "outdoor room" in the neighborhood. It is configured for gatherings both organized and spontaneous, for both ceremonies and day-to-day casual encounters. The size and formality of the central space vary from place to place, and while it most typically takes the form of a square or plaza, it is also possible to give shape to the neighborhood center with just a special "four corners" intersection of important streets. In most climates, shade or other protection from the elements is found at the center.

480 BCE	1573	1909	1929	1940s	1990s
First grid-planned Greek city (by Miletus)	The Laws of the Indies require developments to be divided into grids and main squares	Raymond Unwin's book *Town Planning in Practice* advocates limiting size of developments and creating greenbelts around cities	Clarence Perry develops neighborhood unit	Clarence Stein's interpretation of Perry leads to modern suburban sprawl	Duany Plater-Zyberk reaffirms and updates Perry's diagram

The best centers are within walking distance of the surrounding, primarily residential areas, and typically some gradient in density is discernable from center to edge. Centers possess a mix of uses and the potential for higher-density buildings at a pedestrian scale (four stories maximum for most circumstances, except at the metropolitan core).

Discernible centers are more important than discernible edges because of the center's usefulness in day-to-day life. Paul Murrain has observed that average urban dwellers probably care far less about a well-defined edge for their neighborhood than a well-defined center because the center affects the quality of life by being the place for meeting daily needs and connecting socially. The center is also the place for coalescing of community in response to adversity; we gather at the commons in times of emergency.

Delineating the neighborhood edge by design is more a source of psychosocial comfort than the meeting of a physical need, so the adjustments that are made to the urban fabric at the edge are often subtle.

Walkable Size

The overall size of the neighborhood should be suitable for walking. Neighborhoods range from 40–200 acres.

Most people will walk a distance of approximately one-quarter mile (1,320 feet) before turning back or opting to drive or ride a bike rather than walk. This dimension is a constant in the way people have settled for centuries. Most neighborhoods built before World War II were one-quarter mile from center to edge.

Of course, neighborhoods are not circular in design, nor is that desirable. Neighborhoods tend to elongate along contours and ridges and compress at slopes because the walkability elongates across flat planes. The quarter-mile radius is a benchmark for creating a neighborhood unit that is manageable in size and feel and inherently walkable. We certainly should be willing to walk farther.

Neighborhoods of many sizes and shapes can satisfy the quarter-mile radius test. Large civic spaces such as modern schools with play fields require a great deal of acreage and can be situated where they are shared by more than one neighborhood. When the territory to be settled encompasses more acreage, larger planned communities can satisfy the quarter-mile radius by establishing several distinct neighborhoods or quarters within the community. Significant centers should be spaced about one-half mile apart or less.

Great neighborhoods have a fine-grained mix of land uses and housing types. Any mix of uses dramatically reduces the number of external automobile trips required by residents, and so there is no set minimum to the amount of commercial or office use that should be present. At least three dwelling types are necessary to create architectural diversity.

An assortment of uses gives residents the ability to dwell, work, entertain themselves, exercise, shop, and find daily needs and services within walking distance. An assortment of building types allows people with diverse lifestyles and incomes to live in the same neighborhood without a diminishing of the character or quality of that neighborhood. For instance, in a shopfront building, the business owner or employees could live in a second-floor apartment, or the upper floors could be rented as office space. Nearby row houses and cottages can be located very close to detached homes and even mansions. Naturally, this requires substantial design discipline; designers must work to make sure that compatible building types face one another across unified streets. Most transitions between substantially different building types should occur at the rear lot lines.

It is understood that the amount of nonresidential uses will vary from neighborhood to neighborhood. Some neighborhoods may only have a tiny commercial presence, but every live/work combination, also known as "zero-commute housing," eliminates at least one car from rush-hour traffic. The key is to provide great flexibility in land use even while tightening design controls to ensure compatibility. This shift—from focusing on land use to emphasizing design, from single-use, single-design "pods" to mixed-use, variety-rich neighborhoods—has benefits in three key areas.

First, in transportation, mixing uses is the most powerful way to reduce unnecessary traffic congestion because many auto trips are either shortened or eliminated. Second, the mixed housing scenario is far better socially, since it makes it feasible for householders to put down roots in a community and come to know their neighbors, and housing for families of modest means is included and therefore need not be segregated into concentrations (or pushed to the next county). Third, the occupation of the neighborhood by households with varied schedules and interests not only adds to the vibrancy of a place (as compared to suburbs that are deserted at certain times of the day or days of the week) but adds security as well.

Integrated Network of Walkable Streets

A network of streets allows pedestrians, cyclists, and motorists to move safely and comfortably through a neighborhood. The maximum average block perimeter to achieve an integrated network is 1,500 feet with a maximum uninterrupted block face of ideally 450 feet, with streets at intervals no greater than 600 feet apart along any one single stretch.

A "street network" is of course a connected web of streets, not necessarily a strict Cartesian grid. The street network forms blocks that set up logical sites for private develop-ment, and it provides multiple routes for walking, biking, or driving. The network of streets also provides nonmotorized alternatives to those under the driving age and senior citizens. Small block size and frequent intersections are necessary. When designing streets, we should strive to make them walkable first and then add provisions for cars, trucks, and emergency vehicles.

"Design speed" is the crucial number engineers officially use to configure streets for orderly traffic movement. The chosen design speed must be a low figure, usually less than 25 mph, for a highly walkable environment. The slow design speeds that characterize walkable streets result from the conscious choice of features such as narrow curb-to-curb cross sections, street trees, architecture close to the street edge, on-street parking, and relatively tight radii at the street corners.

The highest quotient of walkability will result when the buildings that shape the street space are set close enough to the front property line to spatially define the streets as public spaces, with a minimum degree of enclosure formed by a building-height-to-street-width proportion of 1:3 or closer.

Special Sites Are Reserved for Civic Purposes

In complete neighborhoods, it is always true that some of the best real estate is set aside for community purposes. These locations are made significant by the geometry of the town plan. Prominent locations, such as a terminated vista seen down a street or at the top of a hill, should be reserved for landmark buildings. These locations are deliberately selected for building sites that will conclude the long view down a street or for anchoring a prominent street corner or neighborhood square. These unique settings within the neighborhoods are the permanent anchors for community pride. Civic buildings, because they serve the entire community, should be accessible and located in areas with greater activity.

Similarly, special sites should be set aside for parks, greens, squares, plazas, and playgrounds. Each neighborhood should have one special gathering space at its center, such as a village green.

Parks are the largest of the open spaces, and contain natural preserves, paths, and trails. *Greens* are smaller but should ideally be large enough for a person to be away from the noise and movement of the street. *Squares* are often used for civic purposes. They are at least one acre in size, located at the intersection of major streets, and shaped by surrounding building frontages. Squares contain landscaping and trees that are deliberately arranged. *Plazas* are used for civic and commercial purposes (such as outdoor cafes) and are primarily hard-surfaced (stone, brick, pavement, etc.). They are smaller than a square and spatially defined by surrounding frontages. *Playgrounds* can be any size, are designed primarily for children, and may be part of larger parks or greens.[1]

Note

1. Duany Plater-Zyberk & Company, SmartCode Annotated, Version 8.0, 2005.

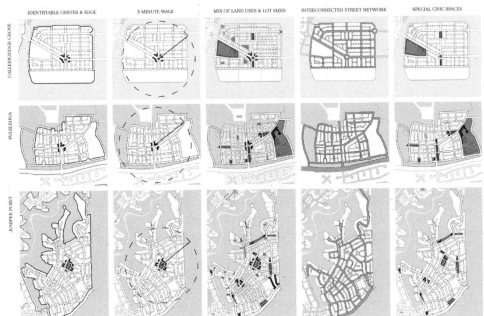

Figure 7-4
Image © Victor Dover.

Table 7-1 Neighborhood Definition		Size (Acres)	% Area Devoted to Center (Acres)		Number of Primary Dwellings	Number of Accessory Dwellings	Net Residential Density (DU/Acre) [2]	S.F. of Commercial Space	Net Commercial Area (S.F./Acre)
Name	Location								
Historic city of Charleston	Charleston, SC	1,015	9%	(88 acres)	5,428 [1]	Unknown [4]	7.6	Unknown [4]	Unknown [4]
Four wards in historic Savannah[5]	Savannah, GA	50	9%	(4.5 acres)	320 [1]	Unknown [4]	9.1	180,200 [3]	3,604
Seaside (original 80 acres)	Seaside, FL	80	5%	(4.1 acres)	330 [1]	Unknown [4]	8.2	153,034 [3]	1,912
The North End Neighborhood	Boston, MA	148	7%	(10.3 acres)	6,600 [1]	Unknown [4]	82.6	708,319 [6]	4,785
Forest Hills Gardens	Queens, NY	142	2.8%	(4.1 acres)	800 [1]	Unknown [4]	7.2	7,500 [3]	52
Callery Judge Grove	Palm Beach County, FL	89	3%	(2.7 acres)	460	350 [7]	9.96	18,000	390
Pulelehua	Maui, HI	108	6.4%	(6.9 acres)	438	101 [7]	11	62,768	1,586
Juniper Point	Flagstaff, AZ	151	9.5%	(14.4 acres)	1739	342 [7]	20	116,200	1,417
Optimum range		40-200	3-10%		400 min[8]				100-400

1. *Source:* US Census, 2000

2. Residential Density = Dwelling Units - Acres (which do not include roads, parks, and public areas); Source: ArcGIS 9 ESRI Data and Maps

3. *Source:* ArcGIS Business Analyst

4. Data unavailable

5. The four wards chosen are bounded to the north by Rt. 25, to the east by Lincoln Street, to the the west by Whitaker Street, and to the south by Oglethorpe Avenue.

6. *Source:* Boston Redevelopment Authority

7. Potential number of units once completely built

8. This minimum is based on 2007 assumptions about conventional retail channels of distribution and per-household purchasing. The number will change as sustainable urbanism advances.

Neighborhood Completeness

Eliot Allen and Doug Farr
Criterion Planners and Farr Associates

Emerging public health research is revealing an ever-clearer understanding of the relationship between neighborhood design and the length and share of all trips that people will willingly make on foot. One central idea that has become very clear is that meeting one's daily needs on foot in a neighborhood is made much more convenient and more likely when many walk-to destinations are clustered close together. The questions raised by this idea are how many destinations are needed and how close together do they need to be to get people to consistently walk?

Criterion Partners has developed a pioneering methodology that can serve as the basis for developing metrics to begin to answer this question. While the criteria in this threshold were developed to assess auto-dependent study areas as large as 500 acres, far larger than a neighborhood or viable pedestrian shed, the tools and methods are immensely useful. The hope is that this tool will be used for research purposes and the number of destinations and clustering distance can be refined to apply to a 40 to 200 acre neighborhood. Once refined, the tool can be used in existing and new communities to identify opportunities for densification and economic development.

The first step is to list all pedestrian destinations that may occur in the neighborhood. The list below, taken from the draft of LEED for Neighborhood Development and amended with sustainable urbanist destinations, serves as the basis for the following examples.

Potential Pedestrian Destinations/Developed Land Uses

Bank	Laundry/dry cleaner	Post office
Child care facility	Library	Restaurant
Community/civic center	Live-work housing	School
Convenience store	Medical/dental office	Senior care facility
Hair care	Park	Share car
Hardware store	Pharmacy	Supermarket
Health club or indoor recreation facility	Place of worship	Third Place
	Police/fire station	Transit Shop

Neighborhood Completeness	=	Number of pedestrian destinations	x	Proportional area balance of all pedestrian destinations in pedestrian shed (Refer to Table 7-2 to determine completeness level).

Table 7-2

Level of Neighborhood Completeness	Percentage of Identified Uses Present in Neighborhood
Excellent	70% or greater
Satisfactory	30–70%
Minimal	10–30%
Poor	Less than 10%

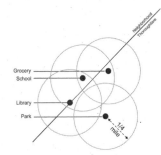

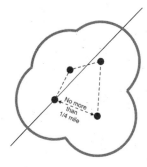

From the list of amenities that has been put together, identify those in the vicinity and their respective walking catchment areas—for example, walking distances of one-quarter to one-half mile. Delineate pedestrian sheds for each amenity (see Figure 7-5).

Identify a critical mass of pedestrian destinations by mapping clusters where destinations are no further apart than one-quarter mile (see Figure 7-6). The number of destinations that meet this proximity threshold is called the critical mass and is the first value in the neighborhood completeness equation.

Use balance is the proportional balance of developed uses in the critical mass pedestrian shed, by land area, expressed on a scale of 0 (low) to 1 (high). This is calculated as follows:

Pj = proportion of developed land uses in the critical mass pedestrian shed (1<j<N)
N = number of unique developed land uses in the study area

The resulting use balance score is the second value in the neighborhood completeness equation.

Figure 7-5
Neighborhood plan showing one-quarter mile catchment areas for each destination. Image © Eliot Allen.

Figure 7-6
Critical mass of four pedestrian destinations clustered and no more than one-quarter mile apart. Image © Eliot Allen.

Sample Completeness Calculations
7 amenities (of 20 possible) in a consolidated pedestrian shed x 0.2 use balance
= 1.4 neighborhood completeness
20 amenities (of 20 possible) in a consolidated pedestrian shed x 0.75 use
balance = 15.0 neighborhood completeness

Neighborhood Completeness Indicator	Value
Excellent	10–20
Satisfactory	5–10
Minimal	3–5
Poor	Less than 3

Neighborhood Housing

Laurie Volk and Todd Zimmerman
Zimmerman/Volk Associates, Inc.

Apologists for the status quo persist in declaring that the automobile-dominated, low-density, single-use pattern of the postwar suburbs is the inevitable manifestation of the ruggedly independent American character. However, the relentless dispersion of housing, shopping and workplaces across the American landscape is far from inevitable.

Purely from a market perspective, if there is any inevitable destiny for American settlement patterns, it will be the reurbanization of our cities and towns rather than the continuation of the slow march toward economic, fiscal, and social entropy. Remaking, reforming, and rebuilding American settlement patterns will be the major real estate story of the first half of the twenty-first century.

The housing market that will drive this urban renaissance is no mystery. We don't have to wait for these urbane citizens to be born or to arrive from abroad; they already live here. The market is simply the convergence of the two largest generations in the history of America: the 82 million baby boomers, born between 1946 and 1964, and the 78 million millennials, who were born from 1977 to 1996.

Boomer households have been moving from the full-nest to the empty-nest life stage at an accelerating pace that will peak sometime in the next decade and continue beyond 2020. In our work in cities across the country, large and small, we have found that since the first boomer turned fifty in 1996, empty nesters have had a substantial impact on urban housing, particularly in downtown areas. After fueling the dramatic diffusion of the population into ever lower-density exurbs for nearly three decades, boomers, particularly affluent boomers, are rediscovering the merits and pleasures of downtown living.

Meanwhile, millennials are just leaving the nest. The millennials are the first generation to have been largely raised in the post-1970s world of the cul-de-sac as neighborhood, the mall as village center, and the driver's license as the main means of liberation. We have found that, as has been the case with predecessor generations, many millennials are heading for the city. They are not just moving to New York, Chicago, San Francisco, and other large American cities; often priced out of these larger cities, millennials are discovering second-, third-, and fourth-tier urban centers.

In contrast to previous generations, the millenials are much more aware of environmental issues and are more actively involved in organizations and activities that promote sustainability. The millenials recycle whenever possible, buy organic products when available, and are very interested in green building and construction.

Boomers and millennials are already the primary purchasers of condominiums; in 2003, for the first time, the national median price of a new condominium exceeded that of a new

Figure 7-7
Rental Loft/Apartments.
Image © Farr Associates.

Figure 7-8
For-sale Loft/Apartments.
Image © Farr Associates.

Figure 7-9
Rowhouses.
Image © Farr Associates.

single-family house. In response, it is the rare regional or national building company that hasn't established an infill housing division. During the mid-decade housing slump, those urban/ infill housing divisions generally accounted for a significantly increased percentage of the parent company's revenue.

The convergence of two generations of this size—each reaching a point when urban housing matches their life stage—is unprecedented. For example, in 2006, there were an estimated 41 million Americans between the ages of twenty and twenty-nine, forecast to grow to 44 million by 2015. In that same year, the population between fifty and fifty-nine also will have reached 44 million, from 38.6 million today. The synchronization of these two demographic waves will mean that there will be 8 million potential urban housing consumers in these age groups eight years from now.

Compared with the postwar flood of households to the new exurban suburbs, the current rediscovery of urban environments is still a mere trickle. But the sheer numbers of urban-oriented households will shift this paradigm.

Over the next several decades, this "demographic imperative" represents the potential for millions of additional urban dwellings, not only in urban infill and downtown locations but also in mixed-use, walkable locations at every scale, from existing urban neighborhoods to new suburban centers.

Zimmerman/Volk Associates groups American households into three general categories: young singles and couples, traditional and nontraditional families, and empty nesters and retirees. These three categories correspond roughly to the major life stages of an individual household. A neighborhood that includes housing types matching the preferences of the potential market, then, could potentially accommodate an individual's housing needs and desires over a lifetime; by extension, that mix of housing types could potentially accommodate several generations of residents over time.

The charts on the accompanying page aggregate sixty recent market studies from among the hundreds prepared by Zimmerman/Volk Associates for public and private sector clients across the country (see Tables 7-3, 7-4, 7-5). They document the range of market potential by household and dwelling types along with the optimal distribution of dwelling types. The averages outline broad national trends, while the ranges demonstrate that housing must reflect local context, site conditions, climate, culture, and tradition, yielding significant variations in the optimal housing mix from location to location.

Urban Detached Housing Types

Figure 7-10
Small lot detached house.
Image © Farr Associates.

Figure 7-11
Large lot detached house.
Image © Farr Associates.

Figure 7-12
Urban detached
Abraham's Lincoln's house.
Image © Farr Associates.

Table 7-3 Optimum Residential Mix by Housing Type for New Traditional Neighborhoods* (New Construction)

		Rental Lofts/ Apartments	For-Sale Lofts/ Apartments Townhouses/ and Duplexes	For-Sale Rowhouses/ Detached Houses	For-Sale Small-Lot Detached Houses	For-Sale Mid-Range Large-Lot Detached Houses	For-Sale Urban	
Percent of all Units	Range	15% to 31%	4% to 17%	2% to 16%	5% to 35%	13% to 34%	4% to 30%	Total %
	Average	23%	9%	9%	24%	22%	13%	100%

*Compiled from 30 market studies conducted between 2000 and 2006.
TNDs range in size from 400 to 4,500 dwelling units.
**Source:* Zimmerman/Volk Associates, Inc.

Table 7-4 Market Potential by Household Types for Downtown and In-Town Neighborhoods**

	Rental Lofts/ Apartments		For-Sale Lofts/ Apartments		For-Sale Rowhouses/ Townhouses/ Duplexes		For-Sale Urban Detached Houses	
	Range	Average	Range	Average	Range	Average	Range	Average
Younger Singles & Couples	33% to 77%	62%	26% to 79%	54%	24% to 70%	47%	17% to 64%	35%
Traditional & Non-Traditional Families	0% to 35%	12%	0% to 26%	8%	0% to 47%	17%	5% to 54%	31%
Empty Nesters & Retirees	9% to 59%	26%	16% to 67%	38%	17% to 56%	36%	15% to 53%	34%
		100%		100%		100%		100%

**Compiled from 30 market studies conducted between 2000 and 2006.
Cities range in size from 3,400 to 900,000 people.
Source: Zimmerman/Volk Associates, Inc.

Table 7-5
Optimum Residential Mix by Housing Type for Downtown and In-Town Neighborhoods**
(New Construction and/or Adaptive Re-Use)

		Rental Lofts/ Apartments	For-Sale Lofts/ Apartments	For-Sale Rowhouses/ Townhouses/ Duplexes	For-Sale Urban Detached Houses	
Percent of all Units	Range	23% to 55%	17% to 36%	15% to 30%	10% to 32%	
	Average	37%	25%	205	18%	100%

Car-Free Housing

Car-free housing is the emerging practice of developing residential buildings that do not provide off-street parking. This practice is the norm in Manhattan and in mixed-use transit-served locations in other large cities. Zoning regulations across the United States adopted over the last fifty to sixty years have required developers to provide one or more off-street parking spaces per dwelling. These parking requirements are probably well suited to the reality of automobile-dominated suburban locations. However, in pedestrian-friendly transit-served locations, they require parking spaces for residents who may not own cars. This requirement can unnecessarily increase the cost of housing by as much as $30,000 to $40,000 per required off-street space and become a self-fulfilling prophecy, inducing car ownership with the "free" parking space the dwelling owner bought. The common practice of selling dwelling units with dedicated parking spaces results in an oversupply of parking. Sustainable urbanism requires that any parking be sold separately from the dwelling unit.

Figure 7-13
Manhattan features block after block car-free housing.
Image © Farr Associates.

Car-free housing is a viable strategy to reduce the cost of housing and to increase development density, walking, biking and transit use. It requires coordination and integration between the location of a development, the municipal regulations that guide the development, and the willingness of banks and developers to bring forward car-free projects. In order to test the market demand and viability of such a concept, a number of projects have set aside a portion of residential units as car-free. The tenancy can be either rental or ownership.

Car-free housing should be developed in concert with either public or developer-provided shared cars (see Car Sharing). Each shared car is thought capable of replacing five to eight private cars. Municipalities have tended to adopt very conservative off-street parking reductions—less than half of the predicted rate of replacement. Car-free housing also requires contractual assurances that residents will not own cars.

The car-free housing criteria on the next page provide guidance regarding the location of potential car-free housing districts and related project requirements (see Table 7-6). The thresholds for regulation of municipal residential parking provide guidance on how to modify existing parking requirements to extend the benefits of reduced residential parking requirements citywide (see Table 7-7).

1913	1940s–1950s	1990s	2003
Henry Ford introduces the assembly line to mass-produce cars	Minimum off-street parking requirements are widely adopted	Milwaukee allows on-street parking to help meet off-street requirements	Gold Dust Apartments in Missoula, Montana, offers car-free units specifically geared toward pedestrians and bikers

Table 7-6 Criteria for Car-Free Housing Districts

Location Criteria

Mixed use	High percentage of neighborhood completeness
Transit service	Corridor with high level of transit service
Connected location	Fine-grained network of pedestrian and bike facilities
Local demographic	See Table 7-11 miminal thresholds for car shares

Project Requirements

Contractual assurances	Renter/owner signs contract agreeing not to own a car
Developer-provided mobility	Transit pass free of charge to each resident
	Minimum one shared car per six to eight dwellings
	Secure indoor bicycle storage
Marketing	All sales or rental solicitations to mention car-free project
Sales	All units are sold unbundled (without parking spaces)
Private parking	None provided, rely soley on on-street and public parking
Public parking	See Table 7-7 below

Table 7-7 Sustainable Urbanist Thresholds for Residential Parking Regulations

Policy	Conventional Practice	Sustainable Urbanism
Off-street parking spaces	Minimum number required per dwelling	Maximum number allowed per dwelling
Reduced parking requirements	Not permitted	Provision for shared car with shared car replaces up to five off-street parking spaces
For-sale parking spaces	Sold with dwelling	Sold separately
Shared-car parking and car	None required	Minimum one per every ten dwellings
On-street parking in front of development	Cannot be used to meet requirements	Can be used to meet off-street or shared car requirements

Neighborhood Retail

Robert J. Gibbs, ASLA
Gibbs Planning Group, Inc.

One of the primary advantages of traditional neighborhood designed (TND) communities over conventional suburbs is the opportunity to walk to shopping and entertainment venues. However, few communities based on new urbanism have successfully implemented retail centers. In many cases, a TND community's retail is not developed until years after the last residential phase is completed.

Often, TND communities' retail centers fail to meet minimal sales necessary for its business owners to earn a reasonable income. The underperforming centers result in businesses that offer limited goods and poor service and thus cannot compete with market-driven retail centers. Many TND developers choose not to build the commercial phase of their community because land values are much higher for residential than retail.

Developing and managing retail centers remains one of the riskiest of all real estate categories. Retailers must respond to ever-changing consumer trends and demands while constantly fending off new competition. As a result, the retail industry relies upon proven methods and techniques to minimize the risk and to earn a market rate of return on their investment. Many of the most desirable historic neighborhoods and TND communities have clusters of successful retailers.

Unlike suburban development, where various commercial land uses are segregated from residential, in a TND community retail and residential are closely intertwined. As a result, the vitality of the TND community's retail can directly impact the surrounding residential areas. In extreme cases, boarded-up storefronts and undesirable tenants such as tattoo parlors and pawn shops can cause the values of adjacent homes to nosedive. Conversely, popular and useful retailers such as coffee shops, cafes, and food markets contribute to the quality of life in the neighborhood. It is in the best interests of the community that the retailers meet or exceed industry sales standards.

Figure 7-14
Traditional corner store.
Image © Gibbs Planning Group, Inc.

Corner Stores

The smallest and most useful retail type, the corner store, ranges from 1,500 to 3,000 square feet. Corner stores are ideally located along major local roads at the busiest entry to the neighborhood. However, in densely populated TND communities, the corner store can be sustainable within the neighborhood when located along its primary street. The store also benefits if it is located adjacent to community buildings, parks, and schools, although schools often dislike corner stores being near their campus because of their appeal as student hangouts (refer to Chapter 7: Neighborhood Completeness).

Approximately one thousand households are necessary to support the average corner store. This represents one corner store per each TND neighborhood, based upon a five-minute walk. However, this number can be reduced significantly if the store is located along a major road with 15,000 cars per day or more. Corner stores that also sell gasoline are supportable with virtually no adjacent homes. Sales from construction trades prior to the completion of an entire neighborhood can potentially support a corner store.

The average corner store will yield approximately $210 in sales per square foot per year, or $300,000 to $600,000. Gross sales will be significantly higher if the store sells packaged liquor or gasoline. Annual rents for the typical corner store will average $14 to $16 per square foot. Rents and sales are significantly higher in dense urban areas. Rent represents only 8–10 percent of most retailers' total operating expenses. Developers will often offer the store owner a significant rental discount in order to have the amenity for the neighborhood. Such a discount is not advised, since if the store is not sustainable from the onset, the business owner will often fail or quit (see Table 7-8).

Convenience Centers

Typically between 10,000 and 30,000 square feet, these centers offer an array of goods and services geared toward the daily needs of the surrounding neighborhoods. These centers are often anchored with a small specialty food market or pharmacy. The balance of the center usually includes five to eight small businesses ranging from 1,500 to 3,000 square feet each.

Each of these small businesses would have a difficult time if located on a stand-alone site. However, by being grouped into a walkable cluster, each business helps to generate impulse traffic and sales for the others.

Convenience centers need about two thousand households, or two TND neighborhoods, to be supportable. These centers must be located along a major road and ideally at the primary entry to both neighborhoods. Their average trade area typically extends up to a one-mile radius. Average sales for convenience center retailers are $225 per square foot per year. Annual rents in centers average $15 per square foot per year, with a range of $12 to $18 (see Table 7-8).

Figure 7-15
New traditional Main Street.
Image © Farr Associates.

Figure 7-16
New urbanist retail center.
Image © U.S. EPA 2003.

Neighborhood Centers

Typically anchored with a supermarket, pharmacy, and video store, neighborhood centers offer a full range of goods and services not available at corner stores or convenience centers. Neighborhood centers generally range from 60,000 to 80,000 square feet in total size (including the supermarket) and typically require 6 to 10 acres of property. Site planning using TND principles can potentially reduce the center's size by up to 20 percent. These centers have an overall blended parking ratio of 4 cars per 1,000 square feet of gross building area. Supermarkets and restaurants will demand higher parking ratios around their business.

These neighborhood centers require 6,000 to 8,000 households to be located within their primary trade area. The typical suburban trade area is 1 to 2 miles. However, in very rural areas it's not unusual for residents to driver over fifty miles weekly to visit a neighborhood center. By contrast, dense urban centers can support a supermarket every few blocks.

Neighborhood center sales and rents vary widely depending on business type. On average, the centers average $245 per square foot per year in sales. Rents range from $7.25 for supermarkets to up to $40 for coffee shops.

Many TND developers and new urbanist planners often try to limit the size of the supermarket to between 20,000 and 25,000 square feet. However, small supermarkets are impractical due to the large variety of goods demanded by the average American household. Today's supermarket must carry a much greater variety of products than it did in the 1960s, when a 25,000-square-foot A&P was considered full-size.

The neighborhood center is a favorite for lending institutions and investment houses. They earn a proven income stream, and it is assumed that families will always need to purchase groceries. Recently the neighborhood center has been threatened by the discount supercenter, estimated to be able to put up to two supermarkets out of business when entering a market. In addition, the popular "green" grocery stores and warehouse clubs are attracting well-educated, higher-end consumers away from the standard supermarket. Retail development is forever reinventing itself (see Table 7-8 below).

Table 7-8

	Gross Retail Area (S.F.)	Dwellings Necessary to Support Retail[1]	TNDs Necessary to Support Retail (6 DU/Gross Acre)	Sales per S.F.	Average Annual Rent per S.F	Average Trade Area	Parking[2]	Urban Form	Anchor Stores
Corner Store	1,500-3,000	1,000	1	$210	$14-16	Neighborhood (5-minute walk)	On-street	Mixed-use corner building	Any small-scale retail
Convenience Centers	10,000-30,000	2,000	2	$225	$12-18	1-mile radius	4.0 cars/ 1,000 S.F of gross building area	Main street	Specialty food market or pharmacy
Neighborhood Center	60,000-80,000	6-8,000	6 to 8	$245	Highly varied from $7.25 to $40.00	1-2-mile radius	4.0 cars/ 1,000 S.F. of gross building area	Mixed-use main street	Supermarket, pharmacy, and video store

1 This number can be reduced significantly if the store is located along a major road with 15,000 cars per day, and reduced nearly to zero if gasoline is sold.

2 Combines on-street and off-street parking

Site Plan and Parking

Convenience-oriented neighborhood businesses must offer a sufficiently high level of amenities in order to be competitive with major shopping centers and big-box stores. The center should be planned to allow for most of the retailers to face the primary road and neighborhood entry street. Ideally, most neighborhood residents will walk or drive through a section of the retail area on their way to and from home. Given that the average household produces ten trips per day, a dwelling neighborhood could produce up to ten thousand daily trips along the shopfronts. Because local businesses mostly rely on the impulse visit and have limited advertising budgets, this exposure is a must.

The corner store or neighborhood center should also be oriented to allow for easy pedestrian access from the surrounding neighborhoods. Surface parking lots should be hidden behind small liner retailers or oriented toward the primary highway. As much as possible, a seamless transition from residential to commercial should be maintained.

Parking remains one of the most critical issues facing any retailer, and this is especially true for neighborhood retailers. Easy-to-use parking is essential. Ample free parking near a store's entry is vital. That being said, parking should not dominate the site plan, and walkable, store-lined streets should be maintained to the greatest extent possible.

In contrast, shoppers will demand parking directly in front of the destination store in a small town or convenience center. Should such a space not be available, the typical shopper will believe that parking is problematic and less convenient compared with the modern shopping center. As a result, this shopper will tend to avoid the location for shopping in the future.

Business Practices

A major weakness of many TND commercial centers is the lack of modern business practices and management. In some cases, retailers have been left to fend for themselves, with little or no required management participation and organization. These practices can result in low sales, high turnover and, eventually a failed center.

One of the most common mistakes in TND neighborhood retail is the lack of required minimum store hours. It's impractical for small independent retailers to maintain extended hours. However, one of the top complaints of many shoppers is the limited hours of small retailers and centers. Approximately 70 percent of all retail sales occur either after 5:30 P.M. or on Sundays. A center that does not keep these hours is limiting itself to one-third of the market share. In addition, good lighting, clean walkways, and well-maintained street furniture are essential for a competitive commercial center. Limited hours and poor maintenance convey a sense of subpar service and lack of value to time-stressed families. Following is a summary of basic recommended guidelines for TND neighborhood center management (see Table 7-9).

Table 7-9   Guidelines for Traditional Neighborhood Business Practices

Management	• Establish a required Common Area Management (CAM) fee as a part of the tenant base rent. This fee is to be used by the shopping center management for maintenance and marketing of the center's common area.
	• Develop a business mix plan that limits overlapping goods and services, while still maintaining healthy competition.
	• Maintain control over interior store plans, merchandising, lighting, and displays.
	• Implement a common marketing campaign for the center and its merchants.
Design	• Require high design standards for storefronts and signage. Adopt a 70 percent minimum clear-glass frontage (as measured between 3 and 8 feet from finished walk) at the first level for all new construction. Avoid suburban shopping center-type signage and storefronts.
	• Businesses should be encouraged to differentiate themselves with signage, color, and façade alterations. Allowing them to reinforce their brand also emphasizes the downtown's wide selection of goods and services. Avoid an overemphasis on continuity of color and form.
	• Reduce the front valance flap height to 8 inches maximum. Only permit canvas-type fabrics; plastic fabrics should be prohibited. Permit two colors for awnings. Small logos or business names on awnings should be permitted.
	• Keep all storefront lights on a central timer to remain illuminated until 10:00 P.M. Large common trash cans should be located in alleys or at the rear of buildings. These containers should be enclosed if possible, and kept clean and free of pests and odors. Restaurant containers should be cooled during warm weather.
Operation	• Maintain minimal hours to 7:00 P.M. weekdays and to 9:00 P.M. at least one evening per week. Suggest 9:00 A.M. to 5:00 P.M. Saturday hours.
	• Cross-merchandise with other downtown merchants by sharing window and interior display props.
	• Highlight holidays and seasons with prominent displays located at the front and center the stores.
	• Require storefront window displays to be updated monthly.
Maintenance	• Paint storefronts and interiors on a regular (one to two year) basis. Clean and paint front doors and windows three to four times per year. Wash store doors 4-5 times daily.

Economic Benefits of Locally Owned Stores

Matt Cunningham
Civic Economics

Many people have strong emotional arguments for supporting locally owned businesses. They list such reasons as better service, unique atmosphere, and a wider choice of goods as reasons to promote local businesses. Recent research has also shown that there is a strong economic reason to shop locally. Money spent at a locally owned business is more likely to stay in the region and have a greater economic impact than money spent at a national chain. This threshold will highlight this new way of thinking about local businesses and show how they help to create a more sustainable economy than national chains.

Local Advantages

A local business has economic advantages over national chains in four main categories: labor, profit, procurement, and charity.

Labor. Spending on local labor accounts for a larger share of operating costs for a locally owned establishment than for an outlet of a national chain. While chains are able to consolidate administrative functions such as bookkeeping and marketing at national headquarters, independents carry out these functions in-house or outsource them within the community. Additionally, economies of scale and carefully engineered store layouts may allow national chains to employ fewer on-site staff than locally based firms.

Profits. A larger portion of profits earned by locally owned stores will remain in the local economy. Purchases of goods, services, and meals at chain outlets generate profits for the corporation, which then either reinvests in global operations or distributes a portion of profits to shareholders. In either case, chain store profits circulating in the local economy are nominal.

Procurement. Locally owned businesses procure a wider array of goods and services in the local marketplace. These include goods for resale, business supplies, and professional services.

Charity. A smaller yet significant share of the local advantage is charitable giving. The owners and employees of local firms generally live in and around their business locations and are more likely to give back to their own communities. National firms may be more likely to donate to charities near corporate headquarters or other large corporate facilities.

Civic Economics knew that in order for cities to create policies to help level the playing field for local businesses against their national competitors, a solid economic rationale would need to be added to the presiding emotional argument. To date, three major studies have been completed to add economic data to the argument.

The first study was conducted in Austin, Texas, during the fall of 2002. Due to a legislative quirk, the city government was to give an incentive package to a new nationally

Figure 7-17
Image © Farr Associates.

based retailer, to be located directly across the street from BookPeople and Waterloo Records, two longtime local landmarks.

Civic Economics spearheaded a study that demonstrated the economic advantages the two locally owned retailers had over nationally based competitors. After reviewing the finances of the locally owned businesses and comparing them to benchmarks for their national competitors, it was determined that for every $100 spent at the local businesses, $45 stayed in the local economy. When the same methodology was applied to the national businesses, only $13 remained local.

The results in Austin demonstrated the economic advantages of supporting local businesses, but it was done on a small scale with just two local merchants. In the fall of 2004 a follow-up study was conducted in the Andersonville neighborhood of Chicago, Illinois. The same basic methodology was applied as in Austin, but for this study the number of local businesses analyzed jumped to ten and the results were categorized as retail, services, and restaurants. The phrase "local premium" was used to label the percentage difference in impact between local and national chain businesses.

The results in Andersonville validated the results from two years earlier in Austin. The overall local premium was 58 percent, meaning that 58 percent more money was left in the local economy after shopping at a locally based business than national chains. Additionally, locally owned stores in our survey actually had higher revenues per square foot of sales than national chains, meaning their local premiums were even higher when calculated on a square-foot basis.

Figure 7-18
Local premium per $100.
Image © Civic Economics.

Figure 7-19
Local premium per square foot.
Image © Civic Economics.

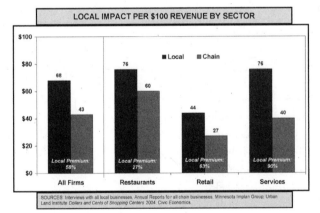

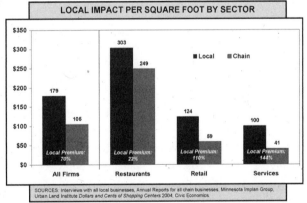

Third Places: Where People Meet, Develop, Trust, and form Associations

Based on the work of Ray Oldenburg

"Third places" is a term coined by Robert Oldenburg, author of *The Great Good Place*. He defined these locations as those outside of home and work and open to the general public where people informally gather on a regular basis. Third places become established by people informally designating them as places to go to see and be seen. Third places need to be easily accessible for a lot of people, comfortable, and open for a minimum of sixteen hours a day, five or six days a week, for people to drop by. Many, but not all, serve food and/or beverages, encouraging people to hang around longer to converse. Coffee shops, tot lots, bus stops, dog parks, pubs, alleys, libraries, laundries, and churches are all examples. Third places are a must-have for a complete neighborhood and a key component of sustainable urbanism.

Oldenburg succinctly describes the social interaction in third places as "meet, trust, and form associations" (from author interview with Ray Oldenburg, September 15, 2006). Third places help to expand people's social networks, facilitating purposeful or happenstance meetings with others they would not normally meet at work or home. Economically speaking, third places can serve as informal markets for services, employment, and entrepreneurship—indeed, the international insurance behemoth Lloyd's of London started in a coffee shop. If your babysitter just quit or you need your kitchen painted, talking it up in a third place might get you a word-of-mouth referral. Socially, the recurring informal contact typical of third places can result in new acquaintances, friends, and even romances.

According to Oldenburg, "The best third places are family-owned and run, ideally by the type of person Jane Jacobs described as a social character—someone who knows everyone in the neighborhood." He believes that locally owned independents know the community and "take an interest" and by contrast, "chain stores don't get involved in the community," often even banning kiosks for posting community flyers and announcements. Traditional third places such as the neighborhood pub are located in walkable urban settings and are much less viable in automobile-dependent locations. In the suburbs, spontaneous meetings are being replaced by scheduled visits arranged by cell phone or text messaging. The criteria set forth in Table 7-10 are meant to aid in both the enhancement of existing third places and the creation of new ones.

Figure 7-20
Intelligensia Café in Chicago is a third place.
Image © Farr Associates.

600 BCE	400 CE	1688	1800s	1940s	1950s	1971
Athenian agora	Arabian coffee shops	Lloyd's of London established in a coffee shop	American taverns	Soda fountains	Shopping malls	Starbucks established in Seattle's Pike Place Market

Table 7-10
Meet, Trust, Form Associations

Third Place Criteria–Outdoor

Target Audience	Needed Facilities	Time of Day 7 · 12 pm · 6 · 11
Dog owners	Dog park	
Preschool children	Tot lot	
Students	Play lawns, hangout space	
Nonworking adults	Lawns, benches, and sitting areas	
Working professionals	Lawns, benches, and sitting areas	
Working parents	All of the above	

Third Place Criteria–Indoor

Categories	Urban	Sprawl
Method of arrival	Walk/bike	Car
Parking	Bike	Free parking lot
Operating hours	16/day	16/day
Opening time	6 A.M.	6 A.M.
Days per week	6-7	5-6
Adjacent uses	Bookstore, laundry	Church, library
Siting	Main Street, preferably a corner	Strip mall
Range	Coffee shop/diner/pub	Coffee shop/diner/pub
Information	Kiosks	Kiosks

The Relative Social Capital of Coffee Shops

Categories	High Social Capital	Low Social Capital
Ownership	Locally owned	Chain
Staff profile	A neighborhood character	Barista
Kiosks	Encouraged	Prohibited
Location	Walk-to	Drive-to

Healthy Neighborhoods

Melanie Simmons, PhD, Kathy Baughman McLeod, MS, and Jason Hight, MS
Healthy Development Inc.

According to the Centers for Disease Control and Prevention's Task Force on Community Preventive Services, an estimated 200,000 to 300,000 premature deaths occur each year in the United States due to physical inactivity. Regular physical activity is associated with enhanced health and reduced risk of mortality. Beyond the effects on mortality, physical activity has other benefits and cost savings. The benefits include reduced risk of cardiovascular disease, stroke, type 2 diabetes, colon cancer, osteoporosis, depression, and fall-related injuries. The direct health care costs of physical inactivity are conservatively estimated to be 2.4 percent of U.S. health care expenditures. Indirect costs of physical inactivity are difficult to estimate. However, indirect costs are believed to be higher because of the costs to employers and insurers from missed work days and disability.[1]

Figure 7-21
Image © Farr Associates.

The recommended amount of physical activity is thirty minutes of moderate-intensity activity five or more days per week. Walking is the most commonly promoted moderate-intensity physical activity; other types can include biking, swimming, mowing the lawn using a push or walk-behind mower, and dancing.

In this example, the built environment's influences on health go beyond individual lifestyle choices. The urban form impacts active transportation and work-related and leisure-time activity (see Table 7-11). Within this context, built environment interventions promote physical activity rather than try to change lifestyle behavior.

The table shows street-scale urban redesigns that are proven effective in promoting physical activity. The studies were conducted on small geographic areas of a few city blocks.

The math in this table should be easy to follow and reproduce. The population affected by the redesigned streets was set at 1,000 people. Projects wishing to use these calculations must adjust the population figures and the level of moderate-intensity physical activity accordingly (use the Behavioral Risk Factor Surveillance System). Then, proposed street-scale urban redesign projects can forecast impacts on physical activity for different populations and locations.

These interventions meet the criteria for being effective physical activity interventions, and so implementing these practices at the community level should be a priority. Community developers should be educated about the value-added aspect of design that promotes healthy communities.

An important way to attract attention and funding from policy makers to support street-scale urban redesign is to highlight the potential health care cost savings. The table demonstrates the potential direct health care cost savings. With effective street-scale urban redesigns, health care cost savings due to greater physical activity would average $92,295 (ranging between $42,192 and $163,494) annually for 1,000 people in a small geographic area of a few blocks. The indirect cost savings are not estimated but are probably much higher.

Table 7-11 Street-Scale Urban Redesign and Physical Activity

Effective Street-Scale Urban Redesigns	Outcome
Greenery: Vegetation along streets, public grounds, private grounds and gardens, and on façades, windows, and balconies, controlling for sex, age, and socioeconomic status[2]	Urban residents were three times more likely to be physically active in high-greenery neighborhoods compared to low-greenery neighborhoods
Walkablity: *High:* higher density characterized by a mix of single- and multifamily residences with nonresidential land uses; mostly street grid with good connectivity. *Low:* single-family residences on curvilinear streets with cul-de-sacs and commercial on outskirts of neighborhood. Both neighborhoods with similar median income[3]	People in high walkable neighborhoods achieve 50 percent more moderate-intensity physical activity than those in to low walkable neighborhoods
Connectivity: Household zones rated on a pedestrian environment scale including ease of street crossing, sidewalk continuity, local street characteristics, and topography[4]	People in highest-rated zones were three to four times more likely to walk to public transit and make other trips by foot or bike.
Lighting: Identified poorly lit areas and improved lighting; compared physical activity before and after lighting improvements[5]	51 percent increase in walking after lighting improvement
Bikeability: Promoted biking, converted four-lane road to two lanes with biking and parking, narrowed streets, and planted trees[6]	23 percent increase in biking after street redesign
Aesthetics: Attractive, friendly, and pleasant walking near home, controlling for sex, age, and education[7]	70 percent increase in walking in neighborhoods with high convenience compared with those with low convenience
Convenience: High neighborhood convenience compared to low neighborhood convenience, with neighborhood convenience defined as shops, park, beach, or bike path within walking distance near home, controlling for sex, age, and education[8]	56 percent increase in walking

Note: Interventions listed under lighting, bikeability, aesthetics, and convenience used similar measures of physical activity and a summary estimate was calculated. The average effect of these street-scale urban redesigns is associated with an average 35 percent increase in physical activity.[9] The interventions should on average increase the existing rate of moderate-intensity physical activity from 45 percent to 61 percent. For a population of 1,000, the number of people active would increase from 450 to 608. Therefore, the number of people engaged in moderate-intensity activity after the street-scale urban redesign would increase by a median of 158 people, with a range from 72 to 279 people.

Medical Cost Savings Calculations

Moderate-intensity physical activity saves $586 per person per year in direct medical costs (2006 dollars)

Median change: 35 percent increase in the number of people engaging in moderate-intensity physical activity

158 more people achieving the recommended amount of moderate-intensity physical activity x $586 = $92,295

savings in direct medical care costs annually

Summary

With effective street-scale urban redesigns, health care cost savings due to greater physical activity would be about $92,295 (ranging between $42,192 and $163,494) annually for 1,000 people in a neighborhood (defined as a small geographic area of a few blocks).

Resources
Healthy Development, Inc.:
www.healthydevelopment.us

Centers for Disease Control
and Prevention: www.cdc.gov/
healthyplaces/hia.htm

National Association of County
and City Health Officials:
www.naccho.org/topics/HPDP/
land_use_planning/LUP_
HealthImpactAssessment.cfm

American Planning Association:
www.planning.org/research/
healthycommunities.htm?
project=Print

World Health Organization:
www.who.int/hia/en/

Notes
1. G. W. Heath et al., "The
Effectiveness of Urban Design and
Land Use and Transport Policies
and Practices to Increase Physical
Activity: A Systematic Review,"
*Journal of Physical Activity and
Health* 3, suppl. 1 (2006): S55–S76.

2. A. Ellaway, S. Macintyre, and X.
Bonnefoy, "Graffiti, Greenery, and
Obesity in Adults: Secondary
Analysis of European Cross
Sectional Survey," *British Medical
Journal* 331, 7517 (2005): 611–12.

3. B. E. Salelens, J. F. Sallis, J. B.
Black, and D. Chen,
"Neighborhood-Based Differences
in Physical Activity: An
Environmental Scale Evaluation,"
American Journal of Public Health
93 (2003): 1552–8.

4. Parsons Brinkerhoff Quade
and Douglas, Inc., *1000 Friends of
Oregon: Making the Land
Use Transportation Air Quality
Connection–The Pedestrian
Environment,* Volume 4A © 1993.

5. K. Painter, "The Influence of
Street Lighting Improvements on
Crime, Fear and Pedestrian Street
Use After Dark," *Landscape and
Urban Planning* 35 (1996): 193–201.

6. A. G. Macbeth, "Bicycle Lanes
in Toronto," *ITE Journal,* April
1999, pp. 38–46.

7. K. Ball, A. Bauman, E. Leslie, and
N Owen, "Perceived Environmental
Aesthetics and Convenience
and Company Are Associated with
Walking for Exercise Among
Australian Adults," *Preventive
Medicine* 33 (2001): 434–40.

8. M. Pratt, C. A. Macera, and
G. Wang, "Higher Direct Medical
Costs Associated with Physical
Inactivity," *Physician and Sports
Medicine* 28, 10 (2000): 63.

9. Heath et al., "Effectiveness
of Urban Design."

Walkable Streets and Networks

Dan Burden
Walkable Communities, Inc.

How to Score the Walkability of a Place

The walkability of a place is shaped by the physical characteristics of both the public right-of-way and the adjacent private development. The spectrum of walkability can be classified in two ways: by the components that make up a place and by its overall look and feel. The following two charts are classified by a list of materials expanded from those found in LEED.

Streets, neighborhoods, and guidelines are flexible. As long as the spirit of a concept is met, quality level designations are met. A weak showing in a row reduces the ability to meet that quality level. A weak showing in one row is offset when other factors indicate high walkability, such as schools or mixed use within one quarter mile of most homes, easy access to nature and open space, the presence of a great park, or a low-automobile-speed environment. Street dimensions are measured curb face to curb face.

LEED Platinum and Diamond levels are intentionally very difficult to achieve. Stone and Bronze levels are of moderate distinction and indicate that the area is somewhat walkable. Criteria for the Platinum level are met only if many pedestrians are seen in most locations twelve to fourteen hours a day (that is, an observer sitting in one place sees a dozen or more people walk by every ten minutes). These levels are marked by population spread in age, ability, and diversity.

Figure 7-22
Image © Dan Burden,
Glatting Jackson Kercher Anglin Inc.

Figure 7-23
Image © Dan Burden,
Glatting Jackson Kercher Anglin Inc.

	Sidewalks and Walkways	Trees and Planter Strips	Connectivity	Street Qualities	Parks and Parking	Driveways/Alleys	Buildings/ Placement
Platinum	Sidewalks 6-8 feet of clear walking space, excellent, well-maintained condition. No barriers. No furniture in main walkway.	Trees in planter strip 8 to 30 feet wide. Trees 3' caliper or more, spaced 15 to 30 feet apart. Trees provide canopy. No utility lines.	Most block connections each 300 to 400 feet. If blocks are longer, trails or other links maintain connectivity.	Streets are 22 to 29 feet wide with parking on both sides. Curbing is used, or no indication cars park to side. Non-mountable curbs.	On-street parking on both sides. Parking permitted 24 hours per day. Parks/plaza or open space within 800 feet of all homes.	Most blocks are alley loaded. No driveways or overhead wires in most streets. Alleys have Accessory Dwelling Units or other means of surveillance.	10 to 20 du/a or more. No garages seen from street. Homes are 10 to 30 feet from street. Good surveillance to street (windows/porches).
Diamond	Sidewalks 5-8 feet of clear walking space, excellent condition. No barriers. No furniture in main walkway.	Trees in planter strip 6 to 8 feet wide. Trees 3' caliper or more, spaced 15 to 30 feet apart. Trees provide canopy. No utility lines.	Most block connections each 300 to 500 feet. If blocks are longer, trails or other links maintain connectivity.	Streets are 22 to 30 feet wide with parking on both sides. Curbing is used, or no indication cars park to side. Non-mountable curbs.	On-street parking on both sides. Parking permitted 24 hours per day. Parks/plaza or open space within 800 feet of all homes.	Most blocks are alley loaded. No driveways or overhead wires in most streets. Alleys have Accessory Dwelling Units or other means for surveillance.	10 to 12 du/a or more. Few garages seen from street. Homes are 10 to 30 feet from street. Good surveillance to street (windows/porches).
Gold	Sidewalks 5 feet of clear walking space, good condition. Few items to walk around. Shrubs, trees maintained, barrier free.	Trees in planter strip 6 feet wide or more. Trees 3' caliper or more, spaced 15 to 30 feet apart. Trees provide canopy. No utility lines.	Most block connections each 300 to 600 feet. If blocks are longer, trails or other links maintain connectivity.	Streets are 22 to 30 feet wide with parking on both sides. Curbing is used, or no indication cars park to side. Non-mountable curbs.	On-street parking on both sides. Parking permitted 24 hours per day. Parks/plaza or open space within 1,000 feet of most homes.	Many blocks are alley loaded. Few driveways, and no driveways cross any portion of sidewalks with cross slopes.	6 to 10 du/a or more. No garages seen from street. Homes are 10 to 30 feet from street. Good surveillance to street (windows/porches).
Silver	Sidewalks 5 feet of clear walking space, fair condition. Very few impediments to walking, but some meandering needed.	Trees in planter strip 4 feet wide or more. Trees 2' caliper or more, spaced 30 to 50 feet apart. Trees provide canopy. No utility lines.	Most block connections are 600 feet. If blocks are longer, trails or other links maintain connectivity. Speeds controlled.	Streets are 28 to 32 feet wide with parking on both sides. Curbing is used, or no indication cars park to side.	On-street parking on both sides. Parking permitted 24 hours per day. Parks/plaza or open space within 1,200 feet of most homes.	Some blocks are alley loaded. Few driveways or overhead wires in street corridor. No driveways cross sidewalks with cross slopes.	6 to 8 du/a or more. No garages seen from street. Homes are 10 to 30 feet from street. Good surveillance to street (windows/porches).
Bronze	Sidewalks 4 to 5 feet of clear walking space, fair or better condition. Some impediments to walking, with some meandering needed.	Trees in planter strip 2 feet wide or more. Trees 2' caliper or more, spaced 30 to 50 feet apart. Trees provide limited canopy, some gaps. Overhead utility lines common.	Most block connections each 60 feet. Some block lengths are longer. Speed is under control, but some complaints possible.	Streets are 30 to 36 feet wide with parking on one side. Curbing is used, or no indication cars park to side.	On-street parking limited to one side. Parking permitted 24 hours per day. Parks/plaza or open space within 1,800 feet of most homes.	Blocks are driveway loaded, no alleys. Driveways are not overly wide, and do not cross any portion of sidewalks with cross slopes.	6 to 7 du/a or more. No garages seen from street. Homes are 30 feet from street. Fair surveillance to street (windows).
Stone	Sidewalks 5 feet placed at back of curb, fair/better condition. Some impediments to walking with some meandering needed. (Note: 4' at back of curb is not walkable.)	No planter strip provided. Some or many houses have trees, but no street canopy is possible.	Block connections sparse, often 600 to 1,000 feet apart. Blocks are a bit high due to long block length.	Streets are 30 to 36 feet wide with parking on one side. Rollover curbs are used. Evidence that some people park by mounting curb.	On-street parking on one side. No overnight parking is allowed. Parks/plaza or open space within 2,600 feet of most homes.	Blocks are driveway loaded. Garages set back, no cars block sidewalks. Some or many driveways cross sidewalks with cross slopes.	3 to 5 du/a or more. Garages seen from street but do not dominate. Homes 50 or more feet from street. Moderate surveillance (windows).

Walkable Neighborhoods
Street, Blocks and Building Forms that Complete the Street– Visual Criteria

	Sidewalks and Walkways	Trees and Planter Strips	Connectivity	Street Qualities	Parks and Parking	Driveways/Alleys	Buildings/Surveillance
Platinum ◆◆◆◆							
Diamond ◆◆◆							
Gold ◆◆							
Silver ◆							
Bronze ◆							
Stone							

Complete Streets

Fred Dock
Meyer, Mohaddes Associates

Street design as a professional practice has developed over the last ninety years to address safety and mobility for the motoring public. The profession is based as much on the physics of moving vehicles as it is on the characteristics of driver behavior. The safety goals of street design have attempted to engineer driver error out of the equation by improving vehicles, the driver-vehicle interface, and the road and roadside environment to remove obstacles and reduce the effects of curvatures. These efforts have led to successively wider roadways—wider lanes, wider clear zones, larger curve radii—which have the effect of promoting faster operating speeds. The mobility goals for street design, originally focused on connecting places, have evolved to focus on minimizing delay while traveling. The results of these joint approaches have been to create a philosophy of wider and faster being better, which separates streets from the land uses adjacent to them and marginalizes pedestrians, bicycles, and transit, modes that are necessary for sustainable urbanism.

Transportation systems that support sustainable communities of compact, walkable neighborhoods and urban centers require multimodal and context-sensitive planning and street design. The idea of context-sensitive solutions (CSS) has developed recently as a process for bringing a collaborative, multidisciplinary design approach to streets that balances the competing needs of the community, the road user, and the environment. CSS requires addressing a wide range of objectives for streets, which include:

- Support for compact neighborhood-oriented development
- Walkability in neighborhoods and mixed-use areas
- Multimodal (transit, bicycle, walking, driving) choices
- Improved compatibility with adjacent land uses
- Provision of high-quality public space for activity and aesthetic values
- Enhanced quality of life
- Protection of environmental quality

The process of sustainable street design integrates the street with the form and function of the surrounding land uses and provides for all travel. The policy approach to this goal is embodied in the Complete Streets movement (www.completestreets.org), which advocates for providing for all travel modes when a street is constructed or rebuilt. The design approach uses a framework that pairs a street typology (modes accommodated, purpose) with a place typology of urban context (levels of activity, location of access, relation to street). This context-based design framework, similar to that

1914	1916	1956	1957	1984	1991	1997	2006
American Association of State Highway and Transportation Officials (AASHTO) started as a highways and roads association	Federal-Aid Highway Program created	Interstate Highway Program funded	Federal Aid Highway Act enacted.	*A Policy on Geometric Design of Highways and Streets (The Green Book)* published by AASHTO	Intermodal Surface Transportation Efficiency Act (ISTEA) passed	*Flexibility in Highway Design* published by Federal Highway Administration	*Context Sensitive Solutions in Designing Major Urban Thoroughfares for Walkable Communities* published by Institute of Transportation Engineers (ITE)

used in form-based coding, is the basis for street design that is described in the 2006 ITE volume *Context Sensitive Solutions in Designing Major Urban Thoroughfares for Walkable Communities.*

The context-based guidance is intended for use primarily in low-speed (under 35 mph) urban environments through the use of a context-sensitive solutions approach. The selection of design controls and design values must follow a rational process that includes consideration of published standards and guidance, particularly that found in the current version of *A Policy on Geometric Design of Highways and Streets* (American Association of State Highway and Transportation Officials, 2001), otherwise known as *The Green Book.*

The CSS approach employs a level of flexibility that is consistent with the policies expressed by the Federal Highway Administration and the American Association of State Highway and Transportation Officials. Policies, guides, and standards used by state and local governments control the design process, and sustainable design must operate within the bounds of those agencies. CSS gives design engineers flexibility to propose alternative ways/strategies for achieving safe designs. Older adopted standards may be inconsistent with some CSS designs. In lieu of updating such standard variances or design exceptions may be obtained to allow the CSS designs to be constructed. The CSS process is designated to provide the technical support necessary to such activities.

Figure 7-24
Low speed urban streets are often the center of neighbor life.
Image © Farr Associates.

Figure 7-25
"Complete streets" are designed to accommodate all travel modes.
Image © 2005 Fred Dock.

Resources
Complete the Streets:
www.completestreets.org

Institute of Transportation Engineers: www.ite.org

Context Sensitive Solutions:
www.contextsensitivesolutions.org

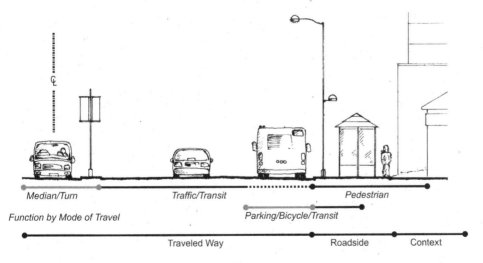

Street Design Realms

Table 7-12 Street Types Appropriate for Low Speed Urban Contexts

Street Types	Maximum Through-Traffic Lanes	Target Operating Speed	Travel Lane Widths*	Transit	Bicycle Facilities	Freight	Median	Curb Parking	Driveway Access	Pedestrian	Intersection Spacing
Boulevard	6	30–35 mph	11–12 ft	Express and local routes	Parallel paths or bike lanes	Regional truck routes	Yes	Optional	Limited	Sidewalk	660–1,320 ft
Avenue	4	25–30 mph	10–11 ft	Local routes	Bike lanes	Local truck routes	Optional	Yes	Yes	Sidewalk	300–660 ft
Street	2	25 mph	10–11 ft	Local routes	Bike lanes	Local deliveries	No	Yes	Yes	Sidewalk	300–660 ft

* Note: On street parking lanes are 7-8 feet in width

Universal Basic Home Access

Eleanor Smith
Concrete Change

Several relatively recent changes drive the need for universal home features that welcome guests and support residents with disabilities:

- *The increased number of older people, both in absolute terms and as a percentage of the national population.* Average life span in the United States has increased by thirty years in the past century, and in spite of improvements in general health, mobility impairment rises dramatically with each decade after age sixty.
- *The greatly increased survival rate of younger disabled people.* For example, in the early 1940s, life expectancy following a spinal cord injury averaged only about one and a half years, while today people with spinal cord injuries typically live for many decades.
- The emergence of a historically unprecedented disability rights movement, raising the expectations of people with disabilities, young and old, to live rich lives and participate fully in community.

Access came first to government buildings, then to commercial buildings such as offices and stores and to public transportation via the ADA of 1990, then to multifamily residences via the federal Fair Housing Amendments Act of 1988 has left single-family houses as the last new buildings lacking any element of basic access.

With the increase in older people has come a steep increase in the number of nursing home residents, at an average cost of more than $60,000 per person per year. Sixty-four percent of these costs are borne by the public coffer. Almost 60 percent of people who move to nursing homes enter directly from hospitals or rehabilitation centers. Although to date no research has been done documenting the extent to which architectural barriers prevent people from returning to their own homes, common sense and anecdotal reports suggest that barriers in homes often force people from their homes and communities into institutions.

Incorporating three designated visitability features upfront improves personal social life and community inclusion. It saves money by decreasing institutionalization and minimizing retrofits, and at the same time costs little at the time of construction—$100 for homes on concrete slabs and $600 for homes with basements or crawl spaces are typical costs when preplanned for design, siting, and grading.

Single-family houses are the only buildings largely untouched by the principle of including people with disabilities. Inaccessible houses exclude people from visiting friends and extended family, waste materials and money through retrofits, and force people out of their neighborhoods and into institutions.

Past	1960s	1990	1991	1990s		2007
New houses offered access only when an identified first occupant currently had a disability	Disability rights movement gains strength	Passage of the Americans with Disabilities Act (ADA) affects public buildings	Fair Housing Amendments Act (FHAA) requires basic access in most multifamily housing	Grassroots disability advocates begin a campaign to change construction habits in single-family houses, bringing	about neighborhoods of accessible new houses across the United States	LEED-ND introduces accessibility into sustainability criteria

Widely incorporating these three specific access features greatly increases the ability to visit others and to remain in one's home after experiencing mobility impairment. These features improve the physical and emotional health of individuals, enhance community diversity, and reduce public financial costs for institutionalization.

Whether termed "visitable," "inclusive," or "universal basic access," three design criteria applied to virtually every new house will create enormous positive change for individuals, diverse communities, and the national fiscal health. Of the many access features one could in corporate, these three are by far the most crucial for visiting, and they provide the basic shell for residing in a house if disability occurs.

Figure 7-26
An attractively designed zero-step entry.
Image © Concrete Change.

- One zero-step entrance on an accessible route
- Passage space of at least 31 inches when the door is open at 90 degrees for all interior main-floor passage doors
- A usable half bath (or preferably a full bath) on the main floor.

The practicality of incorporating these features has already been demonstrated in several U.S. cities where inclusive houses have been built by the thousands, from affordable to high-end. Rather than applying the features to a percentage of houses, the inclusive home standard dictates that the features will be incorporated whenever feasible, which in practice has been more than 95 percent of the time. The 10 or 20 percent approach is impractical because it is not possible to predict in which homes a person will develop a disability. Nor do percentages take into account that eight or more families are likely to occupy any one house over its lifetime, greatly increasing the likelihood that every home will at one time have a resident with a severe long-term or permanent disability. Further, inclusive homes permit disabled people to visit others, a social fluidity taken for granted by nondisabled people.

One Zero-Step Entrance

The zero-step entrance can be located at the front, side, or back of the home, in accordance with the topography. There should be no step from the sidewalk to the porch and no step from the porch to the interior. The grade of the route to the designated entrance should not be steeper than 1:12, and less steep when possible. If a ramp (i.e., a structure with 90-degree drop-offs at the edges) is used, it must be constructed to code. However, the entrance can often be accomplished with a sloping sidewalk rather than a ramp.

On a steep lot where the driveway cannot be graded to a slope less than 1:12, a usable zero-step entrance can proceed from the driveway to the house. A zero-step entrance is nearly always feasible unless all three of the following conditions exist: a steep lot, no driveway, and no back entrance such as an alley. In that and a few other situations, zero-step entrances are impractical.

Preferably, the entry door should have a low threshold of one-half inch. Residential doors with low thresholds are available at low cost and in many attractive styles.

Passable Interior Doors

Thirty-one inches of clear passage space can be achieved with a door measuring 2 feet 10 inches in width. Doors of such size, while not yet available from home improvement stores, are readily available from wholesale suppliers where builders purchase, at nearly same cost as doors two inches narrower. Three-foot doors are also excellent where space permits. Pocket doors are another option.

Usable Bathrooms

In a small bathroom, the door can be hinged out to provide room for the user to shut it. Rectangles of open space at least 30 inches by 48 inches, which can overlap, should be adjacent to each fixture. The FHAA offers useful diagrams for usable small bathrooms.

Resources
Concrete Change: www.concretechange.org

IDEA Center: www.ap.buffalo.edu/idea

Strategies for Providing Accessibility and Visitability for HOPE VI: www.huduser.org/publications/pdf/strategies.pdf

For additional residential universal design features beyond the essential visitability basics, see the *Practical Guide to Universal Home Design:* www.uiowa.edu/infotech/universalhomedesign.htm

Figure 7-27
Homes designed for visibility improve personal social life and community inclusion.
Image © Concrete Change

Managing Travel Demand

Jeffrey Tumlin
Nelson\Nygaard Consulting Associates

Transportation demand management (TDM) is a broad term to describe strategies to change travel behavior. TDM recognizes that there are physical capacity limits to any transportation system, and it seeks to make the most efficient use possible of limited transportation resources.

The need for TDM grew in North America due to the rapid expansion of automobile ownership in the post–World War II era. Throughout the mid-twentieth century, planners' response to increased auto use was primarily to accommodate and encourage demand by providing abundant supplies of automobile infrastructure. This meant creating new and wider highways and adding parking spaces, often by demolishing prewar portions of cities. Minimum parking requirements were invented and spread by a partnership between the American Planning Association and the American Automobile Association.

In response to these concerns, modern transportation demand management became formalized in the United States first during the oil crises in the 1970s, then later under air quality rules in the 1990s. Most programs focus on the 20 percent of total trips that are between home and work, since these trips tend to coincide with peak traffic congestion periods and since they tend to be most amenable to mode shift. The most effective programs, however, cover all types of trips.

TDM is useful in all development contexts, but its effectiveness increases as density increases. Even where transit service is not available, TDM can still achieve 25 percent reductions in traffic by promoting carpooling and "internalizing" some utility trips, for example, by providing concierge services and retail at the workplace. In transit-oriented development (TOD) projects, even at a suburban scale, traffic reductions of 30–40 percent are readily achievable.

There are a variety of tools to calculate the effectiveness of TDM programs, including various traffic models named "3D," "4D," "5D," based on the number of trip generation factors they apply to. The models apply different mathematical formulas to adjust trip generation according to some or all of the following factors:

- *Residential and employment density*. As density increases, trip generation rates decline significantly, since more uses are available within walking distance and transit's market potential increases to the point where frequent service is possible.
- *Diversity of land use types/mix of uses*. Where jobs, housing, and services are within walking distance of one another, auto use declines, particularly for the 80 percent of trips that are non-commute-related.
- *Walkable design*. Where walking is a pleasure, travelers will walk greater distances to reach their destinations.

Ancient world
Congestion levels in ancient cities lead to tolls, restrictions on commoners' use of highways, parking controls, etc.

1908
Henry Ford first markets the Model T

1935
First parking meters installed (downtown Oklahoma City)

Postwar era
American Planning Association and American Automobile Association partner to urge municipalities to adopt minimum parking requirements

1963
Congress passes the Clean Air Act

1991
Washington State passes its Commute Trip Reduction Program

2000s
Congestion pricing reduces traffic by 30 percent in central London

2005
Transportation is the second largest source of U.S. carbon dioxide emissions after electricity generation

- *Access to regional destinations.* The intensity of local transit service and the regional destinations it serves influence travel behavior.
- *Transportation Demand Management.* Parking pricing has greater travel impact than all other TDM measures combined.

	Residential (1)	Non-Residential
Physical Measures		
Net Residential Density	Up to 55%	N/A
Mix of Uses	Up to 9%	Up to 9%
Local-Serving Retail	2%	2%
Transit Service	Up to 15%	Up to 15%
Pedestrian/Bicycle Friendliness	Up to 9%	Up to 9%
Physical Measures subtotal	*Up to 90%*	*Up to 35%*
Demand Management and Similar Measures		
Affordable Housing	Up to 4%	N/A
Parking Supply (2)	N/A	No limit
Parking Pricing/Cash Out	N/A	Up to 25%
Free Transit Passes	25%* reduction for transit service	25%* reduction for transit service
Telecommuting (3)	N/A	No limit
Other TDM Programs	N/A	Up to 2%, plus 10% of the credit for transit and ped/bike friendliness
Demand Management subtotal (4)	*Up to 7.75%*	*Up to 31.65%*

Notes:
(1) For residential uses, the percentage reductions shown apply to the ITE average trip generation rate for single-family detached housing. For other residential land use types, some level of these mitigation measures is implicit in ITE average trip generation rates, and the percentage reduction will be lower.
(2) Only if greater than sum of other trip reduction measures.
(3) Not additive with other trip reduction measures.
(4) Excluding credits for parking supply and telecommuting, which have no limit.

Figure 7-28
Nelson\Nygaard, "Crediting Low-Traffic Developments: Adjusting Site-Level Vehicle Trip Generation Using URBEMIS, Urban Emissions Model, California Air Districts," www.urbemis.com, 2005, page 3.

The Institute of Transportation Engineers' report *Trip Generation and the companion Trip Generation Handbook* are the most definitive available sources for estimating the automobile traffic that different land uses will generate in North America. As noted in the handbook's introduction, however, data for these publications were collected almost entirely at isolated, single-use facilities, where access was primarily limited to automobiles. To address the deficiencies in using *Trip Generation* for TOD and TND projects, URBEMIS (a simplified program for determining trips generated) starts with the ITE standard trip generation rates and offers credits depending upon how far a project deviates from a typical sprawl development. The potential credits for the various measures are summarized in Figure 7-28.

The following sections discuss the most significant various TDM measures.

Density

Residential density provides one of the strongest correlations of any variable with automobile use, but only some of this effect is due to the inherent effect of density alone, as opposed to the other factors for which density serves as a common proxy: parking price, local retail, transit intensity, pedestrian quality, and so on. URBEMIS uses net residential density and applies the formula developed by John Holtzclaw and colleagues.[1]

According to this formula, an apartment building of sixteen units per residential acre would generate 28 percent fewer auto trips than a three-unit-per-acre product. In the densest neighborhoods, density alone can cut trip generation in half.

Parking Supply and Pricing

On the employment side, travel behavior is less strongly correlated with density but very strongly correlated with parking policies. ITE's *Parking Generation* manual assumes that all travelers to an employment site will drive. Accommodating them with parking becomes a self-fulfilling prophecy: abundant parking ensures that parking will be free, that adjacent uses will be farther away, and that transit's market potential will decline. Provided that parking spillover can be managed, reducing the parking supply reduces incentives to drive and produces cost savings that can be invested in transportation alternatives.

Directly related to the supply of parking is the price of parking. Even in locations with little or no transit service, parking charges result in significant changes in motorist behavior, if only to promote carpooling. In locations where direct parking charges are not politically acceptable, parking cash-out programs can achieve similar results. In cash-out programs, employees who do not drive are offered the cash value of the parking spaces given free to employees who do drive. Parking price elasticities vary according to context but generally range from -0.1 to -0.3, that is, every 1 percent increase in parking price results in a 0.1–0.3 percent decrease in parking demand. Parking cash-out programs are somewhat less effective than direct charges. Still, Don Shoup found that solo driving declined by 17 percent on average across several employment sites in the Los Angeles region that introduced parking cash-out.[2]

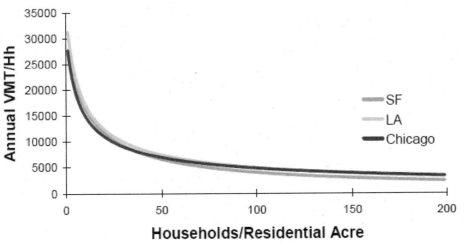

Figure 7-29
John Holtzclaw et al., "Location Efficiency: Neighborhood and Socio-Economic Characteristics Determine Auto Ownership and Use—Study in Chicago, Los Angeles and San Francisco," *Transportation Planning and Technology* 25, 1 (2002): 1–27.

Source: Holtzclaw et. al. (2002).

Transit Service

As transit service intensity and quality increase, driving rates decline. This is especially true where transit is fast, frequent, reliable, and runs all day and into the evening. URBEMIS calculates transit service credits first by calculating a transit service index as follows:

   Number of average daily buses stopping within a quarter mile of the project site

   +

(2X)   Number of daily rail or bus rapid transit trips stopping within a half mile of the site

   +

(2X)   Number of dedicated shuttle trips

   ÷ 900

The benefits of transit service can double in a pedestrian-friendly environment, so the trip reduction benefits of transit are calculated in URBEMIS as follows:

   Transit trip reduction = [Transit service index] x 0.075 + [Pedestrian/bike score] x 0.075

Table 7-11 4D Elasticities

	Daily Vehicle Trips	Daily Vehicle Miles
Density	-0.04	-0.05
Diversity	-0.06	-0.05
Design	-0.02	-0.04
Destinations	-0.03	-0.20

Density	=	Percent Change in [(Population + Employment) per Square Mile]
Diversity	=	Percent Change in {1 – [ABS(b x population – employment)/(b x population + employment)]}
Where: b	=	regional employment / regional population
Design	=	Percent Change in Design Index
Design Index	=	0.0195 x street network density + 1.18 x sidewalk completeness + 3.63 x route directness

Where:

0.0195	=	coefficient applied to street network density, expressing the relative weighting of this variable relative to the other variables in the Design Index formula
street network density	=	length of street in miles/area of neighborhood in square miles
1.18	=	coefficient applied to sidewalk completeness, expressing the relative weighting of this variable relative to the other variables in the Design Index formula
sidewalk completeness	=	total sidewalk centerline distance/total street centerline distance
3.63	=	coefficient applied to route directness, expressing the relative weighting of this variable relative to the other variables in the Design Index formula
route directness	=	average airline distance to center/average road distance to center

Elasticity is expressed as negative numbers. As an example: for parking, price elasticity seems to range from -0.1 to -0.3, meaning that for every 100% increase in price, demand drops by 10% to 30%.

Free Transit Passes

After parking pricing, the operational TDM programs with the greatest effectiveness are free transit pass programs. Where employers provide free transit passes to all employees, or developers or home owners' associations provide free passes to all residents, the trip reduction effectiveness of transit service can be multiplied by 25 percent.

Bicycle and Pedestrian Friendliness

The Florida Department of Transportation, Federal Highway Administration, and other organizations have produced excellent models for estimating how changes to the built environment impact rates of walking and bicycling. Data collection for these formulas can be onerous, however, so URBEMIS uses three of the most important variables:

- *Intersection density.* Small blocks result in significantly higher rates of walking than neighborhoods of superblocks and cul-de-sacs. A grid of 1,300 intersection legs per square mile is ideal, equating roughly to 300-foot-square blocks.

- *Sidewalk completeness.* This refers to the percentage of streets with sidewalks on both sides. However, this measure unfortunately ignores pedestrian quality of service, which examines factors such as the separation between the sidewalk and fast-moving vehicle traffic.
- *Bike lane completeness.* Or, where suitable, adjacent parallel routes.

Together, these factors work equally to allow up to a 9 percent trip reduction credit.

Parking

Eliminate minimum parking requirements, since they serve only to require developers to overbuild parking, resulting in underpriced parking and excessive rates of driving. For employment sites, municipalities should consider parking maximums as a tool for managing congestion.

Development Approvals

Adopt TDM ordinances citywide or as part of TOD or TND overlays. These can require specific TDM measures or simply require projects to meet certain trip reduction targets.

Analysis Tools

Do not use ITE's *Parking Generation or Trip Generation* figures without adjusting them for TOD and TND projects.

Leadership

States and municipalities should ensure that their environmental compliance guidelines, impact fee programs, congestion management programs, transportation funding allocations, and other formulas reward rather than penalize infill development.

Resources
The most thorough online TDM resource is the Victoria Transport Policy Institute's online TDM Encyclopedia at www.vtpi.org/tdm

Notes
1. John Holtzclaw et al., "Location Efficiency: Neighborhood and Socio-Economic Characteristics Determine Auto Ownership and Use—Study in Chicago, Los Angeles and San Francisco," *Transportation Planning and Technology* 25, 1 (2002): 1–27.

2. A summary of many elasticity analyses is found at vtpi.org

Car Sharing

Jeffrey Tumlin
Nelson\Nygaard Consulting Associates

Car sharing is a short-term, membership-based auto rental program. Car-share members typically reserve a car over the phone or online, then walk to a car in their neighborhood and open the door with an electronic key card. Members are billed each month according to how much they drive, much as they would be billed for other utilities such as electric service. Gas, maintenance, parking, and insurance costs are included in the fee.

Shared cars are parked in reserved spaces on the street, in public garages, and in private facilities; such spaces are typically scattered throughout transit-oriented neighborhoods and downtowns or are found at major nodes such as rail stations. Most programs rely on technologies that permit members to identify and reserve the nearest available car, then allow the reserved car to identify and open for the member's unique electronic key. The car reports usage and mileage back to the central office via satellite, automating the entire reservation, use, and billing process.

Car sharing works in locations with sufficient density, transit service, and mix of uses to allow many residents and employees the ability to meet most of their daily needs without the use of a car. It allows members to forgo the costs and hassles of owning, parking, and insuring a car while still maintaining all the mobility benefits of access to a car.

For most motorists, the primary costs of driving, including buying, maintaining, and insuring a car, are fixed; they vary little based upon how much they drive. As a result, motorists have every incentive to drive as much as possible in order to maximize the value of their car. Car sharing shifts all of the costs of driving to variable costs, changing the economic incentives. As a result, car-share programs produce significant transportation and environmental benefits. Each car-share vehicle typically eliminates between six and fifteen privately owned vehicles. Members report an average 39 percent reduction in vehicle miles traveled — even factoring in members who did not previously own a car.

Car shares differ from rental cars in that the former are aimed primarily at short-term rentals from self-accessed, scattered locations. Car-share programs also have the express purpose of reducing vehicle ownership and driving rates.

Locations that meet all of the thresholds in the rightmost column (Large Car-Share Program) of the following table can generally support at least ten car-share vehicles within a half-mile radius of any household or business, offering members a high level of car-share service (see Table 7-13). A modest car-share program with a few vehicles generally requires meeting all of the factors in the middle column (Small Car-Share Program).

Figure 7-31
A company logo identifies
a share-car.
Image © Farr Associates.

1948	1970s	1980s	1987–1988	1998	2004
Sefage program provides shared cars at a housing cooperative in Zurich	Various shared-car pilot programs begin in France, the Netherlands, and the United Kingdom; most fail	Shared-car pilot programs tested in the United States; all fail	Major car-share organizations in Switzerland and Germany are successful, largely because of improved technology	First successful large-scale car-share organization in the United States opens (CarSharing Portland, in Oregon)	More than sixty thousand have become car-share members in the United States, with fifteen successful operators in twenty-two communities

Table 7-13

Minimum Threshold	Small Car-Share Program (2–4 cars)	Large Car-Share Program (10+ cars)
Demographics		
Percentage of one-person households	30%	40–50%
Commute Mode Share		
Percentage driving alone to work	55%	35–40%
Percentage walking to work	5%	15–20%
Vehicle Ownership		
Percentage of households with no vehicle	10–15%	35–40%
Percentage of households with no vehicle or one vehicle	50%	70–80%
Neighborhood Characteristics		
Housing units per acre (minimum)	5	5

Resources
Adam Millar-Ball, *Car-Sharing: Where and How It Succeeds,* Transit Cooperative Research Program Report 108, www.trb.org/news/blurb_detail.asp?ID=5634 (2005).

CarSharing Network: www.carsharing.net

FlexCar: www.flexcar.com

ZipCar: www.zipcar.com

City CarShare: www.citycarshare.com

Philly CarShare: www.phillycarshare.org

Chicago I-Go: http://flexcarnetwork.com/chicago-i-go

For greenfield projects, the market study can help determine the expected number of one-person households, and a thorough transportation demand management study can help estimate walk-to-work rates. In all development projects, car sharing must be considered as one supportive component of a larger TDM strategy.

Chapter 8
Biophilia

Open Space

Among the most neglected realms in town planning are walk-to neighborhood parks and plazas. Because of their prime location—a short walking distance from a large population—they greatly enhance the quality of neighborhood life. Walk-to parks outfitted with benches, playground equipment, and dog runs can serve as intergenerational third places, allowing recurring casual social encounters and the building of social capital. Parks and plazas with a high degree of landscaping, a naturalized stormwater feature, or a view of the night sky play a key role in supporting biophilia. Parks also increase the price home buyers are willing to pay to live close by, providing a very good return on investment for either government or private developers (see Table 8.1).

In master-planned developments, a network of new smaller parks is relatively easy to plan and can be built over time, phased in with the surrounding development. Small parks can be amazingly difficult to develop in existing cities, despite their important contribution to livability. Land prices are often quite high and publicly owned land is rarely located exactly where parks are needed. Many municipal park district policies set a five-acre minimum requirement, which is larger than most vacant land parcels and essentially bars new parks.

Because of these policies, municipal planning often fails to detect and redress the deficiency of walk-to parks (see Figure 8-1). Parks and open space are no less important in commercial and industrial districts. New arrangements for park maintenance and upkeep are also emerging. Neighborhood association volunteers, backstopped with revenue from special taxing districts, can perform upkeep and maintenance.

Filtering stormwater, even in high-density urban locations, is an important aim of sustainable urbanism (see Figure 8-2). In new developments, best management practices

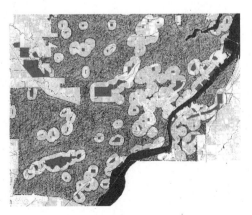

Figure 8-1
Despite a great system of large legacy parks, much of Toledo is underserved by walk-to parks. Grayed areas on the map indicate land more than a 5-minute walk from a park. Image © Farr Associates, data source: Lucas County Auditor, One Government Center Suite 600, Toledo OH 43604.

Figure 8-2
This landscaped plaza serves as a stormwater park filtering runoff water from adjacent streets. Uptown Normal's runoff central roundabout. Image © 2002 Bruce Bondy.

can be designed in at the site, block, and neighborhood scales. In existing built-out areas, stormwater parks are emerging as a promising approach to retrofit the capacity for stormwater filtration. The runoff from city streets combines toxic automotive drippings and concentrates them in stormwater. Such parks can be designed to filter water running off public streets, a widespread municipal discharge currently exempted from regulation under the Clean Water Act.

Consider the following standards:
1. Parks or high quality open spaces should be within a three-minute walk of every dwelling.
2. The minimum park area should be 1/6 acre.
3. The minimum average size of all neighborhood parks should be 1/2 acre.
4. All parks shall be bounded on at least two sides by public rights-of-way.
5. Parks may be fenced and locked at night, if necessary, for security.

Park Types

The Lexicon of the New Urbanism defines various aspects of open space within the neighborhood:

Sports field: an open area specifically designed and equipped for large-scale recreation. Such fields should be confined to the edges of neighborhoods, as their size is disruptive to the fine-grained network required for pedestrian travel.[1]

Table 8-1: Park Proximity Sales Premium

Distance to Park in Feet	Distance to Park in Miles (approx.)	Round-Trip Walk in Minutes	Sales Premium
100	1/50	1	24%
300	1/16	2.5	15%
600	1/8	5	5%
1,300	1/4	10	Insignificant

Source: Miller, Andrew Ross, "Valuing Open Space: Land Economics and Neighborhood Parks."
MIT Department of Architecture Thesis, 2001.

Green: a medium-sized public space available for unstructured recreation, circumscribed by building façades, its landscape consisting of grassy areas and trees, naturalistically disposed, and requiring substantial maintenance.

Square: a public space, seldom larger than a block at the intersection of important streets. A square is circumscribed spatially by frontages; its streetscape consists of paved walks, lawns, trees, and civic buildings all formally disposed and requiring substantial maintenance.

Plaza: a public space at the intersection of important streets set aside for civic purposes and commercial activities. A plaza is circumscribed by frontages; its landscape consists of durable pavement for parking and trees requiring little maintenance. All parking lots of frontages should be designed as plazas with the paving not marked or detailed as parking lots.

Community garden: a grouping of garden plots available for small-scale cultivation, generally to residents of apartments and other dwelling types without private gardens. Community gardens should accommodate individual storage sheds. They are valuable for their recreational and communal role, similar to that of a club.

1 *Source:* Duany Plater-Zyberk & Co. "The Lexicon of the New Urbanism." DBZ, 1999, p. E1.

Public Darkness

Nancy Clanton and Todd Givler
Clanton Associates

Public lighting began as a way to provide some level of safety along rights-of-way for pedestrians and to encourage nighttime activities and commerce. While exterior and right-of-way lighting is required for commerce and public safety, conventional designs often result in extensive, continuous overlighted areas. This can result in glare and light pollution—wasted light from exterior lighting that is directed upward or away from where it is needed. All of this wasted light increases the sky glow effect easily seen in urban areas, reduces the view of stars for citizens as well as astronomers, and wastes energy. Research is now finding that exterior lighting has a harmful effect on flora and fauna and can cause disturbances of human circadian rhythms that have been associated with insomnia and other sleep disorders.

A better approach to lighting design in a neighborhood uses light where it is most useful—at potential vehicle/pedestrian conflict zones, to accent building façades, and to light wayfinding elements. Lighting can be designed to eliminate glare, overlighting, and light trespass. The level of brightness should be based on the type of place being lit, ranging from rural to urban. Rural places will tend to be dark, while higher levels of outdoor lighting are better suited to more vital urban neighborhoods and districts.

Figure 8-3
Los Angeles, 1908.
Image courtesy of International Dark-Sky Association.

Figure 8-4
Los Angeles, 1988.
Image courtesy of International Dark-Sky Association.

1417	1821	1886	1960s	2005	2007
London requires all houses to display a lighted lantern during winter	Paris adopts gas streetlighting	First use of the electric streetlight in the United States (in New York)	Westinghouse manufactures a flat-bottom cobra-head streetlight	Professional lighting societies agree to develop a model lighting ordinance	LEED-ND proposes dark sky criteria for public lighting

Determining Lighting Zone

The lighting zone (L.Z.) is determined based on the ambient light level, population density, frequency of use, and lighting expectations.

Table 8-2: Descriptions and General Lighting Allowances for Lighting Zones

	LZ0	LZ1	LZ2	LZ3	LZ4
Transect Zone	Rural and Reserve	Reserve and Suburban	General Neighborhood	Urban Center	Urban Core
Allowed Initial Lamp Lumens/SF	1.25-1.6*	2.5-3.2	3.3-4.2	7.6-9.7	10.9-13.9
Base Allowance (lumens)	0	17,000	24,000	44,000	60,000
Lighting Design Criteria	No ambient light	Very low ambient light	Low ambient light	Medium ambient light	High ambient light

* This minimal lighting should be turned off most of the time.
Chart data compiled from: Model Lighting Ordinance (draft), Illuminating Engineering Society of North America (IESNA) and International Dark Skies Association (IDA).

Figure 8-5
Pedestrian-oriented lighting.
Image © Clanton & Associates.

Figure 8-6
Automobile-oriented lighting.
Image © Clanton & Associates.

The following targets are proposed to reduce energy consumption and the adverse impact of light on the nighttime environment.

Table 8-3

	Current Practice	2030 Sustainable Urbanist Ideals
Public Expectation	Outdoor brightness	Outdoor darkness
Light Level Regulations	Minimums	Maximums
Control Technology	On-off	Addressable ballasts allow nighttime dimming
Control	Municipally controlled	Block and neighborhood controls
Roadway Lighting	Pole-mounted	Incorporated into roadway fabric
Human Links to Nature	Glare obscures all but a handful of stars	Milky Way visible across North America

According to the International Energy Agency, North America leads the world in consumption of light. Per capita, North Americans used 101 megalumen-hours of light in 2005, compared with 62 in Australia and New Zealand and 42 in Europe. Throughout the world, outdoor lighting consumes approximately 250 terawatt-hours (10^{12} watt-hours) of electricity each year. This accounts for roughly 10 percent of the annual energy used for all lighting.

Stormwater Systems

Jim Patchett and Tom Price
Conservation Design Forum
Contributions from Jamie Simone, Farr Associates

Most contemporary urban, suburban, and rural agricultural land use practices across North America generate substantial amounts of surface water runoff that are directly associated with increased erosion, sedimentation, and flooding, water quality degradation, loss of biodiversity, aquifer depletion, and climate change.

The historic patterns of hydrology that supported the diverse and complex ecology of our lakes, rivers, and streams across North America were predominately groundwater driven. Most of the continent's historical wetlands and aquatic systems, including lakes, streams, and rivers, were sustained from a combination of groundwater discharge and direct precipitation. Nearly all of the continent's endemic wetland and aquatic species, both flora and fauna, are adapted to such stable patterns of groundwater-dominated hydrology and consistent water quality.

Contemporary urban, suburban, and rural land uses have drastically altered the historical patterns of stable hydrology and water quality. Today's environments are dominated by erratic forms of polluted surface water runoff.

Conventional water resource engineering practices directed at the collection, conveyance, and temporary storage of stormwater runoff generally exacerbate downstream flooding, water quality degradation, habitat loss, and system stability due to the cumulative volume and velocity of discharged flows. The collective runoff acts to carve out existing streams and rivers, resulting in deeply incised stream banks subject to constant erosion and sedimentation. The loss of infiltration and groundwater recharge in the surrounding watershed combines with the depression of normal water levels in the stream system to lower the regional water table and starve the stream during periods of drought. At the opposite extreme, intense periods of rainfall, once mediated by landscapes highly capable of absorbing and using the water as a resource, now regularly result in flash floods in areas that were not historically subject to flooding. The economic, environmental, and cultural impacts of flooding are significant, and often catastrophic.

In contrast to traditional stormwater engineering practices, which are designed to direct water away from where it falls, sustainable approaches to site and regional water resource management strive to treat water as a resource, not a waste product. Such measures revolve around the restoration of stable groundwater hydrology on a site-by-site basis through the incorporation of techniques that effectively cleanse, diffuse, and absorb water where it falls, thus restoring the historical patterns of groundwater-dominated hydrology and water quality. This should be the fundamental design and engineering goal of every type and scale of development project, regardless of whether the environment is urban, suburban, or rural. Simply put, the degree to which water leaves land in the form of surface water runoff is the degree to which the area where it fell in the form of precipitation will be in deficit and downstream environments will be surfeited (and generally adversely impacted).

There are many practical, cost-effective design and development innovations that are directed at the restoration of hydrological stability and enhanced water quality in urban, suburban, and rural environments. Innovative design and development techniques that bring water's positive properties to bear, often replicating historical patterns of hydrology, may include one or any combination of technologies that effectively capture, cleanse, recycle, and infiltrate water on-site. Integrated building and site design techniques such as greenroofs, porous paving systems, bioswales and other bioretention measures, rainfall collection and recirculation measures such as storage cisterns, and the incorporation of deep-rooted, highly absorbent native landscape systems are but a few of the multibenefit, cost-effective urban water resource management strategies that may be applied. Such measures are important elements for groundwater recharge, flood reduction, site and regional water-quality enhancement, and the restoration of terrestrial and aquatic ecosystem viability.

The tools and thresholds presented in this section are multidimensional practices that meet traditional water quality and quantity standards as well as achieving planning, urban design, and landscaping objectives (see Figures 8-7 through 8-13 and Table 8-4). The practices address both the quantity and quality of runoff and can be designed and implemented in new developments as well as retrofitted into existing developments in cost-effective ways. The practices discussed here include bioretention, greenroofs, porous pavement, rainwater harvesting and reuse, and native landscaping. It is essential that each practice be designed and engineered based on specific local conditions and land use characteristics. These measures are often most effective when integrated with other building and site development strategies that manage water effectively. Sustainable water management elements can be integrated into roofs, parking lots, streets, driveways, alleys, sidewalks, lawns and landscaped areas, parks and other open spaces, and agricultural fields.

Rainwater is often treated as a waste product in urban and suburban environments, to be eliminated from where it falls as quickly and efficiently as the local jurisdiction allows. Stormwater runoff is typically routed through gutters and storm sewers into detention basins for temporary storage prior to discharge, or directly into local aquatic systems including wetlands, streams, rivers, and lakes. While necessary for some applications, conventional stormwater management measures often contribute to flooding, water quality degradation, habitat loss, and aquifer depletion. Rainwater that flows across driveways, streets, sidewalks, parking lots, turf grass lawns, and other impervious surfaces picks up urban and agricultural pollutants and carries them into our waterways, where they can damage habitat for aquatic organisms as well as render the waterways unsuitable for recreational activities such as swimming, boating, and fishing.

In contrast to conventional collection and conveyance systems, runoff can be directed into bioretention systems that are designed to reduce flow energy and cleanse, convey, and infiltrate water generated from nearby impervious surfaces. Bioretention systems suited for urban contexts include rain gardens, bioswales, dry wells, naturalized detention or retention, and other bioretention structures such as specially designed tree wells, planter boxes, and median strips. For rain gardens and bioswales, porous materials such as sand or gravel are often installed under 18 to 24 inches of amended topsoil to facilitate temporary storage and percolation into the ground. Filtration and water absorption can be enhanced through the incorporation of dense, deep-rooted native vegetation that aids in pollutant removal and infiltration. The resultant reduction in stormwater runoff volume promotes the protection and enhancement of areawide aquatic systems.

left to right

Figure 8-7
Detention basin.
Image © Farr Associates.

Figure 8-8
Bioretention rain garden.
Image © Conservation Design Forum.

Figure 8-9
Bioretention swale.
Image © Bruce Woods.

Figure 8-10
Naturalized detention.
Image © Conservation Design Forum.

Figure 8-11
Permeable paving.
Image © Conservation Design Forum.

Figure 8-12
Extensive greenroof.
Image © Conservation Design Forum.

Figure 8-13
Intensive greenroof.
Image © Conservation Design Forum.

Approach	Horizontal Surface	Stormwater Facility	Brief Description	Area Served by Facility			Rule of Thumb for Sizing Stormwater Facility*
				Lot	Block	Neighborhood	
Conventional							
	Soil	Centralized detention basin	Excavated basin designed to temporarily detain stormwater runoff to meet locally defined allowable release rate.				8% to 12% of site area.
Sustainable Urbanist							
	Soil	Bioretention rain garden	Yard depression planted with perennial vegetation. Includes layer of organic and sand amended topsoil above a gravel drainage layer (where needed).	Yard and adjacent to bottom of downspouts			10% to 15% of roof area – less for permeable sandy soils
	Soil	Bioretention swale	Depressed parking lot or roadside islands planted with perennial vegetation. Includes layer of organic and sand amended topsoil above a gravel drainage layer (where needed).	Edge of paving	Parkways and medians		10% to 15% of impervious area – less for permeable sandy soils
	Soil	Naturalized detention	Detention basin naturalized with shallow side slopes and native wetland and prairie vegetation.			Stormwater parks, parkway medians	8% to 12% of site area. Size may be reduced where upstream bioretention, permeable paving, or greenroofs are utilized.
	Hardscape	Permeable paving	Paving designed to allow water to pass through surface using porous asphalt or concrete or using interlocking concrete permeable pavers. Water can be stored in open-graded stone beneath the surface to meet local detention requirements.	Sidewalks and driveways	Streets and alleys		Not paved area
	Roof	Extensive greenroof	Vegetated roof with drought-tolerant species requiring little or no inputs for vegetative maintenance. Typically 3 to 4 inches of growing medium, depending on vegetation.	Building roof			Net buildable roof area
	Roof	Intensive greenroof	Vegetated roof with a wide range of vegetation, including grasses, shrubs, and even trees. May require irrigation and fertilization. Typically 8 inches and deeper growing medium, depending on vegetation.	Building roof			Net buildable roof area

*Varies based on local stormwater standards and site imperviousness

Food Production

Lynn Peemoeller and Jim Slama, with Cathy Morgan
Contributions from James Gwinner and April Hughes

In the past century, food production has become industrialized and globalized and in effect unsustainable. This is symbolized by the fact that fresh produce travels on average 1,500 miles from field to table in America. That's a lot of fuel consumption! To feed the needs of our ever-expanding communities, family farms have been taken over by big business, sprawl, and agricultural monoculture. Sadly, the farm-as-corporation economic model has become the paradigm for modern food production, with a bottom line of volume and efficiency. This low-cost food is of questionable quality, taste, and safety. Fruits and vegetables from the conventional system harbor residues of multiple pesticides that are toxic to the environment and the body. It's no mystery that a myriad of health problems can be traced back to diet and the current food system, including cancer, diabetes, hypertension, and America's biggest battle, obesity.

Luckily, sustainable solutions are within reach. New economic models for food production are emerging that can feed the world more nutritiously. Organic food is the fastest-growing sector in food production, while sustainable food production and increased food access are being integrated into neighborhoods. Due to the popularity of this movement, the time to act is now. Planners and architects have the opportunity to bring back what years of irresponsible practices have taken away. They can achieve this by integrating food systems in two basic ways: through food production and through food access. Proper zoning regulations will allow for communities and individuals to produce their own food. In communities, points of food access can be created with minimal economic investment and infrastructure. Many towns and villages have begun to strategically plan by conducting a comprehensive needs assessment of the local food system.

Good-quality food is vital to the public health of a population. The economic benefits of community-based food systems include the creation of jobs and self-sustaining markets. Environmental benefits include less energy use, cleaner air and water, and remediated soil. Community benefits include food security, better health, neighborhood beautification, and greater connections between people and the Earth.

Figure 8-14
Image © Kevin Sharp,
People's Food Co-op.

1830	1906	1945	1963	2001	2001	2002	2007
Cyrus McCormick invents the mechanized reaper, enabling agricultural monoculture	Food and Drug Administration created	DDT becomes a mainstay in agriculture	Rachel Carson's *Silent Spring* warns against the rampant use of chemicals such as DDT	Leopold Center for Sustainable Agriculture documents average distance fresh produce is shipped: 1,500 miles	675 million pounds of pesticides used for agricultural purposes in United States	Federal government pays $23.5 billion in crop subsidies to U.S. farmers	LEED-ND introduces food production into LEED system

Food Production

Communities thrive when people are empowered to grow their own food, whether they do it individually or as a community. The number one rule of growing food is clean soil. Clean, nutrient-rich soil will yield safe, high-quality produce. If the site is on a brownfield, the soil must be tested for contaminants such as lead before food can be grown safely. Access to water, sunlight, and good drainage are other important aspects of food production in the urban environment.

Individual	Neighborhood-Based	
● Rooftop gardens	● Community garden	● Urban aquaculture
● Household gardens	● Community orchard	● Edible landscapes
● Household greenhouses	● Community greenhouse	● Community farms

Both public and private land in a neighborhood can be used to grow food. Permanent and accessible community gardens, orchards, and greenhouses can be planned for communities, an approach gaining popularity in sustainably designed communities. Individuals and families can produce food through rooftop gardens, household gardens, and greenhouses. Local food production also offers the potential for recycling food waste— removing organic materials from the waste stream and using it to make soil.

Food Access

It is difficult to access healthy food produced locally. In order to have a steady supply of year-round produce, many retailers buy from national distribution companies instead of local farms. Some of this food is neither fresh nor nutritious. Farmers' markets directly link farmers with consumers, while neighborhood and corner grocery stores can provide increasing access to more nutritious food.

Notable case studies of food access and production are summarized in Table 8-5.

Figure 8-15
Urban garden. Image © 2006 Sustain.

Figure 8-16
Community garden. Image © 2006 Lynn Peemoeller.

Table 8-5: Urban Food Production and Access

Food Production

	Case Study Examples	Approx. area	Food Type	Implementation Time	Jobs	Management
Urban Orchard	Treefolks Urban Orchard Austin, TX	.25 acre	Regionally appropriate fruit and nut trees such as plums, persimmons, pomegranates, pears, peaches, figs, apples, loquats, and pecans	3 to 4 years to get fruit yield	Volunteer	Community planned farm
School Garden	The Edible Schoolyard Berkeley, CA	1 acre	Seasonal organic fruits and vegetables	2 to 3 years	5 full time, 2 AmeriCorps	Private, nonprofit
Market Garden	Gaia Gardens East Lake Commons Atlanta, GA	1.5 acres	Annual vegetables, flowers, orchard	1-2 years	1 full time	Private, business
Urban Agriculture	Added Value, Brooklyn, NY	2.75 acres	Annual vegetables, flowers		85 youth participants	Private, nonprofit
Prairie Crossing	Grayslake, IL	120 acres	Annual vegetables, flowers, hay, pasture	1 year	5 full time, 8 seasonal, 4 part time	Private, foundation

Food Access

	Case Study Examples	Approx. area	Food Type	Implementation Time	Jobs	Management
Kitchen Incubators	Bear River, UT	4,000 sq. ft	Up to 45 customers for value-added food products such as baked goods, pickles, sauces, and candies	Established 2000	45 customers, no jobs	Nonprofit
Food Co-op	Park Slope Food Co-op Brooklyn, NY	19,000 sq. ft.	Wide variety of natural, organic, local, and artisan products	Established 1973	12,800 members, 44 full-time jobs	Cooperative ownership
Farmers' Market	Dane County Farmers Market Madison, WI	8 city blocks (approx. 2,400 linear feet of street)	Up to 160 vendors: vegetables, fruit, flowers, plants, meat, cheese, syrup, jam, bakery, mushrooms	Established 1972	1 full time, 3 part time	Incorporated without stock and as not for profit, with membership fees
Community-Supported Agriculture	Angelic Organics Caledonia, IL	approx. 28 acres	Annual vegetables and fruit	Established 1993	1,300 members, 20-25 seasonal jobs, 5 full-time jobs	Private, some cooperative land ownership

Outdoor Wastewater Treatment

Thomas E. Ennis
Designs4Earth

Wastewater treatment is a complex milieu of environment, politics, culture, and science. The purpose of this threshold is to provide a clearer vision of how to think about wastewater treatment for a sustainable future. It is not intended to be comprehensive; rather, the intent is to give the decision maker enough information to interact with wastewater design professionals in order to work toward a sustainable, site-appropriate design that integrates the reuse of wastes and water in a way that is beneficial to humankind without harming the environment. The field of wastewater treatment design is so broad that often design professionals and even entire consulting firms focus on certain niches of the market.

Society has progressed in the way it manages human wastes (see timeline). Early on, wastes were by and large ignored. As urbanization increased and the source of disease was recognized, sewage treatment began. By the early twentieth century, waterborne diseases were

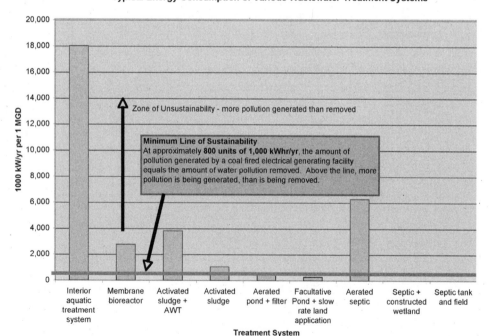

Typical Energy Consumption of Various Wastewater Treatment Systems

Figure 8-17
The graph illustrates the unsustainable fact that many wastewater treatment systems produce more air pollution than the amount of water pollution removed.
Image © 2007 Tom Ennis.

in check and the objective of wastewater treatment was to minimize nuisance conditions noticeable by sight or smell. Primarily the systems were for the disposal of wastes only.

In the latter portion of the twentieth century, systems emerged that viewed the nutrients and the water as resources, rather than waste products. Constituents in treated wastewater effluent, such as nitrogen, phosphorus, and potassium, began to be used for a variety of purposes, including the irrigation of golf courses, green spaces, forests, and farmland; the creation of wetlands and estuaries; and utilization in hydroponics systems. Our understanding of the problems caused by harmful bacteria and viruses increased and enabled science-based designs for beneficial reuse of the nutrients in the sewage. At the same time, knowledge of synthetic contaminants and their effects on humans and the environment continue to challenge designers.

These advances were made with little consideration of the offsetting impact of energy consumption, greenhouse gases, and societal costs. The only limitations were the ability of the society to pay for the construction and operating costs.

Today there are many alternatives for the wastewater planner, but a successful, sustainable project requires a balance of science, site, economics, and regulations.

A critical requirement of a wastewater treatment system is to do no harm to the receiving waters. Our understanding of this will change with time, increasing knowledge, and location. Some areas may be sensitive to thermal discharges, others to nutrients, still others to disinfection by-products. A prerequisite for meeting this standard is to obtain a letter from a local environmental group stating that it has no objections to the project as it relates to a potential change in the receiving stream or groundwater quality.

Sustainable Urbanist Wastewater System Performance Targets

Three additional goals should be pursued in wastewater system design.

1. Reuse of 75 percent of nutrient energy in the waste stream into beneficial uses. This should be calculated on an annual basis.
2. The energy consumption of operation and maintenance, included sludge hauling and disposal, will not exceed 80 kilowatt hours per year per capita.
3. Reuse of 75 percent of water in the waste stream into beneficial uses. This should be calculated on an annual basis.

Figure 8-18
Aeration basin.
Image © 2007 Tom Ennis.

Figure 8-19
Center pivot irrigation.
Image © 2007 Tom Ennis.

1973	1985	1980s–1990s	2000	
Massive reuse for crop production (Muskegon, Michigan)	Direct, potable water reuse pilot (Denver, Colorado)	Natural systems advance	Treatment out of focus: treatment to meet permit	LEED-ND introduces a credit for high performance wastewater treatment

Table 8-6 Typical Acreage Requirements For Wastewater Treatment Systems

	Dwellings Served[1]			
	1000 DU	2000 DU	3333 DU	5000 DU
	(0.3 MGD)[2]	(0.6 MGD)	(1.0 MGD)	(1.5 MGD)
System Type				
Conventional Treatment Systems [3]				
Activated Sludge	0.7	1.4	2.3	3.5
Activated Sludge and Advanced Wastewater Treatment	0.9	1.8	3	4.5
Aerated Pond and Filter Systems [4,5]				
Norh	15.1	30.2	50.4	75.6
Mid-Atlantic	11.3	22.7	37.8	56.7
South	8.6	17.2	28.7	43
Facultative Pond and Slow Rate Land Application Systems [5]				
North	99.3	198.6	331	496.5
Mid-Atlantic	75.6	151.2	251.9	377.9
South	53.4	106.7	177.8	266.8

1 Assumes average 2-bedroom dwellings at 300 GPD. This is a conventional flow rate and may be reduced through water conservation. Specific soils, flows and requirements vary and must be engineered locally.

2 One MGD equals one million gallons per day.

3 USEPA and USAID. *Guidelines for Water Reuse Second Edition*. Washington, DC: USEPA, 2004.

4 Conventionally this system relies on grid electricity to power the treatment process.

5 Reed, Sherwood C., Ronald W. Crites, and E. Joe Middlebrooks. *Natural Systems for Waste Management and Treatment Second Edition*. New York: McGraw-Hill, 1998.

Indoor Wastewater Treatment

John Todd Ecological Design

Eco Machines are ecologically-based wastewater treatment facilities, typically built inside greenhouses, that create clean and reusable water from local wastewater what would otherwise be a monetary and environmental expense for the community, can be turned into resource and an asset.

In a conventional design, wastewater treatment imposes high capital and lifetime operating costs on a community while requiring significant investments in infrastructure and energy for long-distance transport. In this scenario, the wastewater is pumped to a large treatment plant that uses significant amounts of energy and chemicals for treatment and disposal (see Table 8-7).

With Eco Machine technologies, a neighborhood can use its own wastewater to create local green space for varied usage, to grow plants and ecologies that sequester carbon, and to produce clean, chemical-free water for reuse within the community. This can be done in a greenhouse facility requiring a very small above-ground footprint, with sub surface constructed wetlands serving a dual use as a park or orchard (see Table 8-8).

Designed to use wastewater as a local asset, Eco Machines create a variety of positive opportunities for the urban neighborhood. These can include education, flower and fish production, clean water for landscape irrigation, water features, and harvested nutrients for specific purposes.

At the heart of Eco Machines are three principles: ecology, economy, and design. While urban environments are dependent on continuous inputs of energy, food, and materials, they are also great creators of a wide variety of wastes. The Eco Machine is designed to use a substantial portion of the waste created by the urban environment and create opportunities and inputs for various nutrient intensive enterprises within that same environment.

Eco Machines are built for various scales and environments. While this essay concentrates on the sustainable urban neighborhood, Eco Machines are also designed for industrial wastewater, various organic wastes, and crude oils.

The Eco Machine systems built for urban neighborhood wastewater contain the following elements:

- *Collection and distribution*. Small-diameter collection systems with interceptor tanks at each input location minimize pumps, energy, and infrastructure.
- *Pretreatment and equalization*. Underground tanks with biofilters reduce organic loading and ensure that subsequent treatment elements are not overloaded with suspended solids.

- *Constructed wetlands.* Passive, two-foot-deep gravel recirculating beds are planted with functional and aesthetic flora. The treated water flows subsurface, making constructed wetlands an aesthetic green landscape with variable use possibilities. Where space is limited, Advanced Wetland Treatment Systems, which use forced bed aeration to provide oxygen to the root zones, often result in a reduced footprint. Eco Machine Aquatic Cells also further reduce the footprint requirements.
- *Eco Machine Aquatic Cells.* After the constructed wetland or Advanced Wetland Treatment System, secondary treated effluent flows into Aquatic Cells, open, aerobic tank-based systems most often housed in a greenhouse or other light-filled buildings but with possibilities for being outside in warm climates. Each tank is designed through a balance of engineering and ecology to perform a different but critical step in the treatment process. Within each tank is a variety of organisms, each with essential and unique roles in the ecological cycles of water treatment, including microscopic algae, fungi and bacteria, protozoa, snails, clams, fishes, and phyto- and zooplankton; higher plants are grown on suspended racks within each tank. An ideal demonstration of the benefits of ecological diversity, the system is uniquely capable of handling various forms of shock from the waste stream, such as chemical or oil spills. The plants also create a beautiful tropical environment, and the system can be designed for use in flower production or for reseeding local water bodies. Ornamental or native fishes, which perform final polishing, can also be grown for retail or for release into local water bodies.

The tertiary-quality water that emerges from the Eco Machine treatment process can be used for the irrigation of grounds or tree crops, for water features, or for toilet flushing. Narrative signs throughout the system—from toilets to flowers—can provide space for living art, public discourse, and community participation. Eco Machines offer opportunities to use wastewater within the footprint of our neighborhoods and watersheds while creating local value. It is our hope that this local approach will replace the conventional high-energy pump-and-treat paradigm.

Figure 8-20
Eco-Machine.
Image © John Todd Ecological Design.

Figure 8-21
Water quality monitoring in an Eco Machine.
Image © John Todd Ecological Design.

Table 8-7 A Comparison of Alternate Waste water Treatment Systems

	Energy Use kwh/day	Capital Costs $/treated gal.	Sludge Production (lb/day)
Natural System	.05-2	5-12	0-4*
Sequencing Batch Reactor	80-90	4-8	20-25
Membrane BioReactor	3-10	5-20	1-5

*On-site reed drying bed for sludge management

Table 8-8 Rules of Thumb for Sizing Eco Machine Facilities

Scale	Dwellings	Gallons per day (# Dwellings x 250)	Eco Machine Aquatic Cell (in greenhouse)	Conventional Subsurface Constructed Wetland[1]	Advanced Wetland Treatment System[2] (Horizontal Flow)	Advanced Wetland Treatment System[2] (Vertical Flow)
			S.F.	S.F.	S.F.	S.F.
Block	25	6,250	500	12,500	6,250	2,083
	50	12,500	1,000	25,000	12,500	4,167
	100	25,000	2,000	50,000	25,000	8,333
			S.F.	acres	acres	acres
Neighborhood	500	125,000	5,000	5.7	2.9	1.0
	1,000	250,000	10,000	11.5	5.7	1.9
	2,000	500,000	20,000	23.0	11.5	3.8
Duel-Use Opportunities			Flowers, fish, education, etc.	Parks, (community-supported Agriculture), orchards, etc.		

Note: All sizing based on the secondary treatment assumption (30 mg/L BOD and TSS)

1. Conventional subsurface-flow constructed wetlands do not utilize any mechanical components such as pumps. Systems may be oxygen-limited and therefore not capable of nitrogen reduction. However, constructed wetlands can be designed with other conventional or natural components to reduce footprints and increase the ability to remove nitrogen.

2. The Advanced Wetland Treatment System utilizes the patented Forced Bed Aeration System and uses a modest amount of energy. The horizontal flow is a single pass, and wastewater is recirculated in the vertical flow configuration.

Chapter 9
High-Performance Buildings and Infrastructure

The Impact of Planning on Building Energy Usage

Alan Chalifoux

Building Energy Usage: A Primer

Building Energy Usage: A Primer

Building energy simulation programs, specially developed to model building energy usage, can simulate the energy a building will use before it had been built. These results can be used to guide the neighborhood planning process to enable more energy-efficient buildings.

Energy use in a building is determined by two types of heating/cooling loads (the amount of heating or cooling that must go into a building to keep its interior at a reasonable temperature): internal loads—the lighting, people, equipment, and ventilation system inside the building and external loads. The effect of the external loads (also called "skin" loads) is directly influenced by building massing and the building envelope (how the walls, roofs, and windows are constructed).

Different building types use energy in different ways, resulting in distinct energy use profiles. The energy use profile of housing units is characterized by low internal loads. Typically there are not a lot of people living in a house (versus, e.g., an auditorium in a public building). Nor are there many lights or equipment to generate heat inside a home.

Consequently, the external loads drive the energy use profile of housing units. The building envelope (i.e., the way in which the walls, roof, and windows are constructed; the location and size of windows; the use of roof overhangs and fins to shade windows) has a major impact on the energy use profile of housing units. Decisions regarding these building elements are typically made by the design architects. However, many of the most significant design opportunities to reduce building energy use, including building orientation and massing, are actually controlled by the site planner.

Building orientation and massing (the work of the community planner) have significant influence on the energy used by the unit, even before any energy efficiency measures are incorporated into the design of the unit (for example, well-insulated walls, high-performance windows, and other elements that normally fall under the purview of the architect).

In the analysis described here, the residential unit was energy modeled initially as a one-story detached, single-family residential unit, typical of those built annually by the thousands in housing developments (new urbanist and otherwise) across the United States (Option 1 below). It did not have extraordinary windows or overhangs; that is, it was not designed to be a "solar home." Floor plan dimensions were taken to be 25 feet (north and south elevations) by 64 feet (east and west elevations). This 1,600-square-foot unit was then massed, oriented, and stacked differently in the ensuing options. It was rotated 90 degrees (to yield Option 2), then taken to a 40-by-40-foot floor plan (to yield Option 3). Next, the 1,600-square-foot residential space was implemented in three typical two-story town house scenarios (Options 4, 5, and 6). Figure 9-1 summarizes the massing, orientation, and stacking options investigated.

Each residential unit option was modeled in six different geographical regions across the United States:

- Northeast (NE), with weather data from Boston
- Southeast (SE), with weather data from Cape Kennedy, Florida
- North central (NC), with weather data from Chicago
- South central (SC), with weather data from Oklahoma City
- Northwest (NW), with weather data from Billings, Montana
- Southwest (SW), with weather data from Edwards Air Force Base, in California

Energy Modeling Results

The resulting trends were consistent across all these geographical regions. When Option 1 (the detached single-family one-story house) is rotated 90 degrees (to yield Option 2) and the east/west exposures are decreased, energy usage decreases. When Option 2 is subsequently remassed to achieve Option 3's lower surface-to-volume (S/V) ratio, energy usage is further reduced.

Moving from Option 3 (detached single-family one-story house) to Option 4 (two-story town house with one party wall), the energy usage increases slightly. This is due to the general assumption that there will be an increased amount of glazing area in a typical town house wall as opposed to a single-family detached house wall (35% vs. 25%). As Option 4 changes into Option 5 (one party wall becomes two party walls, thereby decreasing the unit's surface-to-volume ratio), energy usage decreases to its lowest point yet in this investigation. Option 6 rotates Option 5 by 90 degrees, making the two exposed walls east- and west-facing; it shows the absolute lowest energy usage of all options.

Option 7 applies exterior shading to Option 5 and shows a resultant reduction in energy usage. Option 8 applies exterior shading to Option 6 and shows another reduction in energy usage. Of special note is the distinct trending in the results between northern climates and southern climates. The units in northern climates tend to be more driven by heating energy and show little to no improvement when external shading is added; it just reduces the amount of solar energy they can harvest (compare Option 5 and Option 7). However, the units in southern climates exhibit a marked reduction in energy when external shading is added (compare Option 6 and Option 8).

The modeling results (showing relative annual energy use) are summarized in Figure 9-2.

Figure 9-3 shows the percentage reduction in annual energy usage (by geographical region) moving from Option 1 to Option 6. Options 1 through 6, while making now architectural changes (walls and windows were left the same, and there were no external shading devices added). Options 7 and 8 added external shading to the windows.

The results from a planner's perspective are obvious:
1. Reduce surface-to-volume ratio as much as possible.
2. Reduce south-facing glass that receives direct sunlight.

Figure 9-1
Building massing and orientation options.
Image © Alan Chalifoux

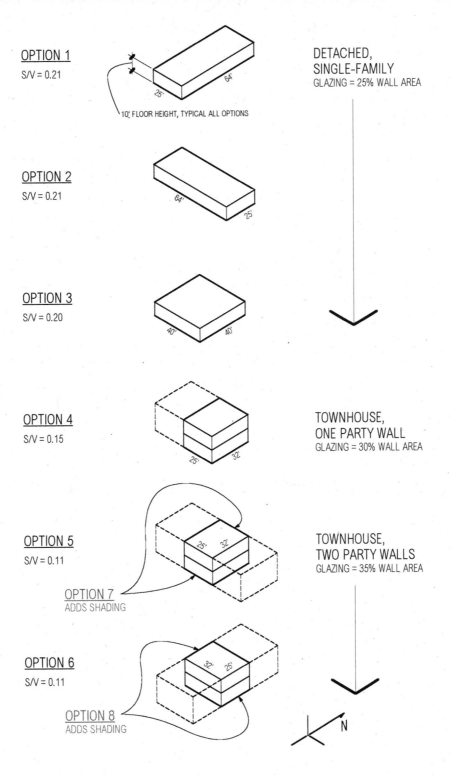

OPTION 1
S/V = 0.21

10' FLOOR HEIGHT, TYPICAL ALL OPTIONS

25'   64'

**DETACHED,
SINGLE-FAMILY**
GLAZING = 25% WALL AREA

OPTION 2
S/V = 0.21

64'   25'

OPTION 3
S/V = 0.20

40'   40'

OPTION 4
S/V = 0.15

25'   32'

**TOWNHOUSE,
ONE PARTY WALL**
GLAZING = 30% WALL AREA

OPTION 5
S/V = 0.11

25'   32'

OPTION 7
ADDS SHADING

**TOWNHOUSE,
TWO PARTY WALLS**
GLAZING = 35% WALL AREA

OPTION 6
S/V = 0.11

32'   25'

OPTION 8
ADDS SHADING

N

Reducing the surface-to-volume ratio will have to be addressed on a case-by-case basis, taking into account the other issues affecting neighborhood planning (such as the desired mix of detached houses versus town houses). Reducing unshaded south glazing should be addressed in concert with the architect. In addition to the unit orientation investigated herein, designers may want to incorporate roof overhangs, external shades, and external trees as means of reducing the amount of direct sunlight received by south-facing glass.

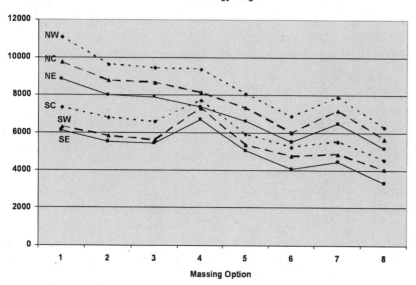

Figure 9-2
A summary of the modeling results, showing relative annual energy use. Image © Alan Chalifoux.

Figure 9-3
This shows the percentage reduction in annual energy usage (by geographical region) as the planner has moved from Option 1 to Option 6, while making no architectural changes (e.g., walls and windows were left the same, there were no external shading devices added).
Image © Alan Chalifoux.

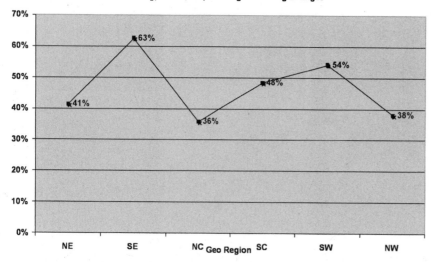

The 2030 Challenge

Ed Mazria
Taken from http://www.architecture2030.org

Slowing the growth rate of greenhouse gas emissions and then reversing it over the next ten years will require immediate action and a concerted global effort. As Architecture 2030 has shown, buildings are the major source of demand for energy and materials that produce greenhouse gases as by-products. Stabilizing emissions in this sector and then reversing them to acceptable levels is key to keeping global warming to approximately one degree centigrade (C) above today's level.

To accomplish this, we are issuing the 2030 Challenge, asking the global architecture and building community to adopt the following targets:

- That all new buildings, developments, and major renovations be designed to meet a energy consumption performance standard of 50 percent of the regional (or country) average of the fossil-fuel-derived, greenhouse-gas-emitting energy used for that building type
- That at a minimum, an equal amount of existing building area be renovated annually to use 50 percent of the regional average of fossil-fuel-derived, greenhouse-gas-emitting energy they are currently consuming, a goal to be accomplished through innovative design strategies, the application of renewable technologies, and/or the purchase (20 percent maximum) of renewable energy
- That the fossil fuel reduction standard for all new buildings be increased as follows:
    60 percent in 2010
    70 percent in 2015
    80 percent in 2020
    90 percent in 2025
    carbon-neutral by 2030 (using no fossil-fuel-derived, greenhouse-gas-emitting energy to operate)

We know these targets are readily achievable and that most developments and buildings can be designed to use only a small amount of energy at little or no additional cost through proper planning, siting, building form, glass properties and location, and material selection and by incorporating natural heating, cooling, ventilation, and daylighting strategies. The additional energy a development or building would then need in order to maintain comfort and operate equipment can be supplied by renewable sources such as solar (photovoltaics, hot-water heating, etc.), wind, biomass, and other viable carbon-free sources.

To meet the 2030 Challenge, we must not only design high-performance and carbon-neutral buildings and developments but also advocate for incentives and actions that will ensure that all buildings and developments meet these targets as well.

The building sector is responsible for the largest consumption of fossil fuels and natural resources in the world today. Unless the architecture, planning, and building community acts now and acts decisively, emerging economies will likely follow current design and building practices, leading to disastrous global consequences.

Fortunately, the energy crises of the 1970s spawned a wealth of research and development into advanced glazing technologies, passive solar system designs, and natural cooling, ventilation, and daylighting strategies. Many private-sector and government-funded (and government-monitored) demonstration projects were built at the time, illustrating that energy consumption reductions of 50 percent or more could be readily achieved through design at little or no extra cost.

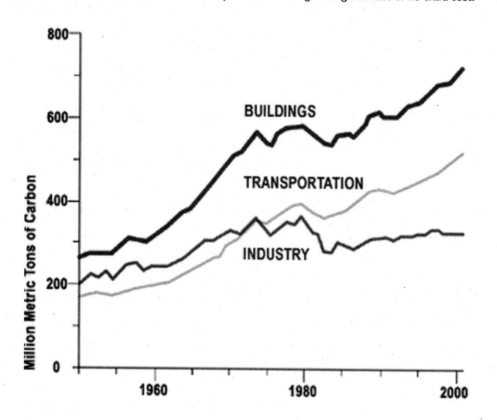

Figure 9-4
The "Buildings" data line on this chart represents the carbon produced by building systems combined with the carbon resulting from off-site electricity production. Image © Architecture 2030 Challenge.

High-Performance Infrastructure

Hillary Brown
New Civic Works, The Design Trust for Public Space

The term "high-performance infrastructure" refers to core best management practices (BMPs) applicable to the typical section of the public right-of-way, encompassing street and sidewalk, underground utilities, stormwater infrastructure, landscapes, and streetscape elements. Considerable opportunity exists for incorporating BMPs into projects of different scales and levels of complexity. Many BMPs will be implemented incrementally through the upgrade and replacement of individual infrastructure components over time. In new developments or major roadway reconstruction projects, a municipality can maximize benefits by employing best practices to coordinate capital investments and to develop integrated designs for the entire roadway system.

Component Optimization

At the single-component level, standard details or specifications may be improved to optimize performance, minimize environmental impact, use materials more efficiently, improve construction practices, or extend lifecycle. Examples of component optimization include:

- Using reclaimed supplementary cementitious materials to increase pavement strength
- Using light-emitting diodes for streetlighting to increase efficiency and reduce energy consumption
- Designing drought-tolerant, water-efficient landscapes to reduce irrigation needs and potable water consumption

Multifunctional Optimization

The density and close proximity of components in the right-of-way can lead to unanticipated damage or degradation. Recognizing the mutual impact of adjacent systems, the guidelines seek to minimize conflicts among parts and, wherever possible, to promote synergies. Undertaking multifunctional optimization strategies could lead to long-term cost savings, improved performance and life cycle, reduced environmental impact, and increased returns on municipal investments. Examples of multifunction optimization include:

- Using structural soils in tree planters to provide load-bearing capacity for sidewalk pavements while offering a better medium for trees to develop deep roots. This practice will significantly enhance tree health and also minimize damage to pavements by preventing upward root growth.

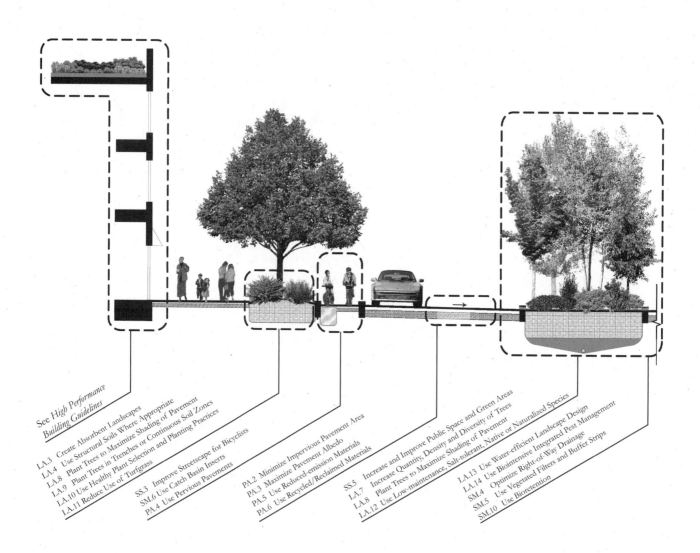

See High Performance
Building Guidelines

LA.3   Create Absorbent Landscapes
LA.4   Use Structural Soils Where Appropriate
LA.8   Plant Trees to Maximize Shading of Pavement
LA.9   Plant Trees in Trenches or Continuous Soil Zones
LA.10 Use Healthy Plant Selection and Planting Practices
LA.11 Reduce Use of Turfgrass

SS.3   Improve Streetscape for Bicyclists
SM.6 Use Catch Basin Inserts
PA.4 Use Pervious Pavements

PA.2   Minimize Impervious Pavement Area
PA.3   Maximize Pavement Albedo
PA.5   Use Reduced-emission Materials
PA.6   Use Recycled/Reclaimed Materials

SS.5   Increase and Improve Public Space and Green Areas
LA.7   Increase Quantity, Density and Diversity of Trees
LA.8   Plant Trees to Maximize Shading of Pavement
LA.12 Use Low-maintenance, Salt-tolerant, Native or Naturalized Species

LA.13 Use Water-efficient Landscape Design
LA.14 Use Biointensive Integrated Pest Management
SM.4   Optimize Right-of-Way Drainage
SM.5   Use Vegetated Filters and Buffer Strips
SM.10 Use Bioretention

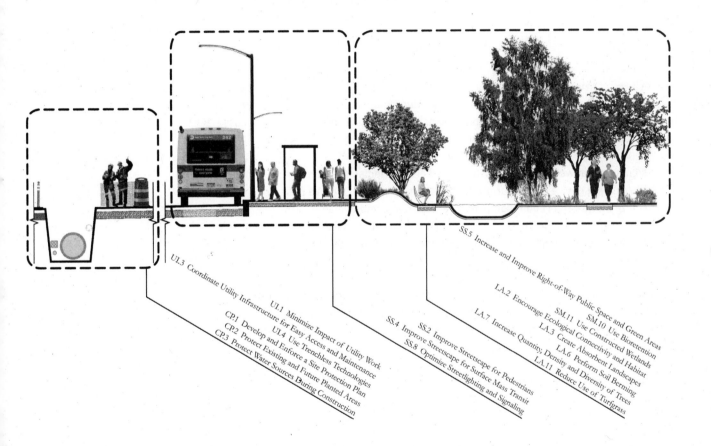

Figure 9-5
Rights-of-way can be designed to reduce long-term resource use and costs. Image © Mathews Nielsen Landscape Architects PC, New York NY; from High Performance Infrastructure Guidelines, October 2005, Design Trust for Public Space (www.designtrust.org) and New York City Department of Design and Construction.

UL3 Coordinate Utility Infrastructure for Easy Access and Maintenance

CP1 Develop and Enforce a Site Protection Plan

CP2 Protect Existing and Future Planted Areas

CP3 Protect Water Sources During Construction

UL1 Minimize Impact of Utility Work

UL4 Use Trenchless Technologies

SS.4 Improve Streetscape for Surface Mass Transit

SS.2 Improve Streetscape for Pedestrians

SS.8 Optimize Streetlighting and Signaling

SS.5 Increase and Improve Right-of-Way Public Space and Green Areas

SM.11 Use Constructed Wetlands

SM.10 Use Bioretention

LA.2 Encourage Ecological Connectivity and Habitat

LA.3 Create Absorbent Landscapes

LA.7 Increase Quantity, Density and Diversity of Trees

LA.6 Perform Soil Berming

LA.11 Reduce Use of Turfgrass

- Using pervious pavement to reduce stormwater runoff and peak demand on stormwater management infrastructure while providing an adequate driving surface for vehicles.
- Utilizing trenchless technologies to repair water-main infrastructure. This will minimize trench cutting and subsequent pavement degradation.

Integrated Design

This systems-oriented approach focuses on improving the performance of the entire roadway system (see Figure 9-5). Design integration requires cross-disciplinary teamwork at the planning, scoping, design, and construction stages. It promotes comprehensive performance improvements, compounds environmental benefits, and potentially offers substantial cost savings. Examples of integrated design include:

- Designing a roadway with a diversely planted center median that functions as both a traffic-calming device and a stormwater bioretention area to improve pedestrian safety, minimize stormwater runoff, dampen street noise, and improve air quality.
- Designing an accessible utility corridor for subsurface utilities within the roadway to allow for easy maintenance, minimization of right-of-way disruption, extended pavement lifecycle, and reduced environmental impact from repeated excavation and disposal of sub-base.
- Designing a right-of-way with reduced impervious pavement area, high-albedo pavements, and maximum shading by trees to substantially help to reduce local urban heat buildup, improve air quality, increase pavement durability, and calm traffic.

Financial Benefits of Integrated Infrastructure Design

In addition to many public health and environmental benefits, financial benefits are also possible. Examples include:

- Decreased first costs
- Decreased operation and maintenance costs
- Decreased energy costs
- Increased real estate values

Large District Energy Systems

Doug Newman, National Energy Center for Sustainable Communities
Robert Thornton, International District Energy Association
With contributions by John Kelly (Endurant Energy) and
Adam Lund (Farr Associates)

District energy systems produce electricity, hot water, steam, and/or chilled water at a central plant and then distribute the energy through underground wires and pipes to adjacent buildings connected to the system. In addition to fossil fuels, district energy systems can utilize a combination of locally available renewable resources such as municipal solid waste, community wood waste, landfill gas, wastewater facility methane, biomass, geothermal, lake or ocean water, and solar energy (see Figure 9-6). They also allow for thermal storage applications that would not otherwise be functionally or economically feasible on an individual building basis. District energy systems improve local economies by increasing energy reliability, stabilizing energy costs, attracting new businesses to the district served by the system, increasing property values, and, ultimately, recirculating energy dollars in the local economy through capital investment and jobs in construction, operation, and maintenance (see Figure 9-6). Electricity is used to energize lights, appliances, equipment, and machinery, while hot and chilled water and steam are used for space heating and cooling and a variety of commercial and industrial processing needs.

From a sustainability standpoint, the essential advantage of a district energy system over a conventional central power plant, transmission, and distribution system is a far more efficient use of the input fuel relative to end uses. Typically, only one-third of the fuel energy input to a conventional fossil-fuel power plant is delivered to the end user as electricity. The vast majority of the energy that is generated is discharged in the form of heat to adjacent rivers and lakes and to the atmosphere, resulting in significant thermal pollution.

By contrast, local district energy systems capture most of the heat energy generated in electricity production and use it to produce steam and hot and chilled water. This process is known as co-generation and is made possible by combined heat and power (CHP) technologies such as gas-fired reciprocating engines, gas turbines, heat exchangers, and absorption chillers.

Such systems generally serve densely populated urban areas, high-density building clusters, and industrial or research campuses. Three rules of thumb for system viability are:

- First, there must be a *high load density*, determined by the thermal load per unit of building floor space, number of stories, and total number of buildings in the area to be served. In greenfield development sites, end users must be located within close proximity to one another. In an existing urban site, there must be a significant vertical density to warrant the considerable cost of constructing the underground network of piping for a district energy system.

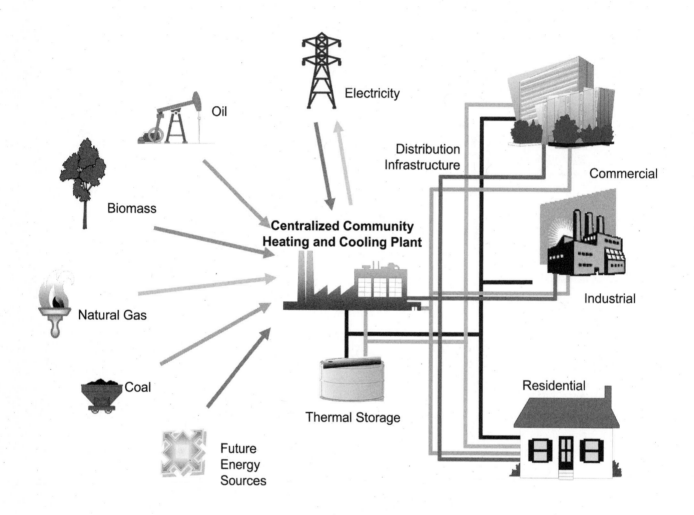

- Second, there must be a *large annual load factor*—the ratio between the actual amount of energy consumed annually and the amount of energy that would be consumed if the peak thermal load were to be imposed continuously for a full year. In other words, thermal energy requirements must be significant enough throughout the year that the capital cost recovery of the plant and piping network is not allocated to a limited period of off-peak demand.

- Third, there must be a *rapid rate of consumer connections* to the system. This last requirement is particularly important, since 50–75 percent of the total district energy system investment is the cost of installing the transmission and distribution network piping.

Thresholds

While there is no universal standard for the configuration of a district energy system that will be applicable in all settings, there are minimum requirements and ranges to consider when investigating the economic and technical feasibility of a district energy system.

Ambient air temperatures. There must be a minimum of 4,000 heating degree-days in a year to make district energy systems economically feasible for space heating. A degree-day unit (referred to as a degree-day) is a measurement of indoor heating requirements affected by outside temperatures. The number of degree-days for any given day is calculated by subtracting the mean outside temperature from 65°F, and the total degree-days for any longer period is the sum of the degree-days of the individual days in that period. Degree-day tables and maps are available from the National Climatic Data Center at the U.S. Department of Commerce. For district cooling systems, customers typically should consume more than 1,000 equivalent full-load hours. In other words, a 200-ton peak-demand building should consume 200,000 ton-hours over the course of a year.

- *Area energy demand.* Each unit of land area to be served by a district heating system must have a high hourly and annual thermal energy demand.
- *Location of thermal plant.* The energy production plant must be located close to the area to be served in order to reduce capital costs and thermal losses in transmission.
- *Transmission distances.* Three to five miles is the maximum distance between a production plant and the end of the distribution network for an economical steam line. Fifteen miles is the maximum distance for a hot-water line when thermal energy is derived from an electrical power plant. Three miles is the maximum distance for a hot-water line when thermal energy is derived from a municipal solid waste incinerator.

- *Cooling load concentration.* Cooling load concentrations must be 150 to 250 tons per 100 linear feet of distribution piping runs.
- *Substantial anchor load.* To mitigate the capital risk, an anchor tenant or initial user located near the plant needs to sign up for at least 20 percent of the initial plant capacity investment. The capital risk is further mitigated when a higher percentage of the capacity is accounted for by additional presubscribed users. An important spatial consideration is that the location of the anchor load should be proximate to the future market density and not an isolated node on a network.
- *Plant footprint.* In cities neighborhoods with high land costs, integrate district heating and cooling plants into urban parking garages.
- *Condenser water sources.* Utilize surface detention ponds for condenser water and/or winter cooling cycles to minimize or eliminate cooling towers.
- *Age of buildings and life cycle.* The opportunity to avoid the capital costs of replacing heating and cooling equipment is the most important factor in a building owner's decision to connect to a district heating and cooling system. In planning such a system for an existing urban site, consideration must be given to the age, type, and life cycle stage for the individual buildings within the proposed service area. Sites predominantly occupied by newer buildings with existing in-building boiler and chiller equipment will not prove to be economical for a district energy system, as owners of these buildings will not be inclined to connect to the system. District heating and cooling systems are viable in master-planned communities and one-owner districts such as college campuses. Retrofitting district systems requires a concentration of built density, all with old mechanical equipment and a high level of building owner cooperation.
- *Utility rates.* In many urban areas where time-of-day rates, load factor ratchet penalties, and high-peak electric demands exist, district cooling systems with thermal or ice storage prove to be very economically attractive.

Resources
International District Energy Association (IDEA): www.districtenergy.org

National Energy Center for Sustainable Communities: www.necsc.us

Global Energy Network for Sustainable Communities: www.globalenergynetwork.org

The 2030 Community Challenge: Economic Growth with Sustainable Urbanism

Our country's almost universal use of the car for daily trips, rather than walking, biking, or riding public transit, has made large segments of the population and entire regions of the country almost completely dependent on cars to meet their daily needs. Consequently, as of 2001 the average American family drives 21,500 miles a year, nearly the circumference of the Earth, largely for mundane trips to work, school, or shopping.[1] The total vehicle miles traveled (VMTs) annually in the United States is expected to grow by 2.5 percent per year.[2] At this rate of growth, Americans will drive one light-year (5.878 trillion miles) per year around 2030.[3] According to a study by the National Institutes of Health, without a change in course, obesity and other side effects of an inactive lifestyle are predicted to shorten life span by as much as five years per American.[4] And the rest of the world is following our lead.

This distinctly American pattern and way of life has been, and for the foreseeable future will continue to be, powered predominantly by carbon-based fuels distilled from oil. The combustion of fossil fuels to power vehicles currently accounts for 32 percent of all CO_2 emissions generated in the United States.[5] Off-the-shelf technology, available today, could greatly improve fuel economy and reduce the CO_2 produced per mile. The federal government should act quickly to require the adoption of these energy efficient technologies, which will lower the cost of driving and paradoxically increase VMT. Sadly, the long-term trend of ever-increasing per capita VMTs, propelled by our automobile-dependent land use patterns, coupled with the projected U.S. population increase to 392 million by 2050 will erase most if not all of the predicted savings.[6] This is consistent with the warning issued by the American Council for an Energy Efficient Economy: "Transportation energy consumption is increasing by 1.8% per year, faster than any other major category of energy use."[7]

The only viable method to meet the challenge of climate change in the transportation sector, while improving community health and well-being, is to greatly reduce the number of miles that American families and businesses need to drive annually and simultaneously implementing sustainable urbanism. Fortunately, these strategies go well together.

Vehicle Miles Traveled Reduction Standard

According to the Pew Center on Global Climate Change, "Between 1969 and 2001, the average annual VMT per household increased from 12,400 to 21,500 (while average household size fell from 3.2 to 2.6 persons, and the average number of vehicles per household grew from 1.2 to 1.9)."[8] In other words, per capita VMTs increased from 3,875 in 1969 to 8,269 in 2001, a whopping increase of 114 percent. The 2030 Community Challenge proposes to reverse this VMT increase by 2030, moving roughly back to what VMT levels were in 1970. This standard can be used by individuals and families to set lifestyle goals and by municipalities and other units of government as targets in their comprehensive planning.

Figure 9-8
Annual VMT growth rates.
Source: Federal Highway Administration status of the Nation's Highways Bridges and Transit, 2002 Condition and Performance Report.
http://www.fhwa.gov/policy/2002.pr/exhibits/9.7.htm

Figure 9-9
The 2030 Community Challenge hopes to restore daily parent-child walks as a societal norm.
Image © Farr Associates.

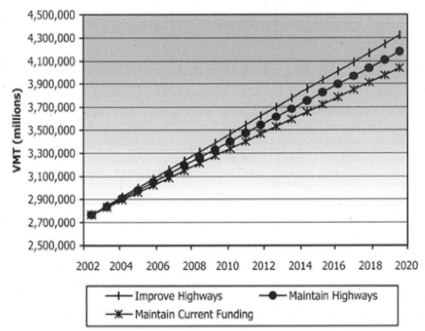

Annual VMT Growth Rates, 1980 to 2020

Legend:
- —+— Improve Highways
- —●— Maintain Highways
- —✳— Maintain Current Funding

(Y-axis: VMT (millions), from 2,500,000 to 4,500,000; X-axis: 2002 to 2020)

2030 Community Challenge—Goals for Per Capita VMT Reduction
in a Given Jurisdiction

Per Capita Vehicle Miles Traveled: Target Reduction
2005: Baseline—8000 VMT per capita*
2010: 10 percent decrease—7200
2015: 20 percent decrease—6400
2020: 30 percent decrease—5600
2025: 40 percent decrease—4800
2030: 50 percent decrease—4000

*2001 U.S. average VMT, to be locally calibrated

Sustainable Urbanism Development Standard
Thresholds in this book have demonstrated that a complete neighborhood can encourage walking, can reduce car trips by up to 10–40 percent,[8] and is associated with reduced levels of obesity, land consumption, and per capita pollution. This standard can be used by companies or governmental jurisdictions as minimum criteria for the percentage of development projects required to meet LEED-ND criteria at the Platinum level.

2030 Community Challenge—Goals for LEED-ND Platinum Certification for Land Developments in a Given Jurisdiction
2010: 20 percent
2015: 40 percent
2020: 60 percent
2025: 80 percent
2030: 100 percent

Notes

1. Marilyn A. Brown, Frank Southworth, and Therese K. Stovall, "Towards a Climate-Friendly Built Environment," www.pewclimate.org/docUploads /Buildings%5FFINAL%2Epdf (accessed September 9, 2006).

2. Federal Highway Administration, U.S. Department of Transportation, "VMT Growth and Improved Air Quality: How Long Can Progress Continue?" www.fhwa.dot.gov/ environment/vmt_ grwt.htm (accessed September 14, 2006).

3. Author calculation based on 2.5 percent annual growth in VMTs.

4. National Institutes of Health, "Obesity Threatens to Cut U.S. Life Expectancy, New Analysis Suggests," *NIH News,* www.nih. gov/news/pr/mar2005/nia-16. htm (accessed September 14, 2006).

5. Pew Center for Global Climate Change, "Innovative Policy Solutions to Global Climate Change," November 2006, www.pewclimate.org/doc Uploads/Buildings%2DInBrief%2 Epdf (accessed February 27, 2007), p. 1 (accessed October 4, 2006).

6. U.S. Census Bureau, National Population Projections, www. census.gov/population/ www/pop-profile/natproj. html (accessed February 27, 2007).

7. American Council for an Energy-Efficient Economy, "Vehicle Fuel Economy Standards: Big Energy Savings at a Modest Cost," www.aceee.org/energy/cafe.htm (accessed February 27, 2007).

8. See Jeff Tumlin, "Managing Travel Demand," in Chapter 7 of this volume.

PART FOUR:
CASE STUDIES IN SUSTAINABLE URBANISM

This part of the book provides a snapshot of the built and visionary work of the sustainable urbanist movement worldwide. Twenty case studies from the United States, Australia, Canada, England, and China aspire to integrate walkable and transit-served with high-performance buildings and adopt very different approaches to do so.

Each project offers different lessons in design, technology, systems integration, and leadership. Among the case studies urban design varies widely, ranging from the studied organic layout of Poundbury to the techno-optimized plan of BedZED. The projects represented here have, or will, come to fruition due to the efforts of a variety of organizations and individuals; in these pages you will find projects initiated by architects, municipalities, environmentalists, and community activists. Traditional urbanist projects embraced a fine-grained street network, while others found virtue in car-free superblocks. A few of the projects from a decade or more ago shaped the sustainable urbanist movement, while others are scheduled for completion in 2030 or 2050 and beyond. Expansive Loreto Bay encompasses 8,000 acres, while tiny Christie Walk packs a photovoltaic array, on-site effluent treatment, and 7,535 square feet of productive landscape into a half-acre infill site.

This collection of case studies reveals that the best sustainable neighborhoods are more than assemblages of energy-saving technologies. Sustainability embraces context. While cookie-cutter subdivisions and nondescript strip malls blanket the country like so many interchangeable parts, the best sustainable urbanism locks in to celebrate place; urbanism taking stock of an area's environmental, social, and economic wealth, and augmenting it through neighborhood and corridor design. Case studies give us the opportunity to see how various participants worldwide have adapted the principles of sustainability to the places they know and love.

The case studies are arranged in four quadrants defined by two pairings: infill/greenfield and built/unbuilt. For the purposes of this book, developments are classified as greenfield if they are located on previously undeveloped land (often agricultural), while infill projects occur within developed areas. A good portion of the infill projects profiled here are actually brownfield developments, dedicated to revitalizing urban spaces by cleaning up contaminated land before building. We use the term *built* to signify a project that has constructed enough of a neighborhood to include at least a modest amount of public space—for example, two houses on either side of a street. *Unbuilt* refers to projects that currently exist only in plans, though they may be nearing the construction phase. A few of these projects, such as Coyote Valley in San Jose, California, are purely conceptual and will never be built.

Developing sustainable urbanism requires a level of design coordination and development sophistication beyond conventional practice. It is not for the faint of heart. Despite these challenges, pioneers have chosen to pursue this approach in projects worldwide. These case study narratives describe the leadership impetus behind each project. Amazingly, many projects needed only one well-placed champion to steer them in pursuit of a sustainable urbanist vision. These leaders can be mayors, planners, developers, activists, or any combination. At this early point in the sustainable urbanist movement, when so many barriers exist, vision and leadership are without doubt the most valuable assets these projects possess.

Chapter 10
Lessons Learned from Sustainable Urbanism

Built Infill

BedZED
South London
England

The BedZED ecovillage in South London is relentless in its pursuit of zero carbon emissions. The unabashedly modern brownfield project, located on the site of an old sewage works in the Borough of Sutton, was born of a partnership between BioRegional, the Peabody Trust, and Bill Dunster Architects. The development team capitalized on favorable conditions that allowed them to buy the land at a below-market rate from the borough, and erected a highly experimental development. Though the project's ambitious technologies have faltered somewhat since its construction, BedZED's founders are still hopeful that the project can attain permanent carbon-neutral status.

The achievement of carbon-neutral status relies heavily on lifestyle factors, not merely efficient buildings. To that end, BedZED incorporates several elements designed to foster a community with a sustainable conscience, reinforcing green building with green behavior. Live/work units offer residents a chance to eliminate the morning commute entirely. Those needing to drive will find it easy to participate in the project's car-share program, which uses solar panels to power up to forty electric cars. Perimeter parking made pedestrian-friendly carfree blocks possible. However, the combination of one parking space per dwelling, perpendicular parking

and back-of-curb sidewalks is far less pedestrian friendly. Community facilities, including playing fields and a village square, are within easy walking distance. Shared building walls and garden spaces promote casual interaction between neighbors and have resulted in such events as a farmers' market, a music festival, and an organic Christmas dinner.

The structures themselves are designed to combine a highly efficient building envelope with usage of 100 percent renewable energy. When possible, construction materials were sourced from within a 35-mile radius of the site, and 15 percent of materials were reclaimed or recycled, such as the reclaimed steel commonly found in the buildings. An airtight building envelope that far exceeds UK requirements for air leakage is the foundation of energy savings. Superinsulation also maintains building temperatures. South-facing living spaces maximize solar heat gain in winter, while north-facing workspaces provide mellow, indirect light and keep office equipment cool. Efficient fixtures and appliances have also reduced usage of potable water and electricity. A wind-driven natural ventilation system uses brightly colored wind cowls to draw fresh air into homes, preheating it as it passes next to warm, stale air leaving the

At a Glance

Master plan: Bill Dunster Architects
Developers: BioRegional Development Group and Peabody Trust
Timeline: Project initiated 1996; built 2002
Dwelling units: 82
Commercial square footage: 26,910 square feet of office space and community facilities
Land area: 4.08 acres

Project Highlights/Benchmarks

- Achieve zero net carbon emissions through the use of alternative energies, including CHP system, photovoltaic panels, and wind-driven natural ventilation
- Reduce potable water consumption by 30 percent
- 15 percent of construction materials reused or recycled
- 50 percent reduction in fossil-fuel consumption from private car use compared with conventional developments in ten years
- Reduce heat consumption by 90 percent
- Within ten years, power 40 electric vehicles using photovoltaic panels

Key Sustainable Urbanism Thresholds

- Food production
- Stormwater systems
- Illustrating density
- Impact of Planning on Building Energy Usage
- Large district energy systems
- Walkable streets and networks
- Managing travel demand
- Car sharing

Figure 10-1
BedZED site plan.
Image © www.zedfactory.com

Figure 10-2
Diagram of sustainable building systems at BedZED. Image © Arup.

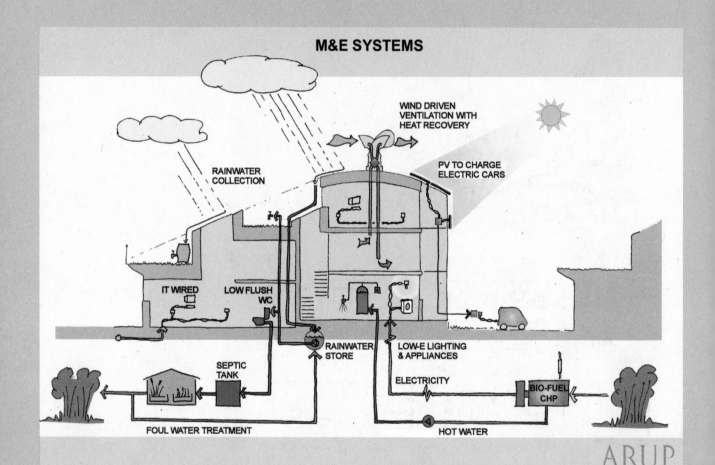

M&E SYSTEMS

WIND DRIVEN
VENTILATION WITH
HEAT RECOVERY

RAINWATER
COLLECTION

PV TO CHARGE
ELECTRIC CARS

IT WIRED

LOW FLUSH
WC

RAINWATER
STORE

LOW-E LIGHTING
& APPLIANCES

SEPTIC
TANK

ELECTRICITY

BIO-FUEL
CHP

FOUL WATER TREATMENT

HOT WATER

ARUP

building. These efficiency strategies have produced savings of 30 percent in water usage, 90 percent in space heating, and 25 percent in electricity in general.

Home efficiency is further augmented by green infrastructure that provides renewable energy. Initially, a CHP (combined heat and power) system was used at BedZED to generate heat and electricity by converting 850 tons of wood chips per year to energy, but that system has since proved unreliable. The development is now investigating a new biomass system to provide heat and power. Homes also draw power from a solar array with a peak output of 109 kilowatts. Rainwater harvesting provides irrigation for landscaping, and stormwater drainage is directed to a roadside pond planted with native vegetation. A now-defunct Living Machine system was originally put in place to treat black- and graywater

using a biological reed bed. New, similar technologies are being discussed for the future. On-site composting and recycling programs make it easy for residents to reduce their household waste.

Social sustainability is addressed by providing fifteen units of social housing (affordable units rented out by Peabody Trust). BedZED also includes 26,910 square feet of office space to promote a job housing balance. BedZED's successes are due largely to the tight-knit community that has formed there through shared facilities and an interest in sustainability. Neighbors are able to support each others' energy-saving habits while creating an inviting place to live. It is to be hoped that the introduction of newer, more reliable green technologies will allow the residents of BedZED to get back on the path to carbon independence.

Figure 10-3
300 mm of rockwool provides superinsulation.
Image © www.zedfactory.com.

Figure 10-4
Southeast aerial view.
Image © www.zedfactory.com.

Figure 10-5
"Sky gardens" maximize private open space.
Image © www.zedfactory.com.

Glenwood Park
Atlanta, Georgia
United States

Green Street Properties envisions Glenwood Park as an antidote to notoriously sprawling Atlanta, soothing traffic congestion and introducing walkability to an automobile-addicted metropolis. Led by Charles Brewer, the development company partnered with Dover, Kohl & Partners and Tunnell-Spangler-Walsh & Associates to create the 28-acre new urbanist community on an abandoned brownfield two miles from downtown Atlanta. Strong developer leadership led to a cohesive product, free of the uncertainty that can plague conceptual projects that must woo developers to actually construct them.

New urbanism is Glenwood Park's forte. Aesthetics are important to the project, and the one thousand newly planted trees lining intimate streets are both beautiful and a practical attempt to reduce the urban heat island effect. The homes are striking as well, incorporating historic southern architectural features that also foster community, such as deep front porches (at least 8 feet deep), closely grouped homes, and varied façades that encourage residents to take leisurely walks and admire their neighborhood. The developer also took care to incorporate historic design features in Glenwood Park's town homes, a rare building type in Atlanta. Automobiles are deemphasized by placing garages along rear alleys and utilizing on-street parking instead of large surface lots. One major goal for the development is to invite civic participation, which is encouraged by a wealth of public gathering spaces. A central, elliptical park provides a playground, community space, and water retention. Two smaller squares are lined with stately trees in the Savannah style. One of them, Brasfield Square, is home to local retailers, restaurants, and office space, an easy five-minute walk from nearly anywhere in the development. Storefronts must be within 10 feet on average from the sidewalk to keep the area friendly and inviting to pedestrians. The increased density of the area (Green Street Properties claims it is four times that of average subdivisions) also makes the neighborhood economically robust. Its mixed-use, pleasant atmosphere invites strolling and attracts people from outside the development to visit and patronize its retailers.

Glenwood Park is also notable for its participation in the EarthCraft Homes program, arguably the strongest regional green building program in the United States. All homes at Glenwood Park are EarthCraft-certified, guaranteeing that a third-party inspector has affirmed that each house meets criteria in several categories, including

At a Glance

Master plan: Dover, Kohl & Partners
Developer: Green Street Properties
Timeline: Began construction 2003; build-out 4–6 years
Dwelling units: 325
Commercial square footage: 70,000 square feet
Land area: 28 acres

Project Highlights/Benchmarks

- EarthCraft-certified homes save 1.3 megawatts of energy per year
- Reduce mileage driven by residents (compared with average driving patterns) by 1,627,500 miles
- 80+ percent of construction waste diverted from landfills
- Offices designed to achieve LEED certification
- Direct access to MARTA rapid transit
- Transformation of a blighted brownfield revitalizes area
- Retail and office space a five-minute walk from anywhere in development
- Stormwater system reduces runoff by two-thirds

Key Sustainable Urbanism Thresholds

- Economic benefits of locally owned stores
- Open space
- Stormwater systems
- Illustrating density
- The integration of transportation, land use, and technology
- The impact of planning on building energy usage
- Walkable streets and networks

Figure 10-6
Glenwood Park site plan.
Image © Loren Heyns,
Dream Studio.

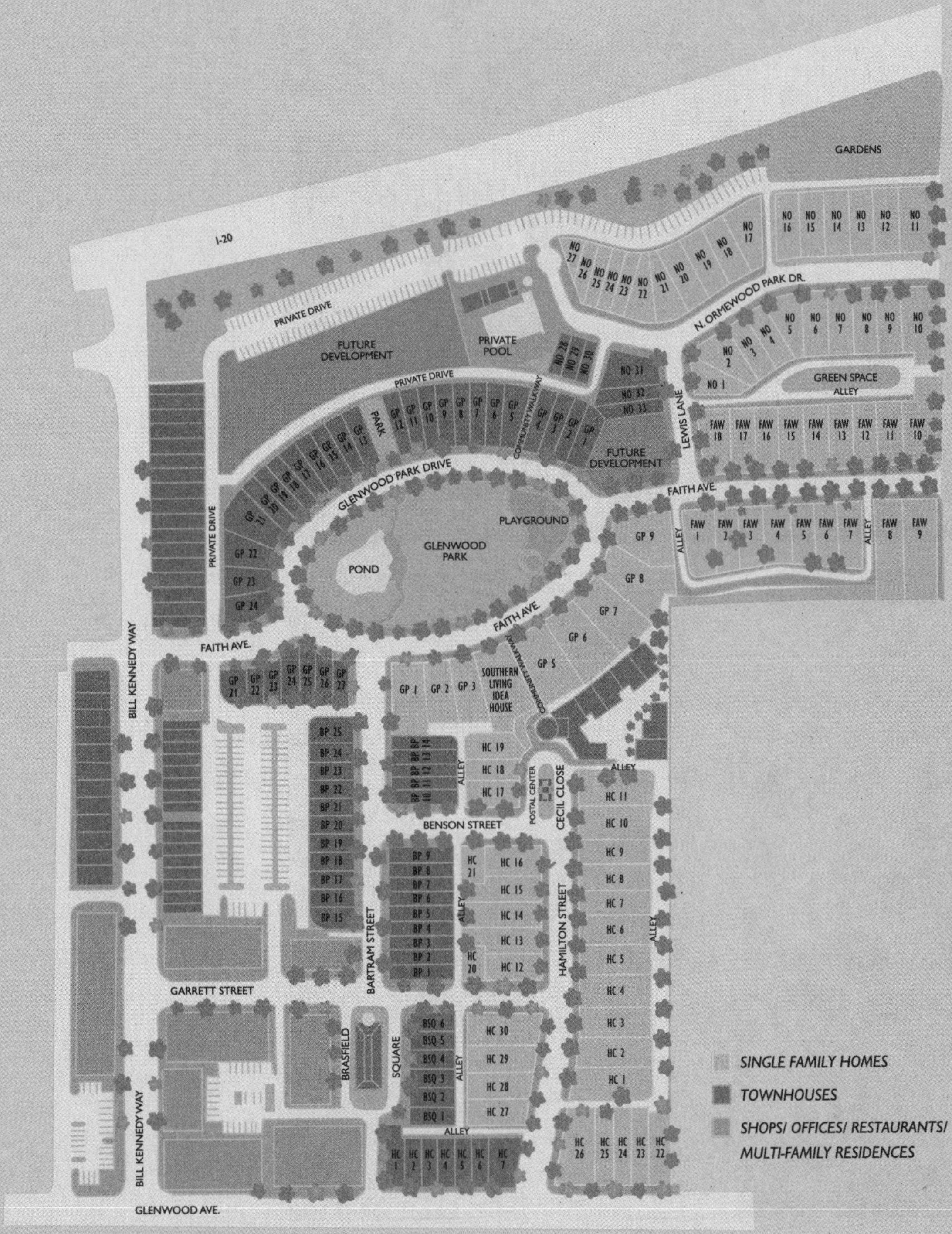

SINGLE FAMILY HOMES

TOWNHOUSES

SHOPS/ OFFICES/ RESTAURANTS/
MULTI-FAMILY RESIDENCES

Figure 10-9
Single-family homes facing
Glenwood Park.
Image © Loren Heyns,
Dream Studio.

indoor air quality, soil erosion prevention, waste management, Energy Star compliance, use of recycled-content materials, and numerous other standards. Many Glenwood Park homes feature recycled-newspaper insulation and boast an energy savings of 1.3 megawatts per year. In addition, no more than 20 percent of construction waste was sent to landfills. For example, 700,000 pounds of granite will be recycled into the central park, while another 30 million pounds of wood chips were converted to electricity at a waste-to-energy plant. Green Street Properties is also pursuing LEED certification for office buildings.

One of the most important elements of sustainable infrastructure at Glenwood Park is the stormwater management system, which reduces runoff by two-thirds. Rainwater is directed to landscaping on individual lots, and excess runoff is captured in the central park, which also includes a sunken area designed to let stormwater soak back into the ground. Using this system, Glenwood Park aims to eliminate the use of potable city water for irrigation entirely. Diverse transit options are also vital to maintaining the walkable nature of Glenwood Park, which features bike paths and direct access to the MARTA rapid transit system. A local elementary school also eliminates the need for children to be transported out of the neighborhood to schools that are already overcrowded.

The site's transformation from an old concrete factory to a thriving, mixed-use neighborhood is dramatic. Increased tax revenue for the area is projected at $4.5 million, turning an eyesore into a success story that may well spur further development in the area. It should be noted, however, that many of the homes are very expensive, despite price points starting in the $160,000 range, and no rental properties are available. The site's flexible design should allow the neighborhood to accommodate the changing needs of its residents, so that they can remain part of the community for years to come.

Holiday Neighborhood
Boulder, Colorado
United States

The Holiday Neighborhood project in Boulder, Colorado, combines sustainable urbanism with an impressive 40 percent affordability rate. It accomplishes this while delivering significant returns on market-rate homes, squelching concerns that its public-sector land developer, Boulder Housing Partners, would not do the site justice as a private developer would. Thoughtful, innovative planning was made possible by an EPA grant won by the Sustainable Futures Society, which pledged to help green Holiday Neighborhood. The funds from the grant were used to arrange a design workshop at which Boulder Housing Partners, the seven developers chosen for the project, and the Rocky Mountain Institute collaborated. The workshop gave the whole team a chance to research and explore sustainable technologies for the site, and in the year following the workshop the Sustainable Futures Society continued to work with developers to pursue new design ideas. This process allowed Boulder Housing Partners and the developers to make smart, informed decisions about what sustainable technologies would be practical and effective for Holiday Neighborhood.

Though the City of Boulder was initially not in favor of density beyond what the zoning specified, Boulder Housing Partners and Barrett Studio Architects (master planners) convinced the city to consider the benefits of additional density in a mixed-use setting: it would prevent Holiday from adding to the city's traffic congestion, and its thirty to forty retail spaces would provide job opportunities to residents. Because affordability was a key goal, homes needed to be smaller and more compact than in traditional residential subdivisions. The city approved a zoning change to allow twenty units per acre to be built in Holiday, up from the site's original ten units per acre.

Another goal of increased density is to favor mass transit over cars, and in support of this the Wild Sage Co-housing portion of the site reduced parking spaces to 1.1 per unit rather than the typical 2. Substantial open space rounds out the community and further encourages walking, cycling, and other alternative modes of transportation. A variety of housing options include single-family homes, carriage homes, town houses, condos, and live/work studios. Community gardens are also included. A refurbished Holiday Drive-In marquee ties the neighborhood together and recalls its heritage as a popular drive-in theater.

Holiday Neighborhood benefited greatly from Boulder's progressive environmental standards. The city already has an established Green Points

At a Glance

Master plan: Barrett Studio Architects
Developer: Boulder Housing Partners
Timeline: Construction began 2002; complete build-out by late 2007
Dwelling units: 333
Commercial square footage: 50,000 square feet
Land area: 27 acres

Project Highlights/Benchmarks

- Density zoned up to 20 units/acre (twice the site's original density)
- Green Guidelines program expands upon Boulder's Green Points program to require ecologically responsible building techniques
- 50 percent reduction in utility bills
- 40 percent affordable housing
- Diverse affordability: emergency transitional housing, subsidized rentals, and for-sale units
- Wild Sage Co-housing pursuing carbon-neutrality 40 percent reduction in water use
- Bus pass provided for all residents

Key Sustainable Urbanism Thresholds

- Open space
- Stormwater systems
- Illustrating density
- The Integration of transportation, land use, and technology
- The impact of planning on building energy usage
- Walkable streets and networks

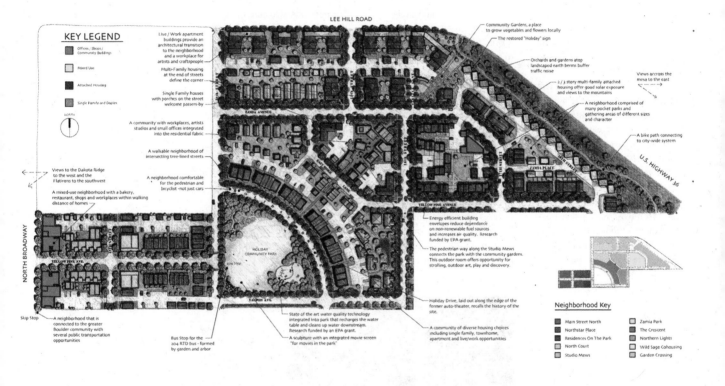

LEE HILL ROAD

KEY LEGEND

Offices / Shops / Community Buildings

Mixed Use

Attached Housing

Single Family and Duplex

NORTH

Community Gardens, a place to grow vegetables and flowers locally

The restored "Holiday" sign

Orchards and gardens atop landscaped earth berms buffer traffic noise

Live / Work apartment buildings provide an architectural transition to the neighborhood and a workplace for artists and craftspeople

Multi-Family housing at the end of streets define the corner

Single Family houses with porches on the street welcome passers-by

Views across the mesa to the east

2 / 3 story multi-family attached housing offer good solar exposure and views to the mountains

A neighborhood comprised of many pocket parks and gathering areas of different sizes and character

ZAMIA AVENUE

A community with workplaces, artists studios and small offices integrated into the residential fabric

A walkable neighborhood of intersecting tree-lined streets

A bike path connecting to city-wide system

ZAMIA PLACE

U.S. HIGHWAY 36

Views to the Dakota Ridge to the west and the Flatirons to the southwest

A neighborhood comfortable for the pedestrian and bicyclist -not just cars

A mixed-use neighborhood with a bakery, restaurant, shops and workplaces within walking distance of homes

YELLOW PINE AVENUE

YELLOW PINE AVE.

NORTH BROADWAY

HOLIDAY COMMUNITY PARK

Energy efficient building envelopes reduce dependance on non-renewable fuel sources and increases air quality. Research funded by EPA grant.

The pedestrian way along the Studio Mews connects the park with the community garden. This outdoor room offers opportunity for strolling, outdoor art, play and discovery.

Holiday Drive, laid out along the edge of the former auto-theater, recalls the history of the site.

Skip Stop

A neighborhood that is connected to the greater Boulder community with several public transportation opportunities

Bus Stop for the 204 RTD bus - formed by garden and arbor

YAMPA AVE.

State of the art water quality technology integrated into park that recharges the water table and cleans up water downstream. Research funded by an EPA grant.

A sculpture with an integrated movie screen "for movies in the park"

A community of diverse housing choices including single family, townhome, apartment and live/work opportunities

Neighborhood Key

Main Street North	Zamia Park
Northstar Place	The Crescent
Residences On The Park	Northern Lights
North Court	Wild Sage Cohousing
Studio Mews	Garden Crossing

program that guides builders in developing efficient, ecologically sound homes. Holiday Neighborhood developers were all required to participate in the Green Points program. In addition, Boulder Housing Partners built upon the Green Points program by issuing its own Green Guidelines to assist developers in attaining the project's sustainability goals. Colorado's 320 days of sun per year allow developers to take full advantage of passive solar heating. The modest-sized home also profit from Colorado's dry climate, which has prompted many developers to use low-cost swamp coolers and whole-house fans to cool homes without central air-conditioning. Drought-resistant native plants provide the bulk of landscaping. In addition, Wild Sage Co-housing is pursuing zero net energy status by incorporating salvaged solar panels, a radiant heat system powered by a central boiler, and efficient appliances. Due to the efforts of Jim Leach (co-housing developer), Jim Logan (co-housing architect), and the future residents of Wild Sage, who were also involved,

residents can expect to drive an estimated 30 percent less than the average American, pay 50 percent less in utility bills, and use 40 percent less water.

Boulder Housing Partners constructed the project's entire infrastructure in 2003 to save on the cost of ongoing construction. Holiday Neighborhood's stormwater management plan, identified as a vital design component at the workshop, focuses on recharging the groundwater supply. Recycling rainwater was the hoped-for ideal but proved impossible because Colorado law states that downstream users have a right to stormwater runoff. Swales and retention areas instead focus on cleansing water before letting it soak back into the ground. Alternative transit options are located near Holiday. Though buses do not run within Holiday, the SKIP bus route runs down adjacent Broadway Street every six to seven minutes. Everyone in Holiday Neighborhood also receives a bus pass funded through home owner association dues.

The affordable housing at Holiday Neighborhood is seam-

lessly integrated into the market-rate housing. Multiple paths to participating in the affordable housing scheme are also offered. Of the 138 affordable units, 49 are for rent through Boulder Housing Partners and target people earning 20 to 50 percent of the median income. Three more are reserved as emergency family transitional housing, and the remaining 86 are for sale to people earning 60 to 80 percent of the median income. In constructing Holiday Neighborhood, Boulder Housing Partners was also careful to select development partners interested in involving the community in producing homes. The Northern Lights segment of Holiday Neighborhood was partially built by community members, and four homes were built by Habitat for Humanity at the Wild Sage Co-housing development. Because Boulder Housing Partners was willing to make less of a profit on land sales than a private entity, it was able to create a truly affordable sustainable community on a site that was originally supposed to be reserved for a big-box retail chain.

Figure 10-11
Shops and homes on Main Street.
Image © Boulder Housing Partners.

Figure 10-12
Community garden.
Image © Boulder Housing Partners.

Figure 10-13
Wild Sage Co-housing is pursuing
carbon-neutral status.
Image © Boulder Housing Partners.

Christie Walk
Adelaide, Australia

Activist-driven from its inception, Christie Walk is pioneering sustainable urbanism in South Australia on the strength of a small team committed to realizing their vision of an "EcoCity." Christie Walk is a response to the daring challenge issued by nonprofit Urban Ecology Australia (UEA) to create an environmentally and socially responsible development in the heart of Adelaide, a sprawling state capital with more than 1 million inhabitants. As a founding member of UEA, architect Paul F. Downton of Ecopolis Architects was able to translate the EcoCity vision into reality through creative use of a unusual T-shaped infill site. As the first development of its kind in South Australia, Christie Walk seeks to tackle sustainability issues with cutting-edge techniques while also modeling an inclusive, organic development process.

Christie Walk's creators—a cooperative essentially consisting of concerned citizens moonlighting as developers—imagined it as a small-scale template for larger urban projects, and so were careful to include all the important elements of good sustainable design. The project packs numerous sustainable features into a modest one-half-acre urban parcel. Christie Walk features the first intensive vegetative roof in South Australia as well as a fully functional community garden. The lush vegetation on the site is supplied with collected rainwater stored in underground tanks. To reduce energy costs, the project employs climate-responsive design technologies, including thermal mass and a user-operated ventilation system. Solar technologies include solar water heating to all residences with heat pumps and to the five-story apartment building, a 5-kilowatt photovoltaic array attached to the power grid, and the first translucent building-integrated photovoltaic system in the state. An ambitious new biologically based, on-site effluent treatment system is the result of negotiations with the state water company, which will operate the system. In return, the water company will get experience working with small-scale systems and the treated effluent will be used to water a nearby city park.

One of the founding principles of Christie Walk is that a true sustainable development engages with the community rather than existing as a separate, privileged enclave. Christie Walk consciously upheld this standard by locating the development in a diverse, lower-income area of Adelaide on a site formerly home to derelict houses and light industry. Because passionate area volunteers were involved from the earliest stages, residents of Christie Walk now reinforce the ties between the cooperative and the rest of the

At a Glance
Master plan: Ecopolis Architects Pty Ltd
Timeline: Development process commenced 1999; final phase built December 2006
Dwelling units: 27
Commercial square footage: 0
Land area: 1/2 acre

Project Highlights

- Alter city parking requirements to allow only 11 spaces for 27 dwellings
- 7,535 square feet of productive landscape and 1,830 square feet of productive roof area
- Retain all stormwater on-site
- Solar hot water for all units
- On-site effluent treatment system
- Site close to all city amenities, including transit, open space, and commerce
- 5 kW photovoltaic array hooked to the power grid

Key Sustainable Urbanism Thresholds

- Food production
- Open space
- Stormwater systems
- Wastewater treatment
- Illustrating density
- The integration of transportation, land use, and technology
- The impact of planning on building energy usage
- Car sharing
- Public darkness

Figure 10-14
Christie Walk site plan.
Image © Ecopolis Architects.

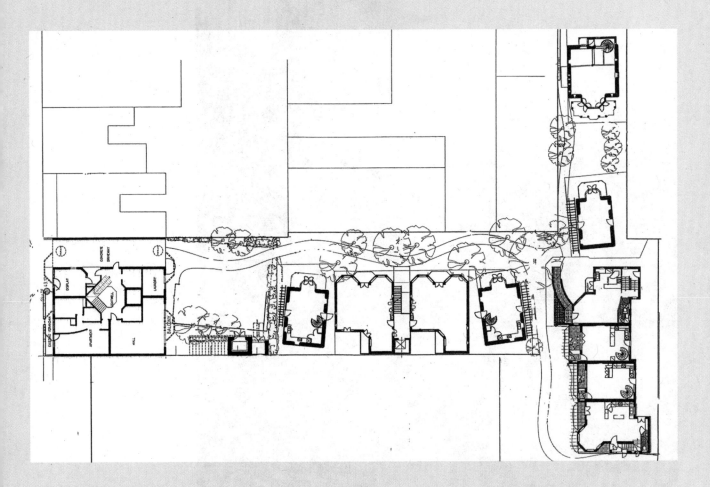

Figure 10-15
Homes face an inner path
lined with greenery.
Image © Ecopolis Architects.

neighborhood. The project also insists that sustainable design has a place in areas supporting affordable housing, because its drastically lower energy costs reduce living expenses. The entire site features walkable paths and open access to the development. This openness facilitates another goal of the project, which is to act as an educational experience. Thousands have visited Christie Walk and it has become a favorite destination of government officials. Christie Walk is just a five-minute walk from a robust central market featuring fresh produce from the Australian countryside, bus routes, tram service, and open parklands.

Christie Walk was always designed to be an educational experience, and it has fulfilled that promise. Volunteers were involved in all stages of the process (most heavily at the beginning). Community members formed a development cooperative called Wirranendi to keep control of the process. For the early stages of the project, they also formed a building company when they could find no builder willing or able to work with environmental design concepts and materials. They trained themselves in order to fill the void, and new on-site educational facilities will allow residents to spread their knowledge and tell their story. An adventurous spirit and willingness to experiment have paid off for the creators of Christie Walk, who have produced a rare community-driven project with applicability to sustainable urban developments worldwide.

Newington
Sydney, Australia

Newington is unlike any other suburb of Sydney, Australia. As home to the athletes of the 2000 Summer Olympics, Newington was in the spotlight from its inception. Developers Mirvac and Lend Lease built a large-scale solar village to house the athletes, with the goal of making the 2000 Games the greenest ever. About half of the planned two thousand units were built prior to the Games, and most of the remaining units are now built. Though Newington was targeted for development years before the Games, the Olympics offered the opportunity to develop quickly and yet still maintain sustainable design principles. The high-profile nature of the project allowed Mirvac and Lend Lease to increase momentum on sustainable technology research, even leading companies to develop new, green products for use at Newington. The end result has been an introduction of new green products into the Australian market following the Games, and a solar village housing approximately five thousand people.

Built on a brownfield site, Newington includes a residential area plus a retail area, business park, and park lands. The retail area, Newington Marketplace, is where the highest-density developments are clustered. The suburb is planned as three park-centered precincts, assuring that all dwellings are within a 5-minute walk of a park. Unfortunately, the plan fails to build neighborhoods, choosing to segregate the commercial uses rather than create walk-to neighborhood centers. An additional 21 acres of the development site was ceded back to the government and incorporated into the Millennium Parklands (at 1,050 acres the largest park in Sydney). Further support for biodiversity exists in the rehabilitated Haslams Creek, formerly a concrete channel and now a natural watercourse. Extensive pedestrian and bicycle networks link the development with these open spaces. Sydney Olympic Park (facilities left over from the 2000 Games) is also adjacent to the site.

Newington's solar suburb concept is particularly unique, and at the time of its construction it was the largest solar village in the world. Solar panels are incorporated into every home; 780 homes have 1,000-watt peak power solar arrays, and 339 homes have 500-watt peak power solar arrays. The collective energy generated by these photovoltaic panels will prevent 1,309 tons of CO_2 from entering the atmosphere per year, the equivalent of 261 cars being taken off the road. Gas-boosted solar hot water is available in every home as well. Window awnings and glazing draw heat inward in winter and provide shade in summer.

At a Glance

Master plan: Cox Group
Developer: Mirvac Lend Lease Village Consortium (a joint venture between Mirvac and Lend Lease)
Timeline: Development began 1997; village complete 1999; further development still occurring
Dwelling units: 2,000
Commercial square footage: Approximately 1 million square feet
Land area: 222 acres

Project Highlights/Benchmarks

- Reduction of landfill waste by 90 percent for hard waste and 60 percent for soft waste
- Solar panels on all homes prevent production of 1,309 tons of CO_2
- 90 percent native plantings for landscape
- Dual water system separates potable and nonpotable water
- Stormwater used to create habitat in parklands
- Homes use 50 percent less energy and potable water than conventional homes

Key Sustainable Urbanism Thresholds

- Open space
- Biodiversity corridors
- Stormwater systems
- Public darkness
- The integration of transportation, land use, and technology
- The impact of planning on building energy usage
- Public darkness

Figure 10-18
Newington site plan.
Image © Mirvac Lend Lease
Village Consortium.

Figure 10-19
View from a Newington balcony.
Image © Rowan Turner.

Figure 10-20
Newington home.
Image © Dean Wilmot.

Up to 90 percent of homes are oriented within 30 degrees east of north and 20 degrees west of north to take maximum advantage of sunlight. All homes have been designed to require 50 percent less energy than conventional developments using elements such as wool insulation, slab construction, and cross ventilation. Water usage (potable and nonpotable) is reduced 50 percent through the use of efficient fixtures, while nonpotable water is supplied for use in toilets and landscaping.

Stormwater runoff is a valuable resource at Newington. It is cleansed on-site with gross pollutant traps and then channeled to water quality ponds in the adjacent Millennium Parklands, providing an important habitat area. Plantings at Newington are 90 percent native species, which ensures that they are compatible with existing soils, require minimal water, and produce few allergens. Substantial green space will also ensure that 40 percent of runoff infiltrates the groundwater supply rather than being conveyed away in sewers. Transit is another important element of Newington's infrastructure that helped Sydney provide a green home for its athletes during the Olympic Games. Bus service runs throughout the development and connects to heavy rail and a ferry. In addition, a corridor was set aside for future light rail. Despite the presence of public transit, the project's failure to rely on it and to develop neighborhoods with walk-to services perpetuates automobile dependence. The developer's choice to allot an average of two parking spaces for many dwellings reveals a business as usual attitude—based on the belief that the average suburban homeowner would be dissatisfied with less. Conscientious construction practices were important to the developers, who carefully monitored construction waste disposal. Waste headed for a landfill was reduced by 90 percent for hard waste and 60 percent for soft waste. Unfortunately, Newington does not make any provision for affordable housing, though a diversity of home types ensures a mix of incomes. Newington's ultimate success is in creating a vast solar village that maintains its mass appeal, proving that green development can be a lucrative venture. Its stimulus of the Australian market for green building is also an important contribution to sustainability.

High Point
Seattle, Washington
United States

High Point is an innovative community redevelopment effort near downtown Seattle, Washington. The project was begun as a HUD HOPE VI vision, and the Seattle Housing Authority cooperated with public and private agencies, developers, and current and former residents to reshape the formerly isolated low-income housing area into a new community that exceeds the HOPE VI program goals for transformation of public housing. The Seattle Housing Authority, Seattle Public Utilities, the Seattle Department of Community Development, the Seattle Department of Transportation, and the architecture, urban design, and planning firm Mithun are just a few of the entities coming together to make this project happen. A total of 1,600 units within a twenty-five-city-block area will accommodate approximately 4,000 residents.

Two bus routes discourage unnecessary car trips, and there are plans to extend Seattle's monorail to the area. The site is near north-south and east-west arterials, and there is also a car-share program. Although there are no bike lanes yet, sidewalks are provided on all streets. While the previous development was a maze of curvy streets, the new High Point relinks with the surrounding street grid. As the site is a ten-minute drive from downtown Seattle, a good number of jobs are within close proximity or easily accessible via transit or car. Within the project a clinic, public library, and neighborhood center all provide local employment while supplying needed services. The housing authority, local garden, and site maintenance association offer additional jobs. An existing elementary school is integrated into the plan as well.

Much thought was put into the project's open spaces. An environmentally critical hillside bordering one edge of the development was retained and one fifth of the total buildable area (20 acres) has been allocated to 21 varied neighborhood parks. In addition, High Point is 10 percent of the watershed for Longfellow Creek, an important salmon habitat. In the interest of protecting the quality of the water that supports those salmon and the residents of High Point alike, narrow streets and bioswales will work together to filter stormwater runoff in landscaped areas. This will reduce runoff by 65 percent, preventing it from gathering too many chemicals from paved surfaces and delivering those contaminants to Longfellow Creek.

Energy efficiency was another design priority for the project. All homes are built to earn a Built Green rating of three stars or better. Energy Star appliances are required, and building envelopes

At a Glance
Master plan: Mithun Architects + Designers + Planners
Developer: Seattle Housing Authority
Timeline: Phase 1 built 2006; Phase 2 begins construction 2007
Dwelling units: 1,600
Commercial square footage: 10,000 square feet
Land area: 120 acre project area; 100 acres buildable

Project Highlights/Benchmarks
- 35 "Breathe Easy" homes reduce factors that contribute to asthma in children
- Increased lighting, small parks within view of homes, narrow streets to slow traffic, and inviting front porches encourage residents to mingle and watch over children
- Housing constructed to Built Green standards
- 20 units already present were deconstructed, and materials sold or reused
- Stormwater management reduces runoff to Longfellow Creek by 65 percent
- Half of the site's 1,600 homes are affordable
- Residents displaced by construction were able to move into the new development and help shape its form
- One fifth of the buildable area is park land

Key Sustainable Urbanism Thresholds
- Healthy neighborhoods
- Open space
- Stormwater systems
- Public darkness
- The impact of planning on building energy usage
- Walkable streets and networks
- Water and the density debate
- Food production

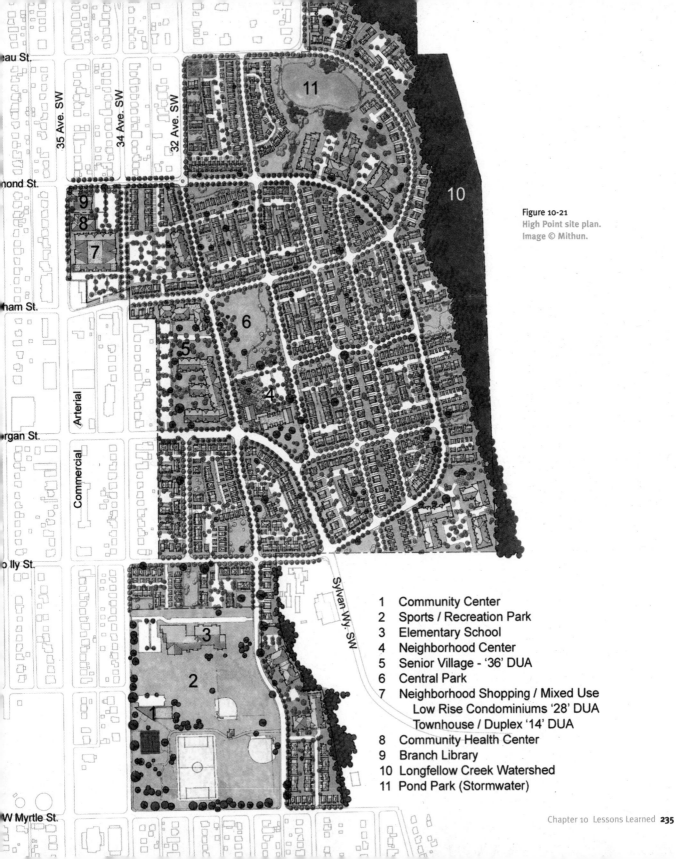

Figure 10-21
High Point site plan.
Image © Mithun.

1   Community Center
2   Sports / Recreation Park
3   Elementary School
4   Neighborhood Center
5   Senior Village - '36' DUA
6   Central Park
7   Neighborhood Shopping / Mixed Use
      Low Rise Condominiums '28' DUA
      Townhouse / Duplex '14' DUA
8   Community Health Center
9   Branch Library
10 Longfellow Creek Watershed
11 Pond Park (Stormwater)

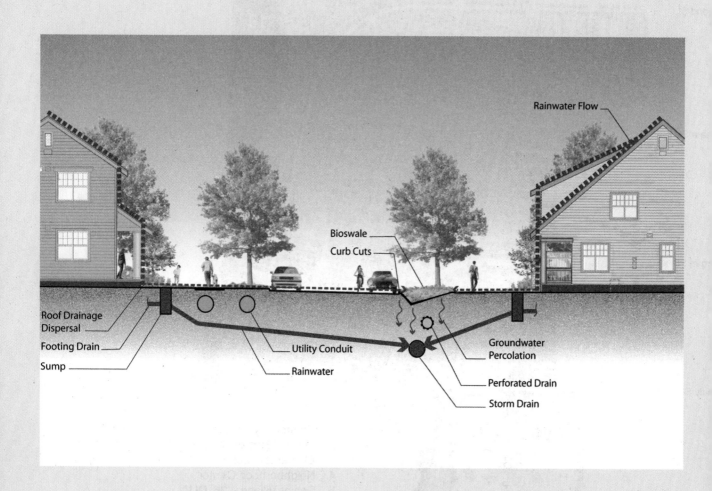

Rainwater Flow

Bioswale

Curb Cuts

Roof Drainage
Dispersal

Footing Drain

Sump

Utility Conduit

Rainwater

Groundwater
Percolation

Perforated Drain

Storm Drain

are kept tight to help to retain heating and cooling within home Tankless water heaters supply hot water for radiant heating that allows residents to heat only rooms in use, saving on energy use. Landscaped swales are interspersed with common turf planting strips to provide stormwater management without sacrificing the aesthetic appeal of a traditional streetscape. In addition, porous concrete sidewalks direct water down into the soil. The project plans also value biodiversity. Seasonal weather was a consideration for the flora chosen; 150 existing trees were kept within the project, and native plant species were included within the landscaping plan. A garden provides fresh produce and is managed though a contract with a group that sells the produce at a local market. In addition, pea patches serve as informal food production for residents interested in small-scale gardening.

One of the design's strengths is the priority given to integrating low-income housing into a mixture of housing types, incomes, and designs. Another design strength is the site's inclusion of features designed to promote interaction among neighbors and a close-knit community. While the previous development had poorly lit, curvilinear streets, the new design leaves porch lights on twenty-four hours per day, with low lighting projecting to the sidewalks. In addition, the city granted the designer permission to use 25-foot intervals for lighting instead of the city's standard spacing of 50 feet. Alleys are lit with garage lights and 12-foot poles. Narrow streets with inviting porches encourage watchful residents to socialize with each other, providing a critical, informal safety net for children playing nearby. High Point is also notable because, during construction, the contractor agreed to hire at least fifty low-income workers and ensure that apprentices, who gained valuable job skills, did at least 15 percent of the union work.

Overall, the project does a great job of addressing social integration through sustainable design. Working within HOPE VI budget parameters, the team was able to mitigate large-scale site impact, in the process protecting a creek, recycling the former development's old-growth timber, and saving more than 150 trees. At the same time, High Point provides meaningful community spaces and new homes for underserved city residents while also integrating them with their neighbors across the street.

Built Greenfield

The Upton development in Northampton, England, marries an abundance of green building technologies to a built form rooted in the traditional English countryside. While some of the eight phases of the project embrace traditional architecture more than others, even the most modern phases incorporate touches such as old-world masonry. One major reason for this continuity is the governing design code developed by English Partnerships, Northampton Borough Council, and the Prince's Foundation. The design code is a unified vision for Upton that guides developers in constructing buildings that will meet the environmental and aesthetic goals of the project. The design code pictures Upton as a warm, welcoming place to live, as well as fertile ground for demonstration of exciting new green technologies.

One important goal for Upton is to create a community that is flexible enough to adapt as residents' needs change. This flexibility was built into the design code by requiring certain features be included in buildings that are likely to be converted to different uses over the years. For example, homes fronting High Street, the main artery, will have high ground-floor ceilings and open layouts that can be converted to offices, shops, cafes, or flats as the market demands. Open space

is also considered in the plan, which includes a country park and playing fields, and also preserves nearby Ashby Woods. Combined with space for public squares, accessible public space in sites A and B totals 51 percent of the acreage. Along with the open space, features such as a bat barn, nesting boxes, and water features promote biodiversity in the development. A mixture of uses will include a substantial number of community buildings, including a medical center, schools, and a day care center, along with residential and commercial development.

Green building standards are high at Upton. Adventuresome exploration of different technologies at each site is designed to educate the community and visitors as well. Homes on every site must meet BREEAM EcoHomes Excellent standards by installing high-efficiency fixtures and appliances, using recycled or local sustainable materials, limiting CO_2 emissions to 25 kilograms per square meter per year, and other similar measures. In later phases of the project, sites will be required to include increasingly complicated and widespread technologies. Sites D1 and D2, for example, will include photovoltaic systems, microcombined heat and power (micro-CHP), rainwater harvesting,

---

At a Glance

Developer: English Partnerships
Timeline: Master plan 2002; sites A and B to be completed 2007; 8 sites total to be finished by 2011
Dwelling units: Approximately 1,000–1,400 (phase 1)
Commercial square footage: 7,535 square feet
Land area: 106 acres (phase 1)

Project Highlights/Benchmarks

- 22 percent of scattered units permanently affordable
- All homes must meet BREEAM EcoHomes Excellent standards; CO_2 emission capped at 25kg/m²/yr
- Mini wind turbines in Site D1
- All developers must secure green energy tariffs
- Extensive sustainable urban drainage system
- Each site required to demonstrate different sustainable technologies
- Twice-hourly bus service started with first residents

Key Sustainable Urbanism Thresholds

- Open space
- Stormwater systems
- The impact of planning on building energy usage
- Large district energy systems
- Walkable streets and networks
- Car sharing

previous page
Figure 10-25
Upton master plan
reestablishes the principles of
place making. Unlike adjacent
conventional cul-de-sacs, it uses
a series of permeable street
networks, blocks, and open
spaces. High-density living and
minimum use of the car create
an attractive urban environment.
Image © English Partnerships &
The Prince's Foundation.

Figure 10-26
Mews looking east in site D1,
designed by Bill Dunster Architects.
Image © www.zedfactory.com.

Figure 10-27
Sustainable urban drainage
system (SUDS) controls stormwater
runoff; neighborhood square
is visible in the background.
Image © English Partnerships.

Figure 10-28
Housing in Upton that responds
to environmental and flooding
challenges sets new standards in
sustainable urban drainage systems
(SUDS). High-quality SUDS design
provides urban amenity for the new
development. Image © Richard Ivey.

Figure 10-29
Many site B homes feature
photovoltaic panels.
Image © English Partnerships.

Figure 10-30
Archway leading to an internal
courtyard.
Image © English Partnerships.

extensive greenroofs, insulation upgrades, solar water heating, high internal air quality, and an NHER (National Home Energy Rating) of 10. Part of site D1 will also add mini wind turbines in an effort to become carbon-neutral, a tip of the hat to the BedZED development in London (architect Bill Dunster worked on both projects). In addition, all developers must secure green energy tariffs (comparable to renewable energy credits in the United States).

An extensive sustainable urban drainage system (SUDS) uses new and existing infrastructure provided by English Partnerships to control the flow and quality of water entering the sewer system. Runoff is directed at bioswales, some of which feature reed beds that also act as animal habitats, and is further controlled with the use of porous paving in courtyards and residential complexes.

Upton is also currently developing a transit strategy. As soon as the first residents moved in, a twice-hourly bus service began running. A car-share program has also been proposed. Upton strives for social sustainability by requiring that 22 percent of housing be permanently affordable. English Partnerships also chose to break with convention and "pepper-pot" the affordable homes throughout the development, rendering them indistinguishable from the market-rate units.

Kronsberg
Hannover, Germany

The Kronsberg District is the city of Hannover's vision for sustainable development in Germany. The city's direction of the decades-long planning process resulted in a development scheme dominated by ambitious energy reduction goals, transit-oriented design, and mixed-income residential areas. Kronsberg's success—by 2001, a 74 percent reduction in CO2 emissions compared with conventional developments—is partly due to the site's development by a government entity rather than private enterprise, which would not have enjoyed the same freedom to pass stringent ecologically minded laws. When the city of Hannover won the bid to host the Expo 2000 World Exposition in 1990, the city made the decision to pursue a sustainable development to both meet growing housing demand and model the Expo's motto, "Humankind—Nature—Technology."

The city of Hannover accumulated the land used for the Kronsberg District over many years, starting in the 1970s. The large site allowed the city to create a plan with a clearly defined residential and mixed-use section following the natural contour of a hill, which itself was designated protected open space. At forty-seven units per net acre, the density of the settlement is able to support a new tram line with three stations in Kronsberg. These are situated so that no resident need walk farther than about one-third of a mile to reach one. The main arterial road is also situated alongside the tram line on the western edge of the development, effectively eliminating through-traffic in the neighborhoods. Car usage is further discouraged because the development allots only 0.8 cars per unit, with the remaining fraction converted to additional public parking spaces. A designated bike street also bisects the length of the site. A cluster of mixed-use buildings—including a health center, a shopping center, a church, and an arts and community center near the central tram stop—provides residents with a pedestrian-friendly community hub. Kindergartens, a primary school, and a high school are also situated within the development.

Kronsberg shines particularly in its application of green technology to individual buildings and in its use of high-performance infrastructure. The city of Hannover accomplished its energy efficiency goals by including efficiency requirements in developer land sale contracts. This is also how the city balanced its desire to contract with numerous developers to create varied neighborhoods with its need to ensure that every residence meet strict green building guidelines.

At a Glance

Master plan and developer: City of Kronsberg

Timeline: City started buying land in 1970s; city council resolved to use sustainable guidelines in 1990; first phase built 1998

Dwelling units: First phase: 3,000, including 300 private row houses; 2,000 additional private houses upon completion

Commercial square footage: Approximately 377,000 square feet

Land area: Total development 395 acres; first phase; 173 acres

Project Highlights/Benchmarks

- Compulsory connection to district heating system reducing CO2 emissions by 23%
- Development of the comprehensive Kronsberg Standard
- Achieved a 74 percent reduction in CO2 emissions in 2001
- All residents within +/– 1/3 mile from tram stop
- 0.8 parking spaces per dwelling
- Designated bike street runs through development
- Green building guidelines built into land contracts
- Two 1.5-megawatt wind turbines
- All excavated soil used within the development
- 47 units per net acre density supports a tram line
- Passive houses use 15 kwh/m²/yr

Key Sustainable Urbanism Thresholds

- Open space
- Stormwater systems
- Illustrating density
- The integration of transportation, land use, and technology
- The impact of planning on building energy usage
- Large district energy systems
- Walkable streets and networks

Figure 10-32
Inner court with water retention
basin. Image © Landhauptstadt
Hannover archive.

Figure 10-33
Solar city courtyard.
Image © Landhauptstadt
Hannover archive.

These guidelines were collected into a single set of principles called the Kronsberg Standard. In addition to the low-energy-use house standards set for developers, energy use was reduced through quality assurance monitoring, an electricity-saving campaign, several solar installations, two 1.5-megawatt wind turbines, a co-generation heating network, and a passive house section featuring energy consumption of 15 kilowatt-hours per square meter per year. Compulsory connection to the district heating network alone reduces CO2 emissions by 23 percent. Rainwater is channeled to landscaped areas and allowed to be absorbed slowly into the ground, recharging the groundwater. All excavated soil was also used within the development for landscaping, eliminating the cost and pollution that would have been involved in removing 100,000 truckloads of soil. The city also instituted a home composting program to complement standard recycling procedures.

The new development offers much-needed housing for a broad social mix. Kronsberg residents working in central Hannover are only nineteen minutes away by rapid transit, which runs every eight to fifteen minutes, and buses run every fifteen minutes. Because all housing except a section of terrace houses is social housing, the city had ample opportunity to shape the demographics of the development. The city exercised its legislative power and raised the income ceiling for occupancy at Kronsberg to twice its normal limit to ensure economic diversity in the population. Developers received subsidies for building social housing. Because their plans had to be cleared with the city's town and ecological planners, the development remains heterogeneous, and housing affordability goals are accomplished without resulting in monotonous design.

Loreto Bay
Baja California Sur
Mexico

With the village of Loreto Bay, the Mexican government has partnered with the Trust for Sustainable Development to reinvent the resort community genre. The 8,000-acre parcel of land—targeted as a new tourist destination by the Mexican tourism agency FONATUR twenty-five years ago but never developed beyond basic infrastructure—will include 6,000 homes, a hotel, a golf course, and 5,000 acres of protected land. Unlike notoriously wasteful traditional resort communities, Loreto Bay's "regenerative design" philosophy aims to actually enhance the ecological health of the area through development.

Life is designed to move at a deliberately slow pace in Loreto Bay. Narrow pedestrian streets will remain unclogged by traffic due to a replacement of gas-powered vehicles with bicycles and electric cars. Intentionally small neighborhoods ensure that most residents are within a few minutes' walk of the neighborhood center. Public and private open spaces are sprinkled throughout the development, including numerous parks, playgrounds, and courtyards with trickling fountains. Because the development will include a number of mixed-use spaces providing shopping, recreation, and gathering areas, it is estimated that at any given time 50 percent of residents will stay almost entirely within Loreto Bay. This further eliminates the need for highway-oriented vehicles and fosters a sense of community among residents.

Loreto Bay Company (a subsidiary of the Trust for Sustainable Development, led by David Butterfield) is currently implementing a highly ambitious sustainability plan that will seek to produce more energy from renewable resources than the development will consume. Homes feature energy efficient fixtures and appliances, as well as reduced-use water fixtures. A planned beach club will be built to LEED Platinum standards. Most homes are constructed out of adobe-like blocks made from local materials (and painted with low- or no-VOC paint), reducing transport costs and providing excellent thermal insulation for the homes. Natural ventilation is also achieved through use of inner courtyards teeming with vegetation and dome-vented kitchen cupolas. Solar hot water units are provided for all homes, and solar technology also powers the fountain and pool pumps. In an attempt to find creative ways to encourage frugal energy use by homeowners, Loreto Bay Company hopes to include an electricity-use monitoring system in homes that will make it simple to keep track of energy consumption.

At a Glance

Master plan: Duany Plater-Zyberk & Company
Developer: Loreto Bay Company
Timeline: Project began 2003; 15-year build-out
Dwelling units: Approximately 6,000
Commercial square footage: 77,000 square feet in Founder's Village (phase 1)
Land area: 8,000 acres (3,000 developed, 5,000 protected)

Project Highlights/Benchmarks

- 20-megawatt wind farm will wean the area from diesel
- 5 miles of restored estuaries
- 5,000 acres protected and restored as native habitat
- Recycling program will send less than 10 percent of residents' waste to landfills
- No gas-powered vehicles permitted; instead, electric cars and golf carts, bicycles, car-share program
- 6,000 permanent jobs created
- 1 percent of all sales and resales fund a nonprofit to support social initiatives
- Electricity use monitoring system
- Solar hot water systems on all homes

Key Sustainable Urbanism Thresholds

- Open space
- Biodiversity corridors
- Stormwater systems
- The integration of transportation, land use, and technology
- The impact of planning on building energy usage
- Water and the density debate
- Walkable streets and networks
- Car sharing

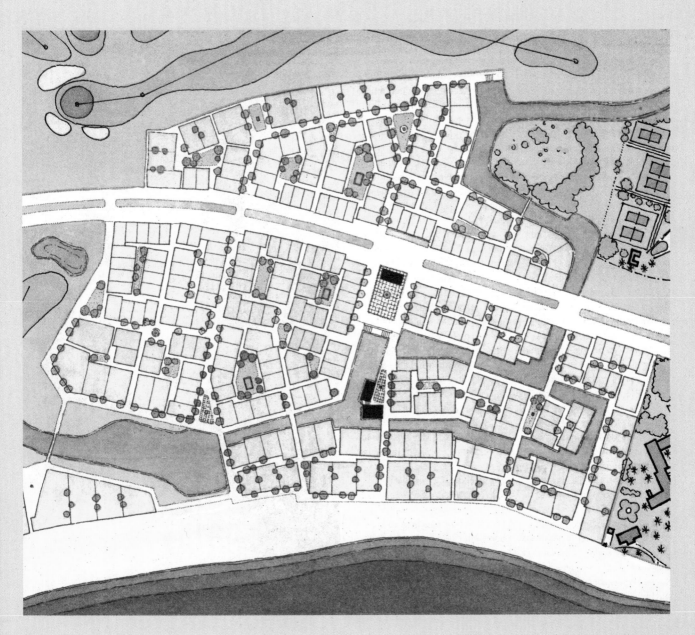

The linchpin of Loreto Bay Company's sustainability program is its high-performance infrastructure whose most exciting element is a proposed 20-megawatt wind farm located near Puerto San Carlos. A recently completed feasibility study suggests that this project is viable for a number of reasons. The wind farm will be located near an existing power station that will allow wind-generated power to be transferred directly to the grid system. Because Loreto Bay is projected to use only 6 to 10 megawatts of power, the surplus will be sold to neighboring municipalities. This situation is extremely beneficial to the greater Baja Sur area because electricity there is currently fueled by diesel, which is very expensive, fluctuates with oil prices, and pollutes the air. The option to expand to a 40- or 60-megawatt wind farm in the future also exists, further cementing the wind farm's promise as a business venture.

Water conservation is vital in the Baja Sur region, and the Trust is going to address it by several means. The first is the restoration of two watersheds. Small dams will slow water flow through natural rainwater channels, giving the water time to soak back into the aquifer. Developing this system will take many years, so the Trust is concurrently pursuing a desalination program using an environmentally safe

reverse-osmosis process. In addition, the golf course is being reseeded with Paspalum grass (a salt-tolerant plant), and a stormwater management plan will be used to direct rain to landscaped areas. Part of restoring the watersheds includes fencing off 5,000 acres of land to protect it from overgrazing and repopulating this area with native vegetation. Five miles of wetland estuaries will be restored as well. This will include the planting of thousands of mangrove trees, which shelter native wildlife. This water conservation system allows Loreto Bay Company to simultaneously pursue its goal of increasing the biodiversity and biomass of the development as whole. To reduce waste, Loreto Bay will use a wet/dry recycling model (proven in other developments to achieve 98 percent participation) that asks residents to separate waste into organic matter, recyclables, and non-recyclables. The organic matter will be composted to provide fertilizer for the community agricultural center (featuring an organic farm and nursery) and the excess will be sold to neighboring communities. The recycling program's ultimate goal is to send less than 10 percent of all waste to a landfill.

As a resort community, Loreto Bay's integration into the surrounding Mexican community is even more critical than most new developments.

Figure 10-36
Outdoor spaces feature prominently
in most Loreto Bay units.
Image © Duany Plater-Zyberk
& Company.

Figure 10-37
Elevated view shows varied
roofline and ocean view.
Image © Duany Plater-Zyberk &
Company.

Loreto Bay Company is pursuing policies designed to make Loreto Bay a good neighbor to surrounding areas, starting with employing a local workforce. It is estimated that about two thousand jobs will be available during the course of construction, with six thousand permanent jobs available by completion (most in the resort industry). Workers generally live in the vicinity, usually five to seven miles away from the development. Loreto Bay Company is also working on a regional affordable housing strategy in concert with the Mexican government to make it possible for workers to live near their place of employment. Currently the plan is to include enough integrated affordable housing in Loreto Bay to accommodate 50 percent of resort employees, with the remainder able to use public transit to reach the community. Loreto Bay Company is committed to providing a generous living wage to workers, and requires subcontractors to do the same. The Trust for Sustainable Development has also created an independent Mexican nonprofit, Loreto Bay Foundation, to address social, educational, and business needs of the surrounding area. One percent of the proceeds of all sales and resales, in perpetuity, will go directly to the foundation to fund sustainability and social initiatives. Money is also being raised for a new, full-service medical center in the town of Loreto. The addition of a regional transit plan in the coming years completes the package of initiatives intended to integrate Loreto Bay successfully into the Baja Sur community.

Civano
Tucson, Arizona
United States

Figure 10-38
Civano site plan. Image ©
Elizabeth Moule + Stefanos
Polyzoides Architects and Urbanists;
Duany Plater-Zyberk & Company;
and Wayne Moody.

The Civano project is a good example of the results achieved when a project is able to capitalize on a sustainable design-friendly political climate. In the 1980s, emerging solar energy technologies caught the attention of Arizona's governor at the time, Bruce Babbitt. With backing from the city of Tucson, plans for a solar village slowly emerged and eventually, years later, expanded to incorporate sustainable principles beyond solar power. Initial plans for the project coalesced through several design charrettes, incorporating the ideas of established new urbanists such as Andrés Duany, and Stefanos Polyzoides, and noted green architect William McDonough, as well as community members.

Civano's strength lies in its integration of sustainable technology and community-focused design. Housing, shopping, work, education, civic facilities, parks, and natural open spaces consciously evoke historical southwestern architecture and pay tribute to the gorgeous Sonoran Desert. The plan shows sensitivity to the site's desert context by harnessing the region's ample sunlight with several solar technologies and aggressively pursuing water conservation. The development agreement between the city of Tucson and the developer cements these goals by pledging to reduce home energy consumption by 50 percent and potable water consumption by 65 percent. Neighborhood 1, designed by architects Moule & Polyzoides in conjunction with Duany Plater-Zyberk & Company and Wayne Moody, is laid out according to the new urbanist transect. Using the transect as a guiding tool, the designers were able to ensure that each neighborhood would feature gathering places, high walkability, a mix of uses, and substantial open space.

As a project begun relatively early on in the sustainable design movement, Civano faced several challenges including finding builders that were familiar with sustainable building practices. Eventually Civano's developers employed an array of creative sustainable techniques in the project, including use of local materials such as straw bales and adobe; an ambitious native plant conservation scheme led by the Civano Nursery and Garden Center, which also acts as a community education center; and energy-saving strategies such as natural cooling towers, use of thermal mass, building orientation, and rainwater harvesting. Most homes have a solar water heater and are ready to install photovoltaic panels, if they are not installed already.

Designing Civano in concert with the desert landscape has allowed the community to drastically

At a Glance
Master plan: Moule & Polyzoides, with Duany Plater-Zyberk and Wayne Moody
Timeline: Initial discussions in early 1980s; project initiated 1996; Neighborhood 1 (of four) began construction 1998
Dwelling units: 2,000+
Commercial square footage: Approximately 1 million
Land area: 1,145 acres

Project Highlights/Benchmarks
The Civano Standard with the following targets:
- Reduce potable water consumption by 65 percent
- Reduce fossil fuel energy consumption by 50 percent over 1995 Model Energy Code
- Reduce internal vehicle miles by 40 percent
- Create one job on-site for every two residences
- Reduce landfill-destined solid waste
- Provide 20 percent affordable housing
- Construction will generate 30 percent less waste than the local average
- 35 percent dedicated open space

Key Sustainable Urbanism Thresholds
- Third places
- Open space
- Stormwater systems
- The impact of planning on building energy usage
- Walkable streets and networks

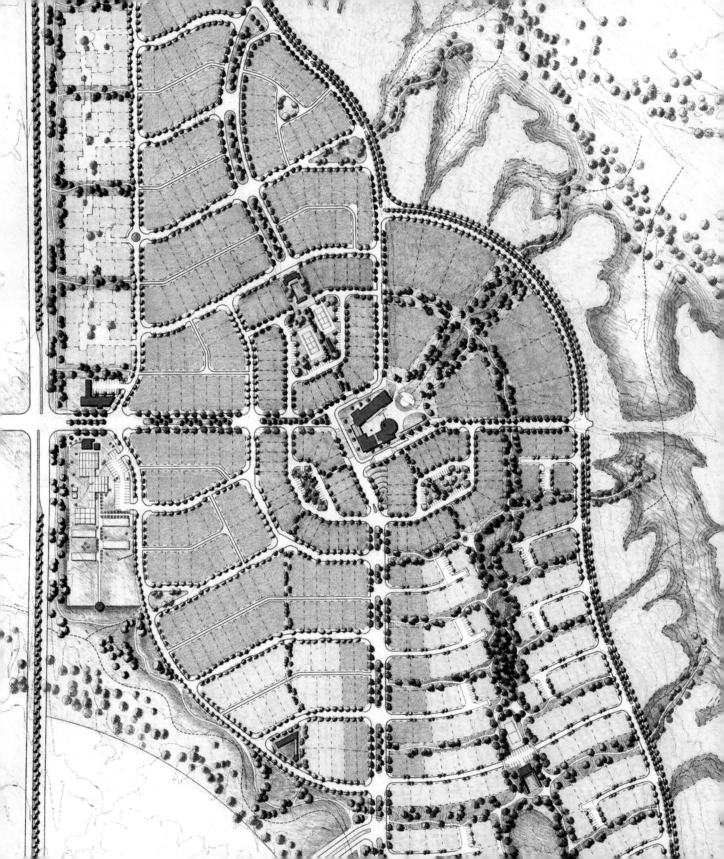

Figure 10-39
Shaded outdoor spaces are an
important design element that takes
advantage of the mild sunny climate.
Image © Moule + Polyzoides.

Figure 10-40
A view of the Civano neighborhood
center with attached cooling tower.
Image © Moule + Polyzoides.

reduce energy consumption. Tucson itself has adopted the project's standard as the city's. As part of its contribution to the project, the city of Tucson has also agreed to extend its reclaimed water line so the whole development has access. This dual water system, separating potable and nonpotable supplies, will be extended to all buildings. In combination with water-harvesting technology and cultivation of native water-storing plants, Civano has implemented a water consumption strategy more in harmony with the desert environment than status quo new developments. Civano's transformation from its original conception as an auto-dependent suburb with solar panels into a walkable urbanist place that seamlessly incorporates green building techniques is a testament to its lead designer. While the original solar suburb concept focused on a single technology, according to its designers, 85 percent of the final plan's sustainability gains can be attributed to urbanist design and only 15 percent to building technology. As the project progresses past the initial Neighborhood 1 and the development responsibility passes to new hands, current residents and former designers hope the original Civano standard will be upheld.

Poundbury
Dorchester, England

Unabashedly traditional Poundbury is the Prince of Wales's grand experiment in sustainable urban design. The development lies on the west end of Dorchester and emulates the town's signature architectural style, which harks back to Dorchester's days as a Roman-era market town. In 1988, the Prince of Wales appointed a well-known proponent of traditional urbanism, Leon Krier, to create a 380-acre master plan to manage Dorchester's growth in the coming decades.

The focus of Krier's plan is creating a strong sense of place. He accomplishes this with traditional Dorset architecture and a human-scaled street network that discourages car use. Through traffic will find it hard to negotiate the constrained streets, and visitors will find far more on-street parking than designated surface lots. Residents contract for private parking spaces, which are usually located in rear-access courtyards, and the original allotment of 2.3 spaces per household has been reduced to 1.5 per household. Higher density than in traditional suburbs supports local retail and offices, putting each resident no further from daily necessities than a five-minute walk. The large percentage of open space (about 35 percent, composed of 100 acres passive space and 30 acres active space) also ensures that any resident can reach it within five

minutes. The development emphatically refers to itself as a mixed-use development, not a residential suburb, proudly mingling offices, light industrial use, and residences. Each of the four neighborhoods (the four phases of the project) will feature all uses. In order to perpetuate the traditional feel of the site, future modifications to the buildings will have to be approved by the Duchy of Cornwall.

The development as a whole is light on green technology and infrastructure, but it incorporates several sustainable design ideas. Most buildings are situated to take advantage of passive solar gain, reducing heating and cooling costs. Shared walls produced by high density also help insulate units. A number of buildings featuring heftier green technologies are planned, and they will aim for an EcoHomes Excellent rating by using features such as photovoltaic panels, rainwater harvesting, solar water heating, and sheep's wool insulation. High-quality historic design is maintained through the use of local materials if at all possible, including slate, stone, and render. The duchy also regulates design aspects such as roof angles and chimneys. Bioswales are located throughout the community to allow rainwater to soak back into the soil. Several transit options eliminate the need for frequent car trips on the narrow,

At a Glance
Master plan: Leon Krier
Developer: Duchy of Cornwall
Timeline: Leon Krier master plan 1988; phase 1 complete 2002; phase 2 in progress
Dwelling units: 2,250
Commercial square footage: N/A
Land area: 380 acres

Project Highlights/Benchmarks
- Creation of 2,000 jobs projected (800 created to date)
- 35 percent of housing affordable
- Parking requirements decreased to 1.5 spaces/unit
- Many homes built to EcoHomes Excellent standards
- Bioswales slow stormwater runoff
- 35 percent open space
- County-wide car share
- Farmers' market with plans for a permanent covered market

Key Sustainable Urbanism Thresholds
- Economic benefits of locally owned stores
- Open space
- Stormwater systems
- Illustrating density
- The impact of planning on building energy usage
- Walkable streets and networks
- Car sharing
- Managing travel demand
- Car-free housing
- High-performance infrastructure

Figure 10-43
Poundbury street development
illustrating how highway challenges
can be incorporated successfully in
the urban fabric. Cars are integrated
within the street design to give
pedestrians priority, and the urban
form is used to achieve traffic
calming. Image © Richard Ivey.

Figure 10-44
Poundbury market. Unlike many
new housing developments,
Poundbury has developed a sense of
community through the physical
design of the town square and
Brownsword. Image © Richard Ivey.

winding roads. A countywide
car-share program is open to
residents, and an hourly bus
provides transportation to downtown Dorchester. Dorchester's
train station is also only a twenty-
minute walk from Poundbury.
A twice-monthly farmers' market
is currently in operation; there
are plans to build a permanent
covered market as well.

One aspect of the development that the Prince of Wales
insisted upon was the intermin-
gling of market-rate and affordable housing. At Poundbury, 20
percent of the units are owned
by a local housing association
and rented to social housing
tenants, while an additional 15
percent of units are maintained
as affordable, using schemes
such as shared equity and
discounted sale price. Some units
are also available for special-
needs residents and retirees. In
addition, eight hundred new jobs
within Poundbury (projected to
be two thousand by completion)
provide the opportunity for
residents of all economic classes
to live near their employment.

Chapter 11
State of the Art in Unbuilt Sustainable Urbanism

Unbuilt Infill

Dockside Green
Victoria, British Columbia
Canada

A reclaimed industrial wasteland will soon be home to the City of Victoria's most ambitious green venture to date. Windmill Development Group and Vancity Enterprises are developing the 15-acre Dockside Green project. The city and developers are aiming for a zero-carbon development and LEED Platinum certification for the entire development, rejuvenating this parcel of waterfront formerly contaminated with petrochemicals and toxic heavy metals. The heart of the project is a "triple bottom line" philosophy that values not only economic profits but also environmental and social results.

The plan responds to its fragmented context by proposing four sections of distinct character. This Radburn-influenced superblock is organized around a central greenway with a creek and dedicated pedestrian and bike ways. Another dedicated pedestrian and cyclist route is offered through the Galloping Goose Trail, a very popular regional trail that reaches the city center. Plans also highlight a waterfront walkway complete with native vegetation to take advantage of the waterfront view. Extensive tree plantings accompany the pedestrian paths and streets. South Plaza and several other mixed-use hubs provide access to office space and nonchain retailers and restaurants, providing incentive for residents to put the pedestrian paths to

good use. A community amphitheater and space allocated for public art further encourage residents of Dockside Green to interact with neighbors and actively enjoy the scenery.

Dockside Green is perhaps most famous for its bold plan to certify all twenty-six buildings in the development as LEED Platinum, in addition to incorporating extensive green infrastructure. Joe Van Belleghem—project lead at Windmill Development Group—and the rest of the development team have even gone a step further and pledged to pay a penalty of up to $1 million CDN if the entire development does not meet LEED Platinum standards, displaying the confidence and drive that have made this project famous. Estimated energy savings for each building will be 45–55 percent less than the Canadian Model Building Code, using a variety of technologies, including a four-pipe fan coil system, low-E double glazing and exterior blinds on west and south building faces, and Energy Star appliances. The efficient appliances will also contribute to a 65 percent savings on potable water consumption. A variety of lighting technologies employed include the use of compact fluorescents, LED lighting in corridors, occupancy sensors, and solar lighting in some landscaped areas. Greenroofs cool the buildings and help channel

At a Glance
Master plan: Busby Perkins+Will
Developer: Windmill Development Group and Vancity Enterprises
Timeline: 10-year build-out; first phase scheduled for completion late 2007
Dwelling units: Approximately 860
Commercial square footage: 242,194 square feet (plus 73,842 square feet of industrial space)
Land area: 15 acres

Project Highlights/Benchmarks
- All 26 buildings LEED Platinum certified
- Estimated building energy savings of 45–55 percent
- Estimated potable water savings of 65 percent
- 11 percent affordable housing
- Biomass co-generation facility
- Biodiesel facility
- Reinvigoration of harbor industry
- Reuse or recycle at least 90 percent of waste on-site
- Dedicated pedestrian and cyclist routes run through the heart of the development

Key Sustainable Urbanism Thresholds
- Neighborhood retail
- Economic benefits of locally owned stores
- Open space
- Biodiversity corridors
- Stormwater systems
- Wastewater treatment
- Illustrating density
- The integration of transportation, land use, and technology
- The impact of planning on building energy usage
- Large district energy systems
- Walkable streets and networks
- Car sharing

rainwater, which will be directed to water features and used in toilets. Builders will use sustainable materials such as low-emissions carpet tiles, low- or no-VOC paints, bamboo flooring and cabinets, cork, and salvaged wood. In addition, the developers intend to reuse or recycle at least 90 percent of construction waste on-site. Residents can reap the full benefits of their superefficient homes by monitoring their own water, electricity, and heat usage with individual sensors (shown in other developments to reduce energy usage by 20 percent).

Total water savings for the development are estimated at 70 million gallons, produced by an on-site sewage treatment facility, efficient fixtures in buildings, and strategic channeling of stormwater. Water features such as the creek are aesthetically pleasing but also help clean the water supply. A biomass co-generation facility will use waste wood to heat homes and provide hot

water. Grease from local restaurants is planned to power a biodiesel facility that will fuel a mini-transit system and shared cars. Mobility options abound, with residents able to choose from the car-share program (which uses exclusively electric or smart cars), the mini-transit, a ferry dock, and possibly a shuttle bus provided by the city. Independent commissioners will assess the performance of these infrastructure features one year after installation to make sure that they are working at full capacity.

Inclusion of 11 percent affordable housing and senior assisted-living facilities will help to ensure resident diversity. First nation workers are being trained in skilled trades to help build the project. The developers were also careful to highlight Dockside Green's unique locale by preserving space for the light industry that has traditionally occupied the area. Boat docks also enhance the maritime feel of the site and recall its context as a harbor neighborhood.

Note: At the time of publication, this project is well underway.

Figure 11-5
Dockside Green takes advantage of its waterfront location by offering access to a launch area for boats and a water taxi. Courtesy Busby Perkins+Will Architects.

Lloyd Crossing
Portland, Oregon
United States

Portland, Oregon's Lloyd Crossing project aims not only to reduce the area's ecological footprint to predevelopment levels but to do so while simultaneously revitalizing a key section of Portland's central city. The Portland Development Commission—the city's urban renewal agency—commissioned the Seattle-based architecture, design, and urban planning firm Mithun to create a vision plan for a thirty-five-block study area in Portland's Lloyd District, a predominantly commercial area. The resultant 2004 Sustainable Urban Design (SUD) plan and Catalyst Project imagines a Lloyd District in 2050 that contains a vital, mixed-use neighborhood of increased density paired with a neutral carbon balance. Aggressive project goals were set using sophisticated predevelopment metrics outlined by Mithun that indicated baseline predevelopment environmental impact in the areas of habitat, water and energy. While the SUD plan outlines a series of long-term goals intended for gradual completion, the four-block Catalyst Project area provides recommendations for a smaller model project that will ignite interest in sustainability and spur further private developments.

The SUD plan emphasizes place-making as an important component of sustainable design. Increased open space in a variety of forms—pocket parks, large parks, habitat corridors—will increase the habitability of the area as well as helping to achieve the project's goal of increasing tree cover from 14.5 percent to 30 percent. Streetscape plans are thick with greenery and downplay automobile traffic by incorporating generously sized sidewalks, designated bike lanes on main streets, significant roadside vegetation, conifer midstreet islands, and street wall setbacks that preserve building character. The plan also focuses on filling gaps in the streetscape with buildings of varied usage and architectural flavor for a more exciting pedestrian experience.

Building-level sustainable design elements are a critical part of the SUD plan, especially as one of the plan's key recommendations is maximizing the usage of allowed floor area ratio (FAR) to keep development as dense as possible. The plan anticipates adding 8.1 million square feet of above-grade building development to existing structures for a total of 10.9 million square feet by 2050. Building efficiency is the first step toward reaching predevelopment standards, and this will be accomplished using efficient fixtures, building orientation, greenroofs, a 10-megawatt photovoltaic array (increasing solar use to 13.7 percent in 2050), and rainwater harvesting for nonpotable use.

At a Glance

Master plan: Mithun
Developer: Portland Development Commission
Timeline: 2001, Lloyd Crossing development strategy commissioned by the PDC; 2004, created the Sustainable Urban Design plan and the Catalyst Project
Dwelling units: At least 1,000 (entire study area); 150–300 for Catalyst Project
Commercial square footage: At least 20,000 square feet of street-oriented retail
Land area: 54 acres

Project Highlights/Benchmarks

- 50-year plan lays out a strategy to reduce environmental impact to predevelopment levels
- Carbon balance reduced from 29,000 tons/year to 2,000 tons/year
- Nearly 90 percent of power will be from renewable sources by 2050
- Goal to live within the site's solar and rainfall budgets
- Catalyst Project will exceed LEED Platinum standards
- 100 percent of nonpotable water provided by rainwater and treated graywater
- 100 percent water treatment on-site
- 10 mW photovoltaic array
- District heat loop allows existing buildings to connect over time

Key Sustainable Urbanism Thresholds

- Neighborhood retail
- Open space
- Biodiversity corridors
- Stormwater systems
- Wastewater treatment
- Illustrating density
- The integration of transportation, land use, and technology
- The impact of planning on building energy usage
- Large district energy systems
- Walkable streets and networks

Figure 11-7
A plan to help Lloyd Crossing
live within its solar budget
relies to a great extent on off-site
wind-generated electricity.
Image © Mithun.

2050 Per Plan Energy Use Conditions

100% **Solar Energy Input**
161,006,000 kWh/yr

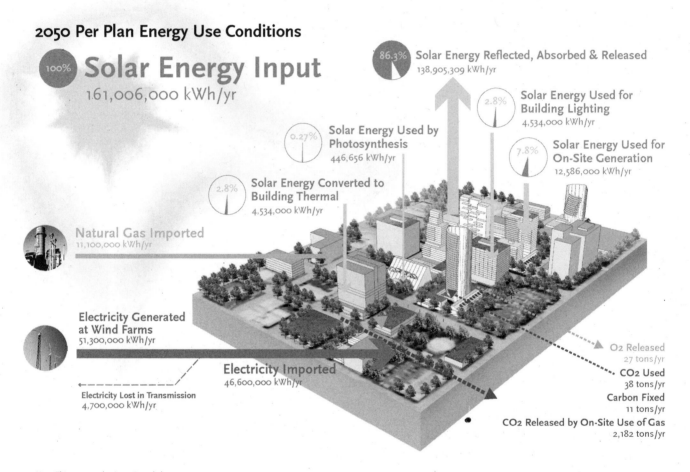

86.3% **Solar Energy Reflected, Absorbed & Released**
138,905,309 kWh/yr

2.8% **Solar Energy Used for Building Lighting**
4,534,000 kWh/yr

0.27% **Solar Energy Used by Photosynthesis**
446,656 kWh/yr

7.8% **Solar Energy Used for On-Site Generation**
12,586,000 kWh/yr

2.8% **Solar Energy Converted to Building Thermal**
4,534,000 kWh/yr

Natural Gas Imported
11,100,000 kWh/yr

Electricity Generated at Wind Farms
51,300,000 kWh/yr

Electricity Imported
46,600,000 kWh/yr

Electricity Lost in Transmission
4,700,000 kWh/yr

O2 Released
27 tons/yr

CO2 Used
38 tons/yr

Carbon Fixed
11 tons/yr

CO2 Released by On-Site Use of Gas
2,182 tons/yr

Note: This concept plan is not intended
to represent specific planned or required
development proposals

Carbon Balance
Net add to atmosphere: 2,144 tons/yr

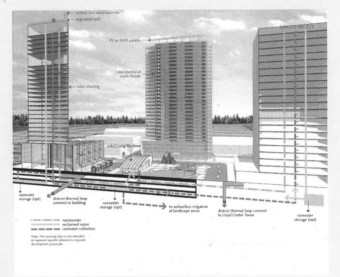

The Catalyst Project includes plans to exceed LEED Platinum standards and thereby surpass the energy performance of current buildings by a factor of at least three. Ambitious materials principles commit to using low-emission, high-performance materials from within 300–500 miles of the project site.

The Sustainable Urban Design plan includes several improvements in infrastructure that support the buildings' technologies. A proposed thermal heat loop would allow buildings to save on heating costs, and buildings would gradually switch to using the heat loop on their own timetables. By integrating building water-saving technology with new community water treatment facilities, the project will reduce potable water consumption by 62 percent and annual fees by 89 percent. This will be accomplished by 30 percent water conservation from efficient fixtures, 100 percent of nonpotable water provided by rainwater and treated black- or graywater, and 100 percent water treatment on-site. Initial suggestions for the Catalyst Project also include space for a living machine water treatment system located near a central park. The site's natural slope toward the nearby

Willamette River makes curbside bioswales viable as well. Habitat corridors will connect patches of vegetation with adjacent wildlife and riparian habitats. Already an area with multiple transportation options, Lloyd Crossing will also include a new streetcar system.

The overarching goal for the site is to create an exceptionally ecofriendly area that also promotes economic development and increases density. Mithun's stated goal to live within the site's rainfall and solar budgets requires substantial capital for infrastructure and building improvements, and the SUD plan outlines several strategies that will help Portland secure the funding. It is also assumed that about 80 percent of savings from energy and water improvements will be reinvested in the development rather than going to residents. The plan's flexibility stems from its long-range nature and the likelihood that it will be implemented incrementally. The gradual process will give technology time to improve further and will allow the Portland Development Commission to assemble a package of incentives, interim retail programs, and partnerships with private developers that will make the plan economically feasible.

Z-Squared
London, England

Z-Squared is a new conceptual project from the nonprofit BioRegional—which also initiated the groundbreaking BedZED—that aims to introduce zero-carbon, zero-waste living to the Thames Gateway. Located east of central London, the Thames Gateway is rapidly being reinvented as a residential area after long industrial usage. Z-Squared will provide two thousand homes in a mixed-use urban development designed to uphold One Planet Living principles. A joint venture between BioRegional and WWF, the ten One Planet Living principles forming Z-Squared's foundation encourage built environments that allow people to live healthy, happy lives without overtaxing the planet's resources. As of this book's publication, a suitable site for the project is in the process of being chosen. Specific site plans will then be developed according to the strategies outlined in BioRegional's comprehensive vision plan, "Z-Squared: Enabling One Planet Living in the Thames Gateway." The vision plan includes detailed analyses of possible project technologies and costs compiled by BioRegional, KBR Engineers, Fulcrum Consulting, and Cyril Sweett.

Z-Squared will promote a localized lifestyle that will allow residents to avoid living at the mercy of the automobile. A mix of uses will encourage residents to shop locally and walk to do so. Promoting local food that has not been transported thousands of miles is an important goal of the project. To accomplish this, a variety of methods including small garden allotments, local organic cafes, and farmers' markets, will be used. The Z-Squared vision plan also introduces the idea of "home zones" that will give priority to pedestrians and cyclists while limiting automobile presence.

All homes will maximize energy efficiency, aiming for a BREEAM EcoHomes Excellent rating. Minimizing waste during the construction process is also important to the development team. Off-site prefabrication of as many building elements as possible will increase control over the waste process. In addition to using recycled materials wherever possible, Z-Squared will avoid using timber by using steel instead. Where timber must be used, it will be certified sustainable.

As a One Planet Living community, Z-Squared acknowledges that infrastructure and lifestyle factors have a profound impact on carbon emissions, perhaps even more than building design. Community-wide services and programs that enable sustainability are the true focus of Z-Squared. On-site energy generation is key, and infrastructure to support district heating will be in place from day one.

At a Glance

Master plan: BioRegional and WWF with concept designs by Foster + Partners

Developer: BioRegional and WWF

Timeline: Vision plan issued 2004; site choice occurring 2007

Dwelling units: 2,000

Commercial square footage: to be determined

Land area: To be determined

Project Highlights / Benchmarks

- Zero carbon emissions, zero waste
- All homes BREEAM EcoHomes Excellent
- CHP system fueled by biogas, biomass
- Energy services to reduce carbon emission by 70 percent energy infrastructure
- Biological wastewater treatment system and rainwater retention on-site
- Dedicated One Planet Living resource center
- Limit on timber construction; only certified sustainable timber

Key Sustainable Urbanism Thresholds

- Food production
- The integration of transportation, land use, and technology
- Wastewater management
- Car sharing
- Walkable streets and networks
- The impact of planning on building energy usage
- Large district energy systems

Figure 11-9
This concept sketch illustrates
the principles of density and
renewable energy usage that will
be part of the Z-Squared project.
Image © Foster + Partners.

The vision plan outlines several renewable energy strategies that compare benefits to a base scenario: a gas-fired CHP will reduce carbon emissions by 70 percent, while a biomass CHP will achieve the ultimate goal of carbon neutrality. Anaerobic digestion will break down organic waste into methane, which can be converted to energy as well. Wind turbines may also be part of the package. They could possibly be located in the Thames estuary to be out of sight, or mini-turbines could be used in the development itself. Given the importance of a reliable renewable energy source to the project, BioRegional will partner with an energy service company to maintain the energy generation technologies. Z-Squared is committed to achieving zero-waste status as well as zero carbon emissions, a goal directly influenced by London's alarming realization that its landfills will reach capacity in five or six years. At Z-Squared, all waste will be either recycled, reused, composted, or converted to energy through the CHP system. The recycling program will be extensive, and include nontraditional recyclables such as textiles. Wastewater will be cleansed through a biologically based system that utilizes a maturation pond and reed bed.

Reduced parking throughout the development, combined with a car-share program, will boost mass transit use. By providing affordable housing, Z-Squared will also ensure that a diverse cross section of Londoners have access to sustainable living.

This project directly addresses the now-famous adage that if everyone in the world lived as the average Briton does, we would need three planets to sustain us. In-depth research and modeling have given BioRegional a sophisticated understanding of where the average UK resident's carbon footprint stems from, and those data inform the plan for Z-Squared. One unique feature of this development is the lasting commitment BioRegional has made to maintain standards of sustainability throughout the project's evolution. As is the case for all proposed One Planet Living communities, Z-Squared will feature an on-site resource center devoted to promoting sustainability. BioRegional representatives will be on hand to monitor the progress of the development and collaborate with residents. It is this kind of hands-on approach that gives Z-Squared a good chance of perpetuating its sustainable mission beyond initial construction.

Figure 11-10
A diagram of the Z-Squared
infrastructure that will increase
renewable energy generation
and decrease waste.
Image © Foster + Partners &
BioRegional.

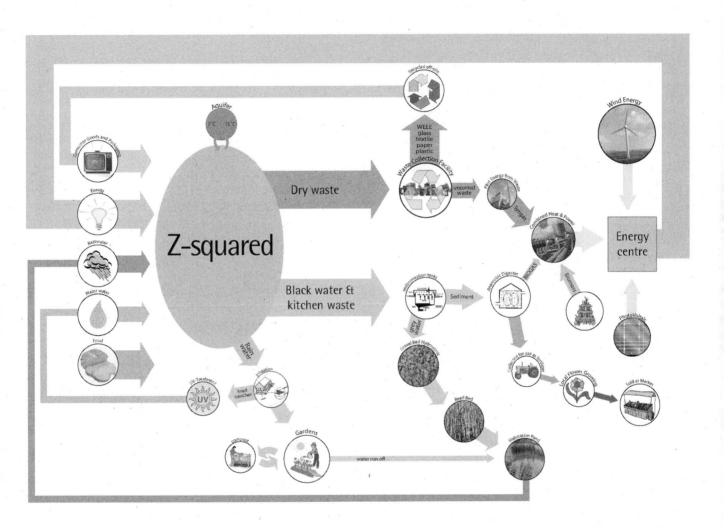

New Railroad Square
Santa Rosa, California
United States

New Railroad Square in Santa Rosa, California, is the first fully conceptualized "transit village" in a proposed string of developments built along the Sonoma Marin Area Rapid Transit (SMART) train line. In anticipation of the new train system, which will run north from San Francisco through rolling wine country, SMART issued an RFP requesting green development on an old railyard near downtown Santa Rosa. What resulted is a plan issued by Railroad Square, LLC (and designed by WRT/Solomon E.T.C.) for a culturally rich, transit-oriented development celebrating the region's superb produce and wine.

New Railroad Square is intended to revitalize downtown Santa Rosa, which has been bisected by increasingly congested U.S. Highway 101. The SMART train line and New Railroad Square are designed to be mutually beneficial, with the SMART line bringing a steady stream of passengers to enjoy the proposed Food and Wine Center, restaurants, and retail, and the 250 units of housing providing a critical mass of residents likely to use the SMART train. Three multistory buildings will provide retail, a child care center, a bicycle center, and other community facilities at ground level, while upper floors will house a mix of residential options. The heart of the development is the Food and Wine Center, which

includes a 30,000-square-foot market featuring fresh local food and space for a culinary school (currently slated to be used by Santa Rosa Junior College). The plan makes the most of the 5.4-acre site, establishing a density of sixty-one units per acre and a floor area ratio of 2.46:1. Pedestrian-only corridors on 4th and 5th Streets and a crescent-shaped public plaza will encourage informal interaction between neighbors and visitors. The rescued infill site will also serve as connective tissue among sections of the city and provide somewhat isolated west side neighborhoods with a vibrant neighborhood core.

At the urging of SMART, the development team outlined a series of building technologies that will help New Railroad Square minimize its ecological footprint. By designing all three buildings to meet at least LEED Silver requirements, the site will reduce water consumption by 40 percent, wastewater production by 50 percent, potable water usage on landscaping by 50 percent, and energy consumption by 30 percent. Energy efficiency will be accomplished using a number of technologies, including passive solar, high-R-value insulation, daylighting, insulating windows, and Energy Star efficient fixtures and appliances. In addition, a 300-kilowatt photovoltaic array

At a Glance

Master plan: WRT Solomon E.T.C.
Developer: New Railroad Square LLC
Timeline: Master plan 2006; construction proposed to begin 2008, to be completed by 2010
Dwelling units: 250
Commercial square footage: 87,950 square feet
Land area: 5.4 acres

Project Highlights/Benchmarks

Designed in harmony with LEED-ND

- Creation of 180 jobs
- Stormwater runoff reduction of 25 percent
- 30,000-square-foot market featuring local food and wine
- All three buildings designed to meet LEED Silver criteria
- Density of 61 units per acre
- 300 kW photovoltaic array
- Preservation of historic water tower and railroad depot style

Key Sustainable Urbanism Thresholds

- Economic benefits of locally owned stores
- The integration of transportation, land use, and technology
- Food production
- Open space
- Stormwater systems
- Illustrating density
- The impact of planning on building energy usage
- Walkable streets and networks
- High-performance infrastructure

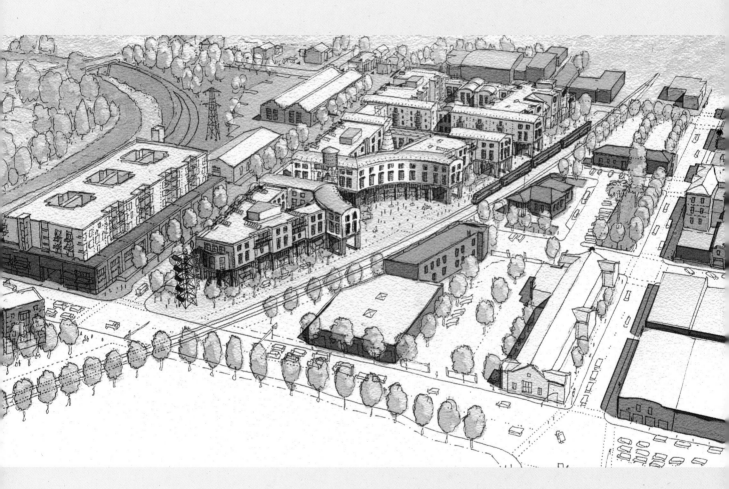

Figure 11-12
New Railroad Square site plan.
Image © WRT/Solomon E.T.C.

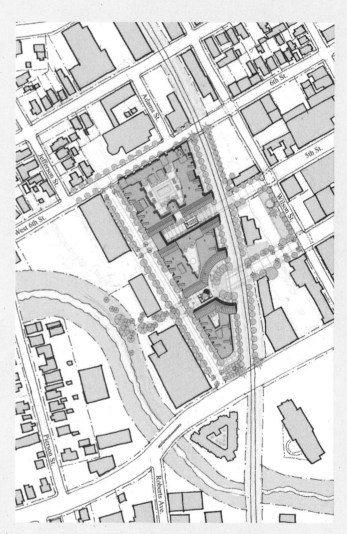

will provide a substantial amount of the site's energy, and solar thermal panels will provide hot water. Construction standards mandate that at least 20 percent of materials must be sourced from within a 500-mile radius of Santa Rosa and 5 percent of the total value of materials must be from materials with recycled content. The central Market Hall includes a distinctive glass thermal chimney that will channel daylight and fresh air into the hall.

An integrated water management system will reduce runoff by 25 percent, using harvested rainwater and stormwater runoff for toilets and landscape irrigation. A restored historic water tower will be relocated to the public square to help filter collected rainwater. Another unique facet of this particular water management system is a flowform-type water feature located at the base of the water tower that will educate the public about water reuse while actively filtering. In addition, photovoltaic panels and bird-safe, low-speed helical wind turbines will power the water tower pumps. Parking management has been thoroughly considered, and the plan includes a subterranean garage that will provide 451 spots for residents, an

auto-dependency of 1.8/dwelling, and 235 for retail shoppers, limiting on-street parking to 65 spaces. An open-air staircase to the garage will also provide much-needed air circulation and daylight. Because food waste is likely to be substantial in this development, the plan proposes a recycling program that transforms food waste into compost for local agriculture. Though the star of the transit network in this development is the SMART railway, a number of other opportunities exist for residents. The site is adjacent to the Prince Memorial Greenway, which follows the path of the Santa Rosa Creek and will provide a regional bicycle network in combination with a SMART bicycle corridor.

A variety of housing options will produce desirable income diversity in the residents. Fifteen percent of the units are set aside as affordable housing. The job housing balance will also be positively affected by the creation of approximately 180 jobs in the various retail outlets. By locating this new development in a central part of Santa Rosa, on top of a transit hub, the developers have funneled growth into an existing community rather than promoting sprawl.

Uptown Normal
Normal, Illinois
United States

Figure 11-14
Uptown Normal redevelopment plan.
Image © Farr Associates.

The Uptown Renewal Project in Normal, Illinois, is a multi-phase redevelopment led by the Town of Normal. The project aims to vitalize and intensify Normal's downtown, whose traditional Main Street layout dates to the post civil-war era. Like similar communities everywhere in the United States, Normal's traditional downtown has been in decline for decades, as a government funded "bypass" road syphoned 95% of all retail activity to national chain stores on the outskirts of town. The town of Normal engaged Farr Associates to master plan and Gibbs Planning Group to assess retail potential for a redevelopment downtown. The revitalizing plan called for a vibrant mix of uses surrounding a new circular park in the newly renamed Uptown Normal.

Enhancing the mix of uses present in Normal's Uptown is a critical component of the redevelopment plan. Currently a limited number of apartments are available above retail, and are usually rented by students from adjacent Illinois State University. After redevelopment, Uptown will feature a substantial increase in housing, at least some of which will be owner occupied. Housing density will be increased by new three-to-five-story mixed-use buildings. Part of the plan is to attract more visitors to Uptown by increasing access to transit and by

providing more public space. A conference hotel will offer convenient lodging and meeting rooms near the site's transit nexus, which includes access to bus and rail service. New civic institutions are also included in the plan, such as a LEED Silver children's museum that is already attracting a lot of visitors. At the heart of the plan is a unique circular intersection that will connect five streets while calming traffic. Peter Lindsay Schaudt Landscape Architects is designing the streetscape and a park within the circular intersection will provide centrally located green gathering space. The park will also include a water feature supplied with cleansed stormwater that will act as both public art and a sustainable demonstration project. The park combined with the connected Gateway Plaza—a larger paved area near the circular intersection—will allow Uptown to comfortably host events such as a farmers' market and the Sugar Creek Arts Festival.

Normal's redevelopment effort includes an unusually progressive sensitivity to environmental impact. In 2000, the Town of Normal became the first municipality in the U.S. to pass an ordinance requiring all new construction over 7,500 square feet occurring in the Uptown district to meet at least minimum LEED certification standards. The ordinance has resulted in several LEED-rated

At a Glance

Master plan: Farr Associates
Developer: Town of Normal
Timeline: Master plan initiated 1999; circular intersection and park to be built 2007–2008
Dwelling units: Around 188 projected
Commercial square footage: 741,000 square feet
Land area: 28 acres

Project Highlights/Benchmarks

- All new construction over 7,500 square feet must be in the plan area LEED certified (first municipality to require LEED for private development 2000)
- Central park and Gateway Plaza provide new public space
- Stormwater system includes retention basin, cistern, and public water feature
- Multimodal center links regional and local transit
- Expanded bus system
- Streetscape design uses runoff to irrigate streets
- First ever USDOT approved circular intersection

Key Sustainable Urbanism Thresholds

- Stormwater management
- Integration of transportation, land use, and technology
- Economic benefits of locally owned stores
- Open space
- The impact of planning on building energy usage

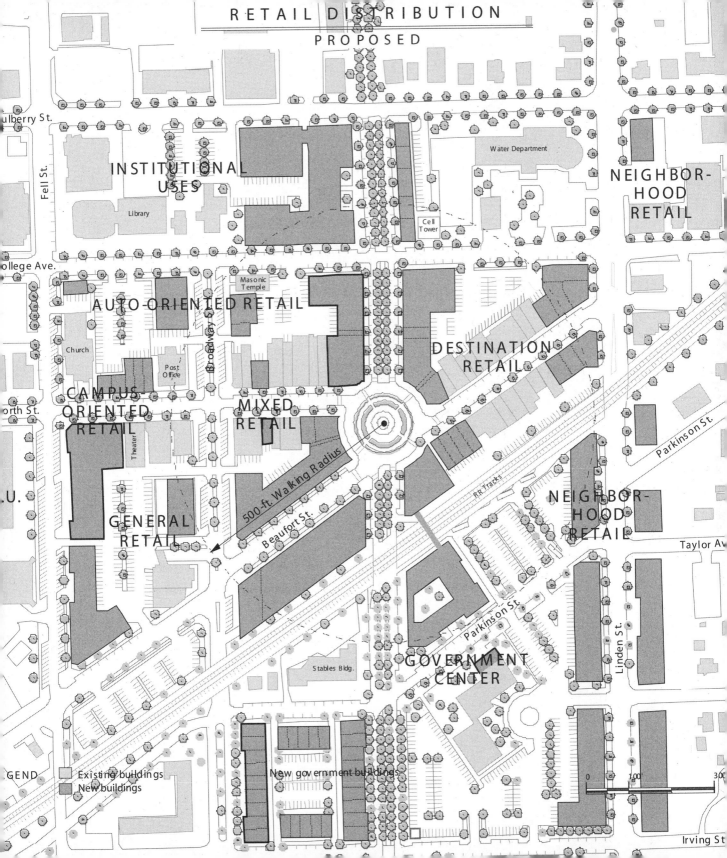

RETAIL DISTRIBUTION

PROPOSED

INSTITUTIONAL USES

NEIGHBOR-HOOD RETAIL

Water Department

Library

Cell Tower

AUTO-ORIENTED RETAIL

Masonic Temple

DESTINATION RETAIL

Church

Post Office

CAMPUS-ORIENTED RETAIL

MIXED RETAIL

NEIGHBOR-HOOD RETAIL

Theater

500-ft. Walking Radius

RR Tracks

Parkinson St.

Taylor Av

GENERAL RETAIL

Beaufort St.

Linden St.

Parkinson St.

GOVERNMENT CENTER

Stables Bldg.

Fell St.

ulberry St.

ollege Ave.

orth St.

.U.

Broadway St.

Irving St.

New government buildings

0   100   300

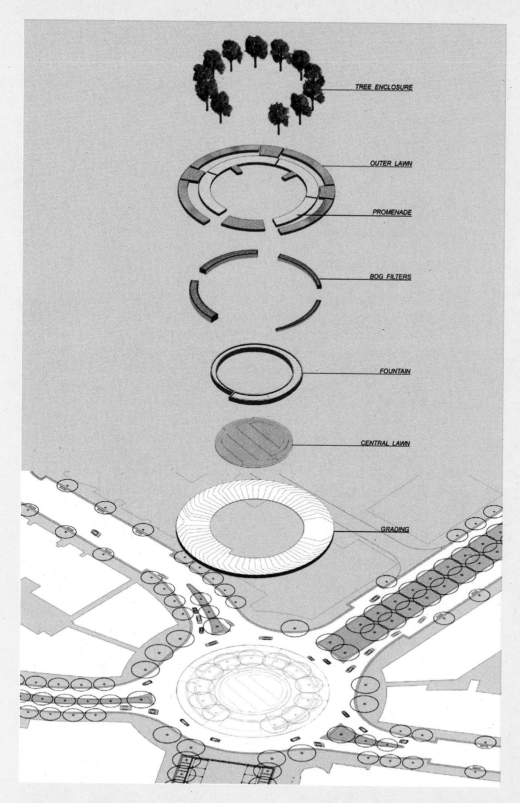

TREE ENCLOSURE

OUTER LAWN

PROMENADE

BOG FILTERS

FOUNTAIN

CENTRAL LAWN

GRADING

Figure 11-15
An exploded view of the functional
layers of the central plaza.
Image © Peter Lindsay Schaudt
Landscape Architecture, Inc.

Figure 11-16
The central plaza will include park
space and a water feature, both
easily accessible to pedestrians.
Image © 2002 Bruce Bondy.

projects, including the Silver-rated children's museum, a bank that is aiming for at least a Silver rating, and an apartment building. By passing this ordinance, the Town of Normal has proven that incorporating sustainable building practices into a redevelopment project need not burden developers or cause investors to be nervous.

Uptown's stormwater management strategy will benefit the environment and the public, which will receive a beautiful new central park from the project. Stormwater will be directed to vegetated basins, where it will be cleansed. From there it will be filtered into an underground cistern made from a converted brick sewer. This water will supply the water feature in the park in the circular intersection, providing an excellent opportunity to attract visitors to Uptown to delight in the usefulness of high-performance infrastructure. Parking in Uptown Normal is also being restructured to encourage the use of public transportation and give priority to pedestrians.

Diagonal street parking spaces are being replaced with parallel spaces, and parking decks will be built instead of increasing free street parking. This strategy dovetails with the plan to revamp local transit, which is one of the project's major goals. The Uptown plan calls for a new multimodal transit center that will be located adjacent to the Amtrak line, capitalizing on Normal's status as the third busiest stop on the St. Louis–Chicago route, currently being upgraded for high-speed server. Local buses will also stop there, and the town hopes to create a more comprehensive local bus system, including express routes attractive to visitors. In addition, the multimodal center could be a departure point for shuttles to Chicago airports, as well as a hub for regional bus service. These improvements will help Normal draw its residents and visitors inward to the busy Uptown district, where they will find a range of shopping, dining, and living options.

Note: At the time of publication, this project is well underway.

Unbuilt Greenfield

Dongtan
Shanghai, China

Chongming Island, site of the forthcoming Dongtan EcoCity, is in a unique position. Starting in 2010, it will take only a forty minute trip to reach the bustling business district of Shanghai, a city now reaching densities four times those of New York City due to its stunning population growth. Yet currently, the island remains largely untouched by anything more disruptive than small-scale agriculture, thanks in part to the slow ferry system that provides the only access from the mainland. The sandy soil is virtually pollution-free, and miles of wetland on the eastern edge of the island provide an internationally recognized avian habitat. China's flagship ecocity will attempt to balance the ecological needs of the delicate and distinctive site with Shanghai's desperate need for more housing. The Shanghai Industrial Investment Corporation (SIIC) is the developer for the site. Arup, a global design, engineering, and consultancy, is working with SIIC to realize their vision for Dongtan by providing a wide array of services ranging from the development of a master plan to business planning to waste management. Arup's long-term commitment to the project and unique methodology has spurred further agreements with Chinese clients to pursue another batch of eco-cities. By 2050, the completed city is expected to

house up to half a million people, with the first ten thousand expected to move into the initial phase of the project in time for the 2010 Shanghai International Expo.

Arup's approach to sustainable design includes not only environmental sustainability but also social, economic, and cultural sustainability. The firm's master plan for Dongtan includes a set of design and sustainability guidelines that are likely to meet international efficiency standards such as LEED and BREEAM. It recognizes that without careful and deliberate planning, precious open space on Chongming Island will succumb quickly to development. In comparison to nearby Shanghai, Dongtan will have much lower housing densities, but its compact design will still achieve densities of 84–112 people per acre, supporting mass transit, social infrastructure, and a range of businesses. Most homes will take the form of six-to-eight-story apartment buildings clustered toward the edges of three "villages" that meet to form a city center. Parks, farms, lakes, and other public spaces will offer breathing room between each of the tightly knit districts. Cycling routes, footpaths, and a canal network will provide convenient connective tissue. While safeguarding nearly 60 percent of the development area is clearly an ecological decision, preservation

At a Glance
Master plan: Arup
Developer: Shanghai Industrial Investment Corporation
Timeline: Phase 1 complete by 2010; entire development by 2050
Dwelling units: Phase 1: 2,500–3,000
Commercial square footage: Not available
Land area: 21,251 acres (86 square kilometers)

Project Highlights/Benchmarks
- Ecological footprint of 2.2 hectares/person, less than one-third that of a typical Shanghai resident
- Preservation of important wetland habitat
- Densities of 84–112 people/acre
- Potable water usage reduced by two-thirds
- On-site waste treatment using anaerobic digester
- Combined heat and power (CHP) fueled by waste
- Solar panels integrated into homes
- Small and large wind turbines
- 60 percent of land devoted to nonurban uses
- Private vehicles banned from the community

Key Sustainable Urbanism Thresholds
- Biodiversity corridors
- The integration of transportation, land use, and technology
- Open space
- Food production
- Stormwater systems
- Wastewater treatment
- Illustrating density
- Car share

eco farming
demonstration

wind turbines

bird park /
large scale
visitor attraction

future dongtan phases
main nodes

future dongtan phases
secondary nodes

other nodes

zero emmissions
road access

waterbus

interchange
to/from shanghai

eco farms

eco farms

eco farms

eco farms

ramsar

ramsar

wetland park

bird
watching

eco park

golf course

national
hotel

eco park

energy centre

New bridge to
Shanghai

horse riding

ferry port
to/from shanghai and pudong

0m   300m   1500m   3000m

of the prized wetland habitat is also expected to draw significant managed tourism to the area. The high-profile eco-city idea, in combination with gorgeous outdoor space that is so rare in Shanghai itself, will draw tourists to this already popular site, strengthening the Dongtan economy.

The long-term vision for Dongtan is to come as close as possible to carbon neutrality. Part of this will be achieved through building-level design elements, such as natural ventilation and superinsulation. The vast majority of homes will be apartments rather than detached homes, designed to maximize energy savings through shared walls and utilities. A range of renewable energy technologies will free Dongtan from fossil-fuel energy sources. Small-scale wind turbines will be located on and near homes, while larger turbines will be sited at the western edge of the development. Solar panels will also provide energy to individual homes. The most ambitious portion of the energy infrastructure is the combined heat and power system (CHP), which will be able to convert waste from a variety of sources into energy, including sewage and compost (converted to biogas in an anaerobic digester) and local sources (including the millions of rice husks that are disposed of daily). By using a dual water system with nonpotable water furnished from collected rainwater and river water, fresh water consumption is expected to drop significantly. The development team understands that Dongtan's proximity to Shanghai could undermine its ecological mission if commuting city-dwellers flood it with cars. Conventional cars will be banned from the city, with car clubs enabling access to clean vehicles, and buses and water taxis running on hydrogen or other clean energy sources. Visitors to Dongtan will arrive via either the suspension bridge or an underground tunnel (projected to be the world's widest). The goal is to encourage visitors to leave cars at the entrance to the city, relying on public transit within its limits. Controlling the number and type of cars in the city will ultimately help foster a community proud of its island's wetland heritage, as well as residents who travel at a pace to enjoy it. A profitable and productive ecocity on this scale will provide an invaluable template for future ecocities throughout China and the world.

Figure 11-18
The canal, lined with small wind turbines, allows residents and visitors to enjoy the wetland flora and fauna.

Figure 11-19
Green space abounds even amidst dense housing.

Galisteo Basin Preserve
Santa Fe, New Mexico
United States

The Galisteo Basin Preserve project—comprising approximately 12,000 acres of open preserve and several compact developments—emerged from a Santa Fe open space program initiated in 2001. The Galisteo Basin Preserve is the flagship initiative of Commonweal Conservancy, a nonprofit organization. Founded in 2003 by the Trust for Public Land's former southwest regional director, Ted Harrison, Commonweal Conservancy sought to challenge the entitled plan to carve up roughly 20 square miles of the Galisteo Basin into 12.5 to 40-acre lots. This project demonstrates how a nonprofit was able to marshal community resources and myriad groups to replan an already approved development into a great sustainable community.

With input from a variety of consultants, Commonweal soon honed the philosophy that has since informed the project's progress— an aggressive conservation plan balanced with thoughtful development as an appropriate alternative to unchecked sprawl. In addition, the Galisteo Basin Preserve project is designed to test the role and capacity of nonprofit developers as leaders in sustainable development. Commonweal's development scheme involves selling lots in three distinct but related communities—New Moon Overlook, West Basin, and the Village—in order to underwrite the conservation of a large preserve that surrounds them. Linking a large-scale conservation program with sustainable neighborhood development serves a dual purpose: it makes the project economically viable while concurrently allowing the residents to take an active part in the land's long-term stewardship and restoration. Residents will also be able to enjoy the land they are helping to protect in a hands-on fashion. A network of walking and bike trails will link neighborhoods within the community, as well as adjoining villages and areas of Santa Fe.

To minimize the project's ecological footprint, the village plan anticipates a wide range of water and energy conservation strategies, including rainwater catchment; community wastewater reuse for outdoor irrigation and other nonpotable purposes; passive-solar-oriented site planning; local energy generation using biomass, solar, and wind resources; and energy-efficient appliance requirements. A robust transit system is the most important infrastructural element in the project due to its less-than-ideal location well beyond the current limits of Santa Fe. Alternative transit options—including a car-share program, a natural-gas-fueled

At a Glance
Developer: Commonweal Conservancy
Timeline: Commonweal Conservancy initiates plans for the project in 2003
Dwelling units: 965
Commercial/civic square footage: 150,000 square feet
Land area: 12,800 acres total (12,332 acres conservation land; 468 acres development)

Project Highlights/Benchmarks

- Over 96 percent of the total land area will be permanently preserved
- 30 percent of homes will be either for local workers or affordable homes (defined as homes for residents earning 50–120 percent of area median income)
- Intensified zoning (from 1 unit/12.5–40 acres to up to 25 units/acre)
- Extensive network of pedestrian/cyclist/equestrian trails
- Charter high school integrated into the village's center
- A natural-gas-fueled bus/van system for local transit
- Comprehensive water plan: conservation using efficient fixtures, wastewater reuse technology, advanced filtration, and cooling towers will reduce water usage for the village to 0.16 acre-foot/year, contrasting with Santa Fe County's 0.25 acre-foot/year

Key Sustainable Urbanism Thresholds

- Open space
- Biodiversity corridor
- Stormwater systems
- Wastewater treatment
- Illustrating density
- Walkable streets and networks
- Car sharing

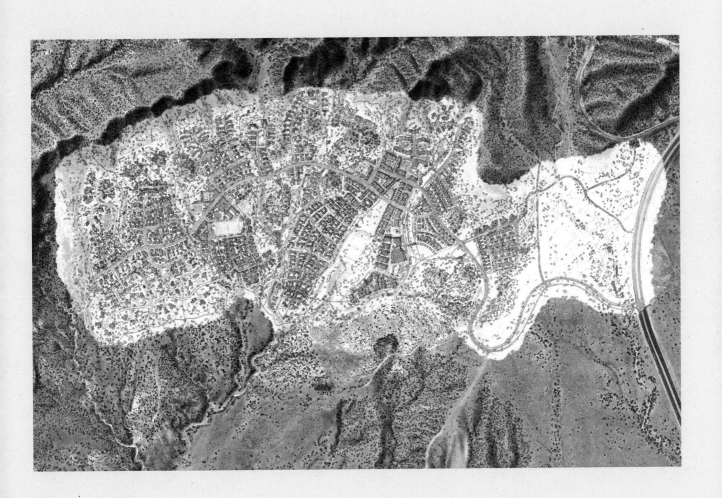

Figure 11-21
The village includes a compact
co-housing development. Image ©
Commonweal Conservancy.

Figure 11-22
This project's particular triumph
is in altering this existing
zoning plan to replace sprawling
development with a dense village
and preserved open space.
Image © Commonweal Conservancy.

bus/van system, and rail service along existing tracks that adjoin the Village site—help to alleviate this problem. Creating a healthy business district in a small community removed from Santa Fe is also challenging, but if successful it will drastically reduce car trips outside the community. The project's design anticipates that a wide array of services will be available, including restaurants, retail, offices, and civic buildings. Commonweal has also taken steps to cultivate a real sense of community in the village by anchoring it with a conservation-focused charter school. Ultimately, the project is defined by its intrepid quest to create a preserve in conjunction with a dense, mixed-use village (densities up to twenty-five units per acre) on land that was destined to be become suburban "ranchettes" on 12.5- or 40-acre lots. Despite the challenges the project faces, it offers a promising alternative to large-lot hypersprawl in rapidly growing regions.

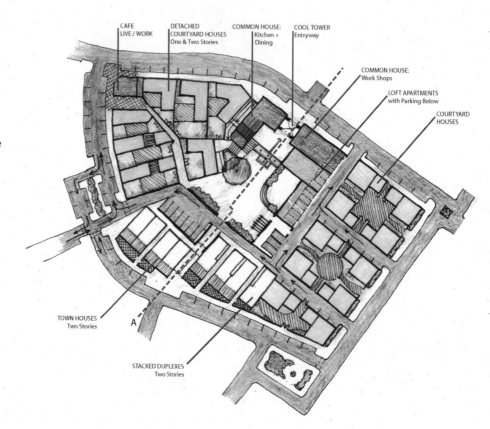

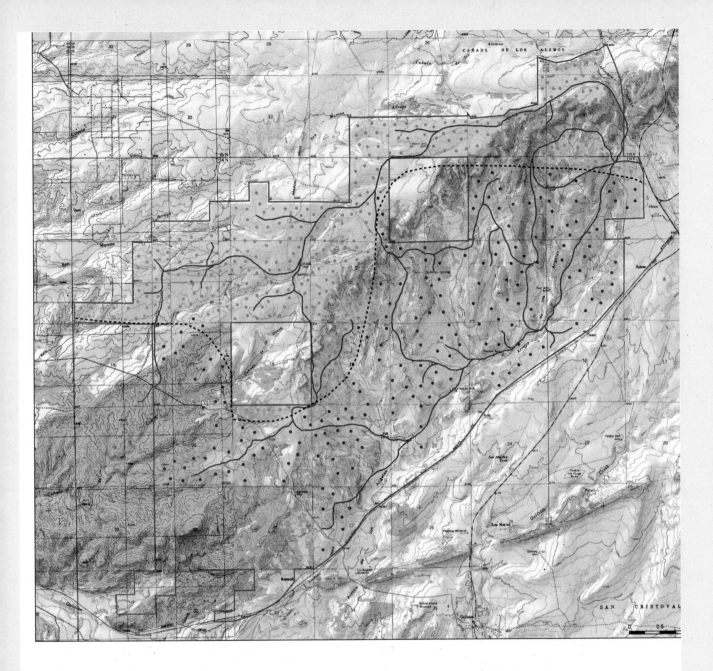

Legend

- - - - - - Santa Fe Hydrologic Zoning (1980)

●   Residential Impact Zone, Homestead (1 per 40 ac)

●   Residential Impact Zone, Basin Fringe (1 per 12.5 ac)

▢   Property Boundary

▨   Development Zones

—   Backbone Roads

Pulelehua
Maui, Hawaii
United States

Pulelehua town was originally conceived by Maui Land & Pineapple, one of the largest employers on the island of Maui, in consultation with Dover, Kohl & Partners. As a company with extensive land holdings, Maui Land & Pineapple was in a unique position to directly address the lack of affordable housing available for its own employees. Collaboration with Dover, Kohl and the community culminated in a vision of Pulelehua as a staunchly new urbanist, walkable, mixed-use community featuring traditional Hawaiian architectural touches.

Pulelehua is designed around three distinct neighborhoods: Crossroads, Kahanaiki, and Mahinahina. Each neighborhood includes a mixture of housing types, ranging from multistory apartment buildings over retail units to the more isolated single-family estate lots. A master Regulating Plan for the town breaks down land use by transect zone, mapping out a dense core at the center of each neighborhood (with the densest area located at the heart of the central neighborhood, Crossroads) and decreasing density approaching the edges of the neighborhoods. Specific unit types are assigned to each transect zone, and the Regulating Plan also indicates certain design elements that must be included to satisfy

requirements. Often these design elements exist to maintain the Hawaiian architectural style, such as requiring terraces or lanais in traditional places on homes. Streets are laid out in a network offering multiple pathways for traffic, to keep congestion down. Residential streets are appropriately narrow, with low speed limits, ample roadside greenery, and generous sidewalks designed to encourage pedestrian use. A system of trails and paths connects the three neighborhoods, winding through green spaces along the way. Each neighborhood is also based on a quarter-mile walking system.

The three neighborhoods of Pulelehua are separated by substantial open space totaling 44 percent of the development. This open space exemplifies the low-tech approach to sustainability taken by the Maui Land & Pineapple Company. A variety of open space types serve different sustainability needs. Gulches are trench-like and have dense vegetation, perfect for helping to capture precious rainfall and channel it back underground. Parks and playing fields ensure that residents are always close to community gathering spaces, and provide a refuge for wildlife. Bioswales also may be incorporated to cleanse rainwater, and permeable pavement is being considered for alleyways. Building orientation in relation

At a Glance
Master plan: Dover, Kohl & Partners
Developer: Maui Land & Pineapple
Timeline: Master plan designed 2004
Dwelling units: 882
Commercial square footage: 168,475 square feet
Land area: 310 acres

Project Highlights/Benchmarks
- 44 percent open space
- 57 percent affordable homes
- Highly organized plan laid out by transect zone
- Hawaiian architecture incorporated throughout
- Community garden space provided
- Biodiversity corridors
- Gulches and bioswales control stormwater

Key Sustainable Urbanism Thresholds
- Open space
- Biodiversity corridors
- Food production
- Stormwater systems
- The integration of transportation, land use, and technology
- Water and the density debate
- Walkable streets and networks

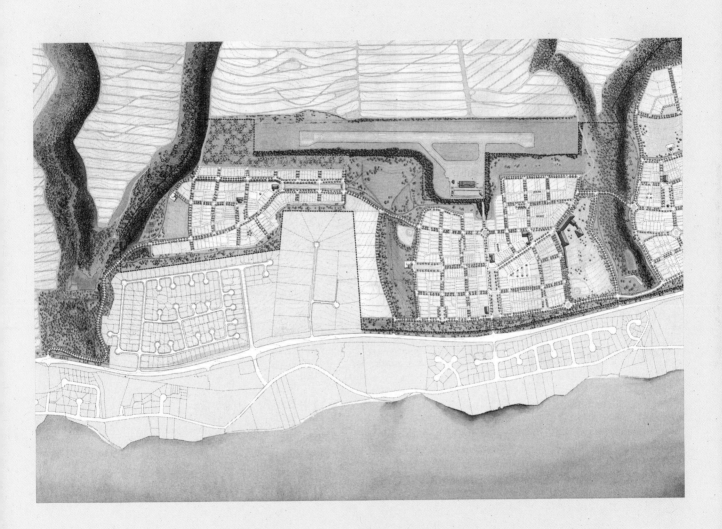

Figure 11-24
Neighbors will find it easy to
get to know each other due to narrow
residential streets and generous
lanais attached to most homes.
Image © Maui Land & Pineapple
Company, Inc./Dover, Kohl &
Partners—Town Planning.

Figure 11-25
Hawaiian-inspired architecture
will help transition seamlessly
between residential and mixed-use
areas. Image © Maui Land &
Pineapple Company, Inc./Dover,
Kohl & Partners—Town Planning.

Figure 11-26
An aerial view shows off streets
filled with greenery and the
neighborhood clusters.
Image © Maui Land & Pineapple
Company, Inc./Dover, Kohl &
Partners—Town Planning.

to the sun was taken into account
to provide plentiful daylight in
residences. Pulelehua also includes
space for community gardens.

The key to Pulelehua's sustainability is in the variety of living and
working options it offers, which
the founders hope will translate
into a diverse population that can
grow with the community rather
than grow out of it. Currently many
of West Maui's workers live an
hour's commute by car away from
the businesses where they work
(including Maui Land & Pineapple).
Pulelehua is located within the
existing grid of West Maui, directly
connecting workers to their place of
employment. Homes are 57 percent
affordable and 43 percent market
rate, with no separation of the
two. A proposed elementary school
would anchor the community, and
shopping in the core areas of each
neighborhood will further eliminate
the need to make short car trips.
The fusion of home and work life
into a traditional community
inspired by Hawaii itself is intended
to begin to alleviate the housing
crunch that West Maui workers face.

Coyote Valley
San Jose, California
United States

Coyote Valley is the subject of much heated debate in its hometown of San Jose, California. In 2002 the City of San Jose announced that development would soon proceed on the 6,800-acre swath of farms and orchards nestled in the city's last significant open space. Controversy reigns, with numerous activist groups, citizens' coalitions, city representatives, and the press weighing in. Out of the discord have come an ambitious new urbanist plan and a fascinating study in the politics of development. Coyote Valley's initial designation as the future site of a research and development campus sparked outrage among several environmental groups, culminating in the preparation of an alternative vision plan by the nonprofit Greenbelt Alliance and WRT/Solomon E.T.C. Completed in 2003, the plan—titled "Getting It Right: Preventing Sprawl in Coyote Valley"—advocates a mixed-use community built densely to accommodate a permanently protected greenbelt in the southernmost section of the site. "Getting It Right" sets major sustainability benchmarks that the Greenbelt Alliance is still using to rate the progress of the city's own Specific Plan for the site, currently under development.

The "Getting It Right" plan has proved a powerful tool in marketing the message of sustainability. In some ways a tutorial in smart growth for city planners, "Getting It Right" enumerates the advantages of a smart growth formula for Coyote Valley. The city's stated goal of twenty-five thousand housing units is met with an average density of twenty-eight units per acre, enough to preserve space for a precious greenbelt buffer. The plan arranges for an ultra dense urban town center, that would house high-density dwellings, pedestrian-friendly retail space, and commercial space. A proposed Caltrain (commuter) rail station and a light rail stop would make it the site's transit hub. The rest of the development is organized around multiple neighborhoods shaped by the site's geography, each including a neighborhood center, a sizable park, an elementary school, and access to transit. Mixed-use areas within each neighborhood fight sprawl and discourage automobile use. Because job creation is a high-priority goal for San Jose, "Getting It Right" includes several employment-oriented districts. These districts are incorporated throughout the neighborhoods of Coyote Valley, satisfying demand for flexible commercial space but not segregating offices in a suburban industrial campus style. The plan is also concerned with civic space, recommending 40,000 square feet for community buildings and 22,000 square feet for libraries. In addition, the plan

At a Glance
Master plan: WRT Solomon E.T.C.
Timeline: City adopts sprawl zoning plan in 2000; "Getting It Right" completed 2003; specific plan draft December 2006
Dwelling units: 25,000 currently, still under debate
Commercial square footage: 16.7 million
Land area: 6,800 acres

Project Highlights/Benchmarks
- Average density of 28 units/acre
- Floor area ratio of 1.00
- Aggressive transit plan, including light rail and Caltrain (commuter rail)
- Ultradense town center (up to 100 units/acre)
- Permanent protection of the Coyote Greenbelt
- Open space network based on existing watershed, providing flood management and biodiversity corridors
- Employment-oriented districts used instead of isolated industrial campuses
- 20 percent affordable housing

Key Sustainable Urbanism Thresholds
- Neighborhood retail
- Open space
- Biodiversity corridors
- Stormwater systems
- Illustrating density
- The integration of transportation, land use, and technology
- Water and the density debate
- Walkable streets and networks

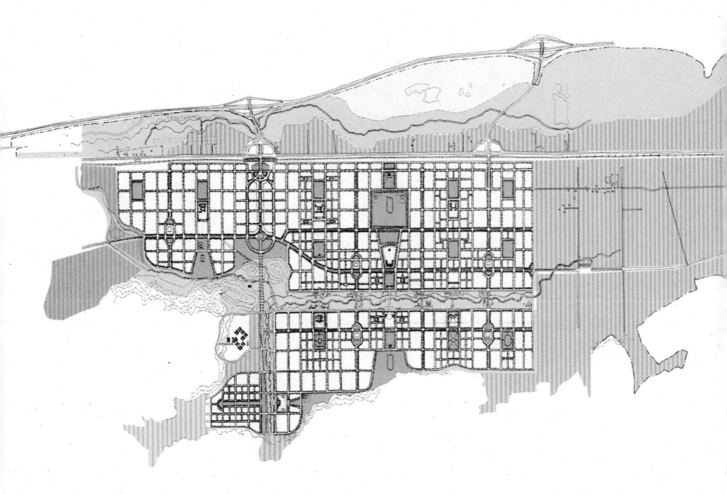

Figure 11-27
This site plan shows how the
"Getting It Right" vision plan is
careful to include green open space in
the form of active parks, passive
parks, and a naturally occurring creek.
Image © WRT/Solomon E.T.C.

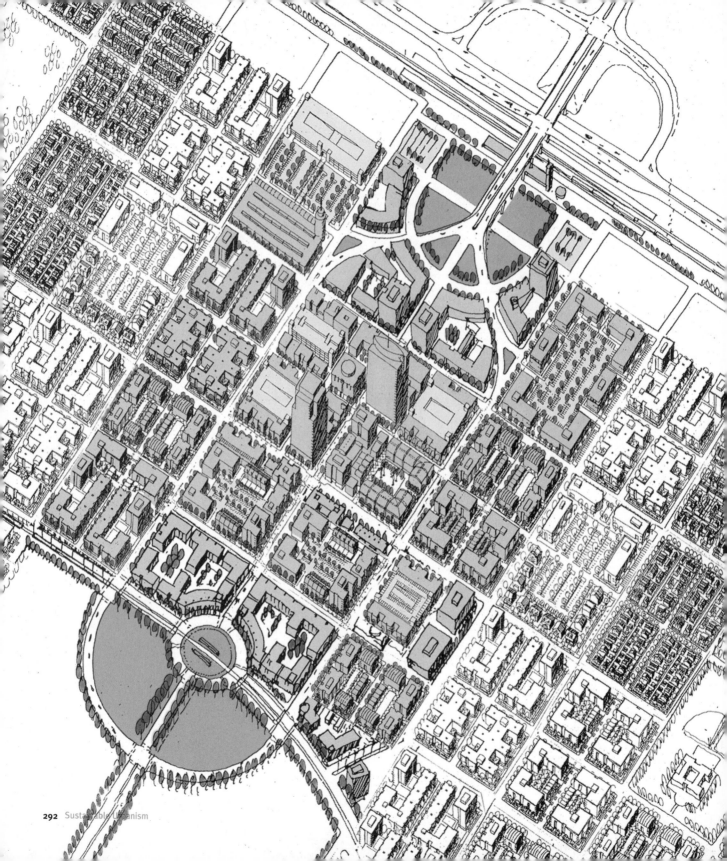

Figure 11-28
This town center rendering illustrates how the superblock system used in the "Getting It Right" plan can be easily subdivided and shaped to allow for multiple uses and traffic patterns. Image © WRT/Solomon E.T.C.

Figure 11-29
A rendering of how typical sprawl would look on the Coyote Valley site—developed haphazardly, with winding streets that limit transit and pedestrian mobility. Image © WRT/Solomon E.T.C.

Figure 11-30
The smart growth land use plan favors streets set to a grid and dense, mixed-use developments that support transit. Image © WRT/Solomon E.T.C.

calls for 20 percent affordable housing, to allow service workers in the community to live within Coyote Valley.

Environmentally sound infrastructure is developed according to specific ecological needs of the site. Two creeks run the length of the development, and these are preserved in "Getting It Right" as part of a network of parks and waterways that provide natural flood management. Green building practices are also encouraged in "Getting It Right," which suggests that at minimum all commercial spaces should meet LEED certification standards.

"Getting It Right" also addresses implementation strategies, aware that any development in Coyote Valley must be approached delicately. The plan recommends that interim low-density development be allowed in the town center in order to smooth the transition from rural

lot to urban core. "Getting It Right" also calls out provisions in the city's initial development plan that it views as unsustainable, including a 50-acre lake that complicates transit and is not based on valley ecology; an untested transit system that may not inspire enough use; winding, suburban-style roads; and a conspicuous absence of affordable housing provisions. In its first Coyote Valley Specific Plan draft, released in December 2006, the city addresses some of these concerns but not all. Though progress on the site is currently slowing due to political turnover and collective caution, the new draft is obviously more engaged in a dialogue about sustainability than it was formerly. The advocacy for smart growth on the part of the Greenbelt Alliance and its numerous partners and supporters has fundamentally changed the local conversation about the future of San Jose.

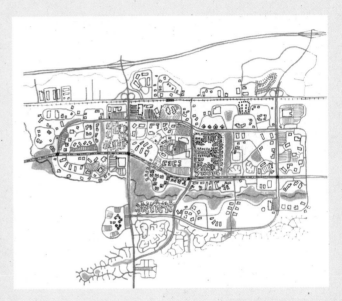

Scales of Intervention

Bethel Commercial Center (Chicago, IL)
1/4 acre

Christie Walk (Adelaide, Australia)
1/2 acre

BedZED (London, England)
4 acres

Dockside Green (Victoria, Canada)
15 acres

One of the most promising signs for the emerging practice of sustainable urbanism is the variety of scales at which projects have been built. These projects pursue sustainable urbanism through a variety of strategies, including walkable urbanism, high-performance infrastructure, and high-performance buildings. There is no one right size for a project. Instead, there are many scales of intervention: the built-out city with no redevelop- ment sites can implement sustainable urbanism by transforming a street repaving into a high-performance infrastructure demonstration project; a small-town mayor can pursue a moderately sized project on an available infill site; areas of fast greenfield growth can plan and zone entire transit-rich sustainable corridors. This section is designed to display the range of scales at which sustainable urbanism can be implemented.

Figures 11-31 to 11-37
Bethel Commercial Center images © Farr Associates; Christie Walk images © Ecopolis Architects; BedZED images © www.zedfactory.com; Dockside Green images courtesy Busby Perkins+Will Architects; High Point photograph © 2005 Doug J. Scott; High Point site plan © Mithun; Green Line Initiative © Farr Associates.

High Point (Seattle, WA)
120 acres

1 Community Center
2 Sports / Recreation Park
3 Elementary School
4 Neighborhood Center
5 Senior Village - 36' DUA
6 Central Park
7 Neighborhood Shopping / Mixed Use
   Low Rise Condominiums '28' DUA
   Townhouse / Duplex '14' DUA
8 Community Health Center
9 Branch Library
10 Longfellow Creek Watershed
11 Pond Park (Stormwater)

Green Line Corridor (Chicago, IL)
6000+ acres

Sustainable Urbanist projects organized by size

Project Scale	Type of Construction	Sample Project with Select Sustainable Systems	Project Image
Less than 1/4 acre	Single building	**Bethel Commercial Center** ● Transit-oriented design ● Mixed-use, multimodal center ● Green roof	
1/4–1 acre	Multiple buildings	**Christie Walk** ● Solar hot water ● Community gardens ● Thermal mass construction	
1–5 acres	An urban block	**BedZED** ● Natural ventilation ● Combined heat and power system (CHP) ● Passive solar design ● Car share	
5–40 acres	Fraction of a neighborhood	**Dockside Green** ● All buildings LEED Platinum ● Biomass co-generation ● Biodiesel facility	
40–200 acres	Neighborhood	**High Point** ● Seamless integration of affordable housing ● Community gardens ● Streets relinked to Seattle grid	
200+ acres	Corridor	**Green Line Initiative** ● Complete neighborhoods developed ● Transit-oriented design ● Density concentrated in mixed-use buildings near transit stops	

Epilogue

Our founding mythology casts Americans as civilizing settlers, subduing nature and claiming our patch of God's green earth. The modern translation of this myth is dystopian. We buy vegetated land on which to build, and then we denude it. We use land as a fungible asset to be scraped clear, developed, and polluted largely as we see fit. We like to be surrounded by "open space" to buffer us from conflicts and even contact with other citizens in our democracy. We hate density. We drive everywhere. We are inactive, indoors, obese, and on a path to a shorter life span. This has been the American way, our American dream (see Figure E-1). Happily, our times demand that we challenge ourselves to take a new approach to our built environment and our lifestyle. That new approach—its what, where, and how—is focus of this book.

The rest of the world is way ahead of us. On a per capita basis, Europe, India, and China consume a fraction of the land, resources, oil, and energy that we do. While we drive, they walk, bike, and ride transit. Americans will gladly share a cup of sugar with their neighbors, while the rest of the world shares cars, walls, and floors. They have local, state, and national leaders who are thinking about the future and steering their societies on a different course from that being taken by the United States. Some European countries essentially require the sustainable urbanism this book advocates. They have signed the Kyoto Protocol and follow Agenda 21. Planning is done competently and is granted more authority over private property. Germany taxes stormwater as it leaves a site. Steep gas taxes discourage driving and encourage the funding of transit. Denmark aims to have 40 percent of its cities use district energy systems. Sweden aims to be carbon-neutral. The typical new development in Beijing is designed at fifty units to the acre (see Figure E-2). All these countries' citizens are more physically active and weigh less on average than we do.

I believe firmly that there is a parallel between this book's advocacy for sustainable urbanism and the moon shot of an earlier generation. Then President John F. Kennedy set an audacious goal that challenged the nation. It had a beginning and an end. It took years of struggle and trial and error. It required inventiveness and our best and brightest. The parallels end there. Sustainable urbanism, against enormous odds, requires the improbable: that the base of the pyramid—millions of us—"get it" and act in concert. National leadership is absolutely essential, if only to end the destructive subsidies and the regulations that make sustainable urbanism illegal. What this book calls for is something that no one person can effect—a change in our political culture.

Changing the built environment in the ways called for in this book seems like an impossible undertaking. In truth, the entire built environment gets renewed or rebuilt every few generations, and we just need to do it differently. The far bigger challenge is changing the values, perceptions, and dreams that cause us to persist on the wrong course when we all know better. I believe that the time is ripe for the United States to turn the page and adopt sustainable urbanism as our generation's moon shot.

Figure E-1
An American single-family home with plenty of yard space.

Figure E-2
New development in Beijing is designed for 50 units per acre.

Glossary

Accessory Dwelling Unit (ADU): A self-contained housing unit incorporated within a single-family dwelling (not within accessory structures, except with a special permit) that is clearly a subordinate part of the single-family dwelling.

Accessory Use: A building or a usage of land that is additional to its primary use. A garage apartment or granny flat located behind a main house is an example of an accessory use.

Agricultural Preservation Restriction Program (APR): A voluntary program that is intended to offer a nondevelopment alternative to farmers and other owners of "prime" and "state-important" agricultural land who are faced with a decision regarding future use and disposition of their farms. Toward this end, the program offers to pay farmers the difference between the fair market value and the agricultural value of their farmland in exchange for a permanent deed restriction that precludes any use of the property that will have a negative impact on its agricultural viability.

Annexation: A change in existing community boundaries resulting from the incorporation of additional land.

Biodiversity: The variety and essential interdependence of all living things; it includes the variety of living organisms, the genetic differences among them, the communities and ecosystems in which they occur, and the ecological and evolutionary processes that keep them functioning.

Blight: Physical and economic conditions within an area that cause a reduction or lack of proper utilization of that area. A blighted area is one that has deteriorated or has been arrested in its development by physical, economic, or social forces.

BMP: Best management practice refers to the practice considered most effective to achieve a specific desired result for protection of water, air, and land and to control the release of toxins.

Brownfield: A site that is underutilized or not in active use, on land that is either.

Built Environment: The urban environment consisting of buildings, roads, fixtures, parks, and all other improvements that form the physical character of a city.

Capital Improvement Program (CIP): A community's plan for matching the cost of large-scale improvements—such as fixing roads and water and sewer mains—to anticipated revenues, such as from taxes and bonds.

Carrying Capacity: The level of land use or human activity that can be permanently accommodated without an irreversible change in the quality of air, water, land, or plant and animal habitats. In human settlements, this term also refers to the upper limits beyond which the quality of life, community character, or human health, welfare, and safety will be impaired, such as the estimated maximum number of people that can be served by existing and planned infrastructure systems, or the maximum number of vehicles that can be accommodated on a roadway.

Catch Basin: A conventional structure for the capture of stormwater utilized in streets and parking areas. It includes an inlet, sump, and outlet and provides minimal removal of suspended solids. In most cases a hood is also included to separate oil and grease from stormwater. Catch basins are differentiated from drainage inlets, which do not contain sumps or hoods.

Character: The image and perception of a community as defined by its built environment, landscaping, natural features and open space, types and style of housing, and number and size of roads and sidewalks.

Charrette: A planning session in which participants brainstorm and visualize solutions to a design issue. The term *charrette* comes from the French term for "little cart" and refers to the final intense work effort expended by architects to meet a project deadline. At the École des Beaux Arts in Paris during the nineteenth century, proctors circulated with little carts to collect final drawings, and students would jump on the *charrette* to put finishing touches on their presentations minutes before their deadlines.

Cluster Development: A pattern of development in which industrial and commercial facilities and homes are grouped together on parcels of land in order to leave parts of the land undeveloped.

Compact Building Design: The act of constructing buildings vertically rather than horizontally.

Comprehensive Plan: A municipal document or series of documents that serves as a guide for making land use changes, preparation of capital improvement programs, and the rate, timing, and location of future growth. It is based upon establishing long-term goals and objectives to guide the future growth of a city. It is also known as a master or general plan. Elements of a comprehensive plan include:

- Economic development
- Environment
- Housing
- Land use
- Recreation and open space
- Transportation

Conservation Areas: Environmentally sensitive and valuable lands protected from any activity that would significantly alter their ecological integrity, balance, or character, except in cases of overriding public interest.

Context Sensitive Design (CSD): A collaborative, interdisciplinary approach that involves all stakeholders to develop a facility that fits its physical setting and preserves scenic, aesthetic, historic, and environmental resources. CSD is an approach that considers the total context within which a project will exist.

Corner Store: A small retail establishment (3,000 square feet maximum) located in a residential area. It may include a single residential unit. This land use is limited to areas with adopted neighborhood plans that specifically permit them.

Deed Restriction: A legally binding restriction on the use, activity, and/or limitation of property rights, recorded at the registry of deeds.

Density: The average number of people, families, or housing units on one unit of land. Density is also expressed as dwelling units per acre.

Detention Pond: Also called extended detention basins, an area surrounded by an embankment, or an excavated pit, designed to temporarily hold stormwater long enough to allow solids to settle. It reduces local and downstream flooding.

Downzoning: A change in zoning classification to less intensive use and/or development.

Ecosystem: The species and natural communities of a specific location interacting with one another and with the physical environment.

Eminent Domain: The legal right of government to take private property for public use, provided the owner is offered just compensation for the taking of property.

Endangered: Species that are in danger of extinction. It also is a category that denotes protection under federal law (The Endangered Species Act).

Eutrophication: The natural aging process of water bodies by siltation and organic decomposition, which reduces both water volume and oxygen levels. Surface runoff or airborne deposition of nitrogen and phosphorus accelerate this.

Fiscal Impact Analysis: The analysis of the estimated taxes that a development project would generate in comparison to the cost of providing municipal services demanded by that project.

Flood Hazard Area: The total stream and adjacent area periodically covered by overflow from the stream channel. The area contains (1) the floodway, which is the channel itself and portions of the immediately adjacent overbank that carry the major portion of flood flow, and (2) the flood fringe, the area beyond the floodway that is inundated to a lesser degree.

Flood Plain: The nearly level area adjacent to a water body, subject to inundation under heavy rain or blockage condition. Also called the overflow area.

Flood Zone, 100 Year: The land along a creek, dry wash, river, lake, seaside, swamp, bay, estuary, or in a low-lying area or depression that has a 1 in 100 chance of flooding every year.

Floor Area Ratio (FAR): The total floor area of all buildings or structures on a lot divided by the total area of the lot.

Garage Apartment: A single-unit apartment located above a garage and sited behind the main house.

Granny Flat: A freestanding, single-unit (usually single-story) apartment building located behind the main house in a residential area.

Green Building or Green Design: Building design that yields environmental benefits, such as savings in energy, building materials, and water consumption, or reduced waste generation.

Greenfield: Newly developed real estate on what was previously undeveloped open space.

Greenway: A linear open space; a corridor composed of natural vegetation. Greenways can be used to create connected networks of open space that include traditional parks and natural areas.

Groundwater: All water below the surface of the land. It is water found in the pore spaces of bedrock or soil, and it reaches the land surface through springs or can be pumped using wells.

Habitat: The living environment of a species, providing whatever that species needs for its survival, such as nutrients, water, and living space.

Habitat Fragmentation: The division of large tracts of natural habitat into smaller, disjunct parcels.

Impact Fees: Costs imposed on new development to fund public facility improvements required by new development and ease fiscal burdens on localities.

Impervious Cover: Anything that stops rainwater from soaking into the ground, including roads, sidewalks, driveways, parking lots, swimming pools, and buildings.

Inclusionary Zoning: A system that requires a minimum percentage of lower- and moderate-income housing to be provided in new developments.

Infill Development: A type of development occurring in established areas of a city.

Infrastructure: Water and sewer lines, roads, urban transit lines, schools, and other public facilities needed to support developed areas.

Jitney: Privately owned, small or medium-size transport vehicle usually operated on a fixed route but not on a fixed schedule.

Land Development Code (LDC): Rules, regulations, and ordinances that govern how and where certain types of development may occur.

Land Use: The manner in which a parcel of land is used or occupied.

Leapfrog Development: Development that occurs beyond the limits of existing development and creates areas of vacant land between areas of developed land.

Level of Service (LOS): A qualitative measure describing operational conditions within a traffic stream in terms of speed and travel time, freedom to maneuver, traffic interruptions, comfort and convenience, and safety. Level A denotes the best traffic conditions, while Level F indicates gridlock.

Location-Efficient Mortgage: A lending program that allows home buyers to borrow more money based on the transportation cost savings of living near mass transit.

Low-Impact Development (LID): An approach to land use planning that attempts to maintain the predeveloped ability of a site to manage rainfall.

Mixed-Use (MU): A development that combines residential, commercial, retail, and/or office uses, either in a vertical fashion (in a single building) or a horizontal fashion (adjacent buildings).

● A neighborhood urban center that allows a variety of residential types (condos, apartments, townhouses) and commercial, office, and retail uses clustered together in a development of less than 40 acres.

● A neighborhood mixed-use building that allows residential uses above ground-floor commercial uses.

Multifamily: A building that is designed to house more than one family. Examples are a fourplex, condominiums, or an apartment building.

National Environmental Policy Act (NEPA): A comprehensive federal law requiring analysis of the environmental impacts of federal actions such as the approval of grants; it also requires the preparation of an environmental impact statement (EIS) for every major federal action significantly affecting the quality of the human environment.

Neighborhood Planning: A two-phase process by which members of the community develop plans to manage future development in their neighborhoods. The first phase of the process involves establishing goals and objectives and the actions required to address neighborhood issues. The second phase implements the land use and zoning changes recommended in the neighborhood plan in the form of a Neighborhood Plan Combining District.

Neotraditional Development: A new development built to emulate a traditional neighborhood, where a mix of different types of residential and commercial developments form a tightly knit unit.

New Urbanism: Neighborhood design trend used to promote community and livability. Characteristics include narrow streets, wide sidewalks, porches, and homes located closer together than typical suburban designs.

NIMBY: Acronym for "not in my backyard." Describes the sentiment that exists among some people who do not want any type of change in their neighborhood.

Nonpoint Source Pollution (NPS): Pollution that cannot be identified as coming from a specific source and thus cannot be controlled through the issuing of permits. Stormwater runoff and some deposits from the air fall into this category.

Open Space: An area set aside or reserved for public or private use with very few improvements. Types of open space include:
- Golf courses
- Agricultural land
- Parks
- Greenbelts
- Nature preserves

Pedestrian-Scaled: Development designed so a person can comfortably walk from one location to another, providing visually interesting and useful details such as:
- Public clocks
- Benches
- Public art
- Drinking fountains
- Textured pavement such as bricks or cobblestones
- Shade
- Interesting light poles
- Trash bins
- Transit system maps
- Covered transit stops
- Street-level retail with storefront windows

Performance Zoning: Establishes minimum criteria to be used when assessing whether a particular project is appropriate for a certain area; ensures that the end result adheres to an acceptable level of performance or compatibility.

Plan: A statement of policies, including text and diagrams, setting forth objectives, principles, standards, and proposals for the future physical development of the city or county.

Planning: The process of setting development goals and policy, gathering and evaluating information, and developing alternatives for future actions based on the evaluation of the information.

Quality of Life: Those aspects of the economic, social, and physical environment that affect whether a community is considered a desirable place in which to live or do business.

Recharge: Water that infiltrates into the ground, usually from above; it replenishes groundwater reserves, provides soil moisture, and affords evapotranspiration.

Redevelopment: The conversion of a building or project from an old use to a new one.

Rezone: To change the zoning classification of particular lots or parcels of land.

Riparian Area: Vegetated ecosystems along a body of water through which energy, materials, and water pass. Riparian areas characteristically have a high water table and are subject to periodic flooding.

Runoff: The water that flows off the surface of the land, ultimately into streams and bodies of water, without being absorbed into the soil.

Siltation: The process by which loose soil is transferred and builds up in streams, rivers, and lakes, causing changes in the features' boundaries and depth.

Sprawl: Sprawl defines patterns of urban growth that include large acreage of low-density residential development, rigid separation between residential and commercial uses, leapfrog development in rural areas away from urban centers, minimal support for non-motorized transportation methods, and a lack of integrated transportation and land use planning.
- Residences far removed from stores, parks, and other activity centers
- Scattered or "leapfrog" development that leaves large tracts of undeveloped land between developments
- Commercial strip development along major streets
- Large expanses of low-density or single use development such as commercial centers with no office or residential uses, or residential areas with no nearby commercial centers
- Major form of transportation is the automobile
- Uninterrupted and contiguous low- to medium-density (one to six du/ac) urban development
- Walled residential subdivisions that do not connect to adjacent residential development.

Streetscape: The space between the buildings on either side of a street that defines its character. The elements of a streetscape include:
- Building frontage/façade
- Landscaping
- Sidewalks
- Street paving
- Street furniture
- Signs
- Awnings
- Streetlighting

Sustainability: A concept and strategy by which communities seek economic development approaches that benefit the local environment and quality of life.

Traditional Neighborhood Corridor: The combination of an activity center and the transportation connections linking it to the rest of city. These links may be made by frequent public transit service, walking, cycling, or car. The major throughway into a traditional neighborhood corridor should be wide enough to accommodate all modes of vehicular transportation and on-street parking, and provide space for safe and inviting sidewalks for pedestrian as well. A traditional neighborhood corridor is characterized by a mixture of various uses and densities such as stores, offices, and different types of housing.

Traditional Neighborhood Design (TND): A basic unit of the new urbanism containing a center that includes a public space and commercial enterprises; an identifiable edge, ideally a five-minute walk from the center; a mix of activities and variety of housing types; an interconnected network of streets, usually in a grid pattern; and a high priority on public space, with prominently located civic buildings and open space that includes parks, plazas, and squares.

Transit-Oriented Development (TOD): A form of development that emphasizes alternative forms of transportation other than the automobile—such as walking, cycling, and mass transit—as part of its design. Transit-oriented development locates retail and office space around a transit stop. This activity center is located adjacent to a residential area with a variety of housing options, such as apartments, townhouses, duplexes, and single-family houses. It is similar to a traditional neighborhood development.

Urban Growth Boundary: A line drawn around a city that prohibits development outside that boundary. Designed to slow or prevent sprawl, UGBs are meant to accommodate growth for a designated period of time and are used to guide infrastructure development. Portland, Oregon, is the most commonly cited example of an urban growth boundary.

Watershed: The geographic area from which water drains into a specific body. A watershed may contain several subwatersheds.

Wetlands: An area having specific hydric soil and water table characteristics supporting or capable of supporting wetlands vegetation.

Zero-Lot-Line Development: A development option in which side yard restrictions are reduced and the building abuts a side lot line. Overall unit densities are therefore increased. Zero-lot-line development can result in the increased protection of natural resources.

Zoning: The classification of land in a community into different areas and districts. Zoning is a legislative process that regulates building dimensions, density, design, placement, and use within each district.

Wiley Books on Sustainable Design

For these and other Wiley books on sustainable design, visit www.wiley.com/go/sustainabledesign

Alternative Construction: Contemporary Natural Building Methods
by Lynne Elizabeth and Cassandra Adams

Cities People Planet: Liveable Cities for a Sustainable World
by Herbert Girardet

Design with Nature
by Ian L. McHarg

Ecodesign: A Manual for Ecological Design
by Ken Yeang

Green Building Materials: A Guide to Product Selection and Specification, Second Edition
by Ross Spiegel and Dru Meadows

Green Development: Integrating Ecology and Real Estate
by Rocky Mountain Institute

The HOK Guidebook to Sustainable Design, Second Edition
by Sandra Mendler, William O'Dell, and Mary Ann Lazarus

Land and Natural Development (Land) Code
by Diana Balmori and Gaboury Benoit

Sustainable Construction: Green Building Design and Delivery
by Charles J. Kibert

Sustainable Commercial Interiors
by Penny Bonda and Katie Sosnowchik

Sustainable Design: Ecology, Architecture, and Planning
by Daniel Williams

Sustainable Healthcare Architecture
by Robin Guenther and Gail Vittori

Sustainable Residential Interiors
by Associates III